SILENCE AND THE WORD

Negative theology or apophasis – the idea that God is best identified in terms of 'absence', 'otherness', 'difference' – has been influential in modern Christian thought, resonating as it does with secular notions of negation developed in recent continental philosophy. Apophasis also has a strong intellectual history dating back to the early Church Fathers. *Silence and the Word* both studies the history of apophasis and examines its relationship with contemporary secular philosophy. Leading Christian thinkers explore in their own way the extent to which the concept of the apophatic illumines some of the deepest doctrinal structures of Christian faith and of Christian self-understanding, both in terms of its historical and contemporary situatedness, showing how a dimension of negativity has characterised not only traditional mysticism but most forms of Christian thought over the years.

OLIVER DAVIES is Reader in Philosophical Theology in the University of Wales and has written a number of studies of Christian mystical writers, including *Meister Eckhart: Mystical Theologian* (1991). The first volume of his Systematic Theology appeared as *A Theology of Compassion* (2001), and a second volume, *On the Creativity of God*, is currently under preparation.

DENYS TURNER is the Norris-Hulse Professor of Philosophical Theology at the University of Cambridge and former H. G. Wood Professor at the University of Birmingham. He is the author of *On the Philosophy of Karl Marx* (1969), *Marxism and Christianity* (1983) and *The Darkness of God* (Cambridge, 1995). He is currently working on a book on Thomas Aquinas and the doctrine of God.

SILENCE
AND THE WORD

Negative Theology and Incarnation

EDITED BY

OLIVER DAVIES AND DENYS TURNER

PUBLISHED BY THE PRESS SYNDICATE OF THE UNIVERSITY OF CAMBRIDGE
The Pitt Building, Trumpington Street, Cambridge, United Kingdom

CAMBRIDGE UNIVERSITY PRESS
The Edinburgh Building, Cambridge CB2 2RU, UK
40 West 20th Street, New York, NY 10011-4211, USA
477 Williamstown Road, Port Melbourne, VIC 3207, Australia
Ruiz de Alarcón 13, 28014 Madrid, Spain
Dock House, The Waterfront, Cape Town 8001, South Africa

http://www.cambridge.org

First published 2002

Printed in the United Kingdom at the University Press, Cambridge

Typeface Baskerville Monotype 11/12.5 pt.   *System* LaTeX 2$_\varepsilon$ [TB]

A catalogue record for this book is available from the British Library

Library of Congress Cataloguing in Publication data

Silence and the Word: negative theology and incarnation / editors
Oliver Davies and Denys Turner
p.   cm.
Includes bibliographical references and index.
ISBN 0 521 81718 8
1. Negative theology – Christianity – Congresses.   I. Davies, Oliver, 1956–
II. Turner, Denys, 1942–
BT83.585 .S55 2002   230 – dc21   2001052404

ISBN 0 521 81718 8 hardback

In memory of Herbert McCabe

καί ὡς διὰ θυσιαστηρίου τοῦ νοός, τὴν ἐν ἀδύτοις πολυύμνητον τῆς ἀφανοῦς καὶ ἀγνώστου μεγαλοφωνίας σιγήν τῆς θεότητος, δι' ἄλλης λάλου τε καὶ πολυφθόγγου σιγῆς προσκαλούμενον.

Through the altar of the mind he summons the silence of the unseen and unknown call of the deity much hymned in the innermost sanctuaries, by another silence that speaks, rich in tone.

Maximus the Confessor, Mystagogy

Contents

Notes on contributors

OLIVER DAVIES is Reader in Philosophical Theology in the University of Wales and has written a number of studies of Christian mystical writers, including *Meister Eckhart: Mystical Theologian* (SPCK 1991). The first volume of his Systematic Theology appeared as *A Theology of Compassion* (SCM Press 2001), and a second volume, *On the Creativity of God*, is currently under preparation.

PAUL S. FIDDES is Principal of Regent's Park College, Oxford and University Research Lecturer in the University of Oxford. His previous books include *The Creative Suffering of God* (Oxford University Press 1988), *Past Event and Present Salvation* (Darton, Longman and Todd 1989) and *The Promised End* (Blackwell 2000).

DAVID F. FORD is Regius Professor of Divinity in the University of Cambridge and Chairman of the Management Committee of the Centre for Advanced Religious and Theological Studies. His recent writings include *Self and Salvation: Being Transformed* (Cambridge University Press 1999), *Theology: a Very Short Introduction* (Oxford University Press 1999) and (editor) *The Modern Theologians* (2nd rev. edn Blackwell 1997).

BERNARD MCGINN is Naomi Shenstone Donnelley Professor in the Divinity School at the University of Chicago. He has written extensively on apocalyptic thought and Christian spirituality and mysticism. He is currently engaged in a five-volume history of Western Christian mysticism under the title *The Presence of God* (Crossroad and SCM Press, three volumes published between 1991 and 1997).

HERBERT MCCABE joined the Order of Preachers after studying philosophy at the University of Manchester. From 1964–7 and 1970–9 he was editor of *New Blackfriars*. He lectured in philosophy and theology at Blackfriars, Oxford, and in the Department of Theology and

Religious Studies at the University of Bristol. In 1987 he published *God Matters* (Geoffrey Chapman). Herbert McCabe died on 28 June 2001.

MARK A. MCINTOSH, Associate Professor of Theology at Loyola University Chicago, is the author of *Christology from Within: Spirituality and Incarnation in Hans Urs von Balthasar* (University of Notre Dame Press 1996), *Mystical Theology: the Integrity of Spirituality and Theology* (Blackwell 1998) and *Mysteries of Faith* (Cowley Publications 2000). He also serves as Chaplain to the House of Bishops of the Episcopal Church, USA.

JANET MARTIN SOSKICE is a University Lecturer in the Faculty of Divinity at Cambridge University and a Fellow of Jesus College. She is the author of *Metaphor and Religious Language* (Oxford University Press 1985) and is presently working on a book on *Naming God*.

DENYS TURNER is the Norris-Hulse Professor of Philosophical Theology at the University of Cambridge and former H. G. Wood Professor at the University of Birmingham. He is the author of *On the Philosophy of Karl Marx* (Sceptre, 1969), *Marxism and Christianity* (Blackwell, 1983) and *The Darkness of God* (Cambridge University Press, 1995). He is currently working on a book on Thomas Aquinas and the doctrine of God.

GRAHAM WARD is Professor of Contextual Theology and Ethics at the University of Manchester. He is author of *Barth, Derrida and the Language of Theology* (Cambridge University Press 1995), *Cities of God* (Routledge 2000), and is editor of *The Postmodern God* (Blackwell 1997) and *Companion to Postmodern Theology* (Blackwell 2001). He is currently working on a project concerning Christian polity and the world wide web.

ROWAN WILLIAMS is Bishop of Monmouth and the Archbishop of Wales. He has been Dean of Clare College, Cambridge and Lady Margaret Professor of Divinity in the University of Oxford. His recent publications include *Arius: Heresy and Tradition* (Darton, Longman and Todd 1987), *Teresa of Avila* (Geoffrey Chapman 1991), *Sergii Bulgakov* (1999) and *On Christian Theology* (Blackwell 2000).

Preface

This book originated in a colloquium that was held at the University of Birmingham in Spring 1999. The contributors represented different fields of interest in Christian theology, but a common theme in their work was an engagement with what is often termed 'spirituality', that is to say with Christianity as an existential and dialectical religion. There was a further consensus that the dimension of negativity, or apophasis, which is most often associated with the canon of Christian mystical texts, belongs also to mainstream Christianity and can be found in theological works not normally considered to be of a 'mystical' kind. In the resulting volume, each contributor is exploring in his or her own way the extent to which the concept of the apophatic illumines some of the deepest doctrinal structures of Christian faith, and of Christian self-understanding in terms both of its historical and contemporary situatedness. It is hoped that the resulting conversations between contributors will reach out beyond the ranks of those who ordinarily study the 'mystical' and will creatively engage those for whom such concerns may appear limited or marginal.

The editors wish to express their thanks to the Department of Theology at the University of Birmingham for offering financial support for the original colloquium, as they do to Kevin Taylor and the staff of Cambridge University Press for their kind and efficient collaboration in the production of this volume. Most of all however the editors wish to express real gratitude to the contributors themselves for their generous, inventive and whole-hearted engagement with the topic, and for giving such solid flesh to the insubstantial outline of what seemed an interesting idea.

The Select Bibliography at the end of the volume contains items which are repeatedly used by contributors and those which touch more generally on the nature of the apophatic, with regard also to Christian doctrine and culture. It is neither a complete listing of bibliographical material referred to in the chapters nor is it intended to survey the extant literature on Christian mystical texts.

OLIVER DAVIES
DENYS TURNER

Introduction

Oliver Davies and Denys Turner

The classical Christian apophatic tradition, which is made available to us principally in a number of Greek patristic and Western medieval texts, feeds into three distinct currents of contemporary thinking. In the first place, it appears to offer a point of contact with the pervasive mood of atheistic secularism in modern society. Language which pivots around denials about God and a rhetoric of absence seems meaningful in the context of a widespread scepticism about traditional religious beliefs and values in a way that the increasingly exasperated or despairing repetition of kerygmatic affirmations does not. But it can seem defeatist, at best, to preach a God of the gaps to half-empty pews rather than a God who is Lord and Creator of all. Secondly, and more challengingly, negative theology can be used creatively to explore affinities with an intellectual environment in which negation – as difference, absence, otherness – is frequently judged to be more interesting than affirmation. In 1968 Gilles Deleuze wrote that difference 'is manifestly in the air', and the thinking of difference has broadly characterised continental philosophical development down to the present day, in the writings of thinkers such as Deleuze himself, Lyotard, Derrida, Bataille, Foucault, Lacan, Levinas and Ricoeur.[1] If decline in religious observance reflects a real disruption of traditional patterns of belief as much as it does a mood of social iconoclasm, then the 'turn to difference' is more than just a fashionable rejection of the metaphysical systems of the past. As Deleuze has pointed out, there is already a constructivist element at work in Kant's First Critique which serves to 'dissolve the cogito' and 'fragment the self', thus liberating forces which in later thinkers will become powerfully deconstructionist.[2] Nietzsche is still widely read in our society, and the 'postmodernity' fathered by French readings of Nietzsche during the

---

[1] Gilles Deleuze, *Difference and Repetition* (trans. Paul Patton, London: Athlone Press, 1994), p. xix.
[2] Ibid., p. 86.

nineteen sixties and seventies has successfully portrayed itself as representing what is most radical and engaging in contemporary thought.[3]
Negation then has captured something basic to the spirit of the times,
reflecting reality as process, which is disjunctive, fissured and ultimately
resistant to any schematisation. But thirdly, negative theology resonates
positively with a deeply rooted trend in contemporary religiosity towards
the privatisation and internalisation of religion, whereby faith is translated into transcendence or 'religious experience' which is indifferent
or even hostile to traditional religious beliefs and practices. The term
'spirituality', which is widely and generally uncritically used in our society as a hallmark for the modern *homo religiosus*, captures this sense of
an individual relation with the divine mediated through exciting experiences of a 'mystical' kind. Here in turn 'mystical' texts come into play
which articulate a *via negativa* or disruptive discourse about God that
can seem, in modern contexts, to challenge the conventions of religion:
the tedium of church attendance and dull rehearsal of moribund and
formulaic belief.

All three points of contact between negative theology and contemporary society, through religious scepticism, philosophical engagement with
radical difference, and the turn to 'experience', serve to pull Christian
apophasis away from its matrix in Christian cultic belief and practice.
But the very texts that communicate negative theology in the modern
world are themselves the product of times and places in which the dis-
continuity between 'mysticism', belief and practice did not obtain. This
can be shown from the two principal streams of negativity in medieval
Christianity. The first is that of a formation of the self in suffering and
dereliction under the weight of the divine presence. This is most frequently, though not exclusively, apparent in texts written by religious
women, who creatively explored a spiritual responsivity of abandonment and alienation. Such works, frequently of a visionary character,
are embedded in strongly Christocentric devotional practices in which
the physical and emotional suffering of Christ in powerlessness seemed
to offer a particularly expressive model of sanctity for those for whom
imitatio of Christ as king, priest and teacher was less easily accomplished.
The intense spiritual reformation of the self described in these works is
not a 'religious experience' at an angle to Christian belief however but
is clearly deeply grounded in and structured by the primary Christian

---

[3] See David B. Allison, ed., *The New Nietzsche* (Cambridge Mass. and London: MIT Press, 1985;
originally published by Dell Pub. Co., New York, 1977).

doctrines of death and resurrection. It is the second stream of negativity, that of a more formal – and generally male – negative theology, which can be more easily misconstrued. This is a tradition which begins essentially with the *Mystical Theology* of pseudo-Denys, a fifth or sixth-century text, which originally belonged to a broader discussion on the possibilities and limits of speaking about God. It shows both a liturgical and biblical background, as marking the interpenetration of the human and the divine, and functions as an apophatic corrective to the exuberant excess of the *Divine Names*. There, as in other works, the same author draws out the extent to which language, primarily biblical in origin, authentically mediates and communicates the divine nature. The interdependence of the *Mystical Theology* and the *Divine Names* shows the dialectical pulsation between affirmations and negations that characterises the enterprise of Christian negative theology as whole. Here negation is not free-standing, but secures the theological character of the affirmative speech patterns in address to God or speech about God. Being cancelled in this way, these are shown not to be ordinary language use at all but speech that is burdened to the point of excess: as exhausted as it is full. This same dialectic or 'constructive deconstruction' is to be found in an internalised form in Bonaventure's *Journey of the Mind to God*, in which a transcendental epistemology of ascent is again inscribed throughout with the distinctive structure of Christian credal belief, as death and resurrection. In the case of Meister Eckhart the affirmative context can be seen both in the role played by the motif of 'divine birth' in his transcendental anthropology, and in the social context of his preaching. The fourteenth-century Rhineland saw an explosion of Eucharistic and visionary piety particularly among the women's communities for which Eckhart, as a leading Dominican, held pastoral responsibility. His internalised, abstracted and cognitive understanding of the life of faith functioned as a counterpoint to the externalised concretions of visible piety. A fourteenth-century vernacular text such as the *Cloud of Unknowing* also retains Dionysian cycles of a dialectical affirmation and negation in the passage from the senses to contemplation. Once again a movement of negation, as 'forgetting', is held in tension with a movement of affirmation or spiritual 'practices', and each informs the other. Contemporary appropriations of negative theology, for all their vitality, tend to set Christian negation apart from its affirmations, thus changing it from a negation of experience within a Dionysian dialectic to an experience of negation as such which has cut free from the liturgical and ecclesial contexts that originally supported it. This is to risk trading a mechanism of correction which maintains the truly theological and transcendental character of Christian affirmations for an ineffable 'experience' which seems to validate the individual in his or her sublime independence of communal structures and commitments.

The contributors to this volume are united in their belief that negativity plays a central role within the Christian tradition, together with a sense that the specific problematic of the relation between negative theology and mainstream Christian tradition is one which has received insufficient attention in recent time. This broad unity of view survives the wide diversity of approach and subject matter which otherwise distinguishes the contributions, and the subtle conversations between contributors regarding the specific locus of the negative and its distinctive character which the careful reader will note. Addressing the scholarly deficit in reflection upon the negative within tradition necessarily calls into question some of the ways in which Christian apophatic texts are read today. But it also poses questions about the nature of the traditions which we have received from the past and which may of themselves invite more deconstructionist readings, with a new potential for liberating the reader from outmoded ways of thinking and believing. This can be an exploration of new ways of appropriating tradition itself, as it can become a resource for responsible, creative dialogue with other religions, in which silence and negation are frequently also key motifs which are foundational to the dynamic of their own distinctively religious ways of speaking. Not least, such a focus upon 'negative theology' can also become a means of conducting a dialogue with much in contemporary secular intellectual culture which is powerfully influenced by concepts of otherness, absence and difference.

The contributions are printed here following the chronological order of their subject matter, with the exception of the first and last chapter, which serve as a point of entry into and departure from the volume as a whole. In 'Apophaticism, idolatry and the claims of reason', Denys Turner sets the scene for a discussion of apophasis and incarnation in Christian tradition by pointing to the deep opposition between theism and atheism which is a defining problematic of modernity. Uses of negation in contemporary 'postmodern' discourse stand in a precarious relation with both traditional forms of Christian negative theology and with modern denials of the existence of God. As a possible route out of the impasse of a sterile and oppositional thinking about God, in which both theisms and atheisms mutually define each other, Turner proposes readings of Thomas Aquinas on God, language and theology which show that he is 'a theist who knows nothing of "deism", an apophaticist whose negativity is rooted in rational foundations, and a rationalist whose conception of reason is as distanced from that of the Enlightenment as it is possible to be'. The crux of thomist rationalism and metaphysics is seen to reside in an ever deeper discovery of the foundation of the natural order as being *created*, thus revealing the Creator as one whose existence is known but whose nature always remains beyond the reach of human cognition. This presents a view of theological reason which contests any easy appropriation of a rationalist natural theology as it denies a fashionable postmodern rejection of reason and its operations. Grounded in a thoroughgoing and ultimately medieval theology of creation, this chapter points in the direction of an understanding of reason as intrinsically belonging in and ordered to a divinely created world.

In his study 'The quest for a place that is "not-a-place": the hiddenness of God and the presence of God', Paul Fiddes addresses the theme of Old Testament wisdom as the background to Christology and to a rethinking of the Trinitarian relations. Divine wisdom was hidden on account of its limitlessness, while human wisdom – as participation in God's wisdom – was both limited and flawed. Fiddes draws a parallel here between the non-place of biblical wisdom, as excess and ubiquity, with the revisiting of Platonic *khora* in postmodern texts, as a rhetoric of absence, the 'trace' and the Totally Other. Against both a postmodern transcendentalism of absence and a Christian dialectic of presence and absence, Fiddes proposes the hiddenness, or 'concealed presence' of God, in four sites or modalities. The first is the creation itself in which God is present, though not in a way that suppresses 'the otherness of created beings'. The second is the 'no-place' within the self which is the metaphorically structured place of encounter between God and the self. The third is the sphere of interpersonal relations, in which God is 'hidden' as a possibility of love, which Fiddes links with an argument for the hypostasisation of relations within the Trinity itself. The fourth modality of divine hiddenness is that of objects in the world which can come to mediate divine presence. But the incarnation itself represents the consummate form of the hiddenness of God, in that – like wisdom itself – the non-localised pleroma which indwells Christ invites us not to comprehension but to participation.

In 'The gift of the Name: Moses and the burning bush' Janet Soskice argues that the widespread rejection of the attributes of God as infinite, omniscient and all-powerful constitutes in fact a denial of the God of the Enlightenment, and that that God has been disseminated as much through the deconstructionist texts of modernity as by traditional readings. An analysis of the revelation of the divine name in Exodus, especially 3:14, which has often served as a proof-text for the God of the attributes, appears on closer analysis to be God's self-placing as the God of Israel's history. Moses is to know that what he meets is the God of Israel's past (of Abraham, Isaac and Jacob), of its present (who sees its suffering) and of its future (the God who will lead them from slavery to the promised land). We discover in Augustine however a way of apprehending the divine attributes which is entirely dynamic, since Augustine knows God as presence within history, including the intimacy of his own particular history. The sense of the presence of God in life and history which we find in Augustine reverses the attempt to control God through a human naming, which is the object of the current critique of the attributes. In contrast Augustine, the rhetorician, understands that his ability to speak of God at all is grounded in God's prior calling, from within experience and history, and so is formed as prayer, which is the creative human response to the divine gift.

In 'Aquinas on the Trinity' Herbert McCabe sets out Thomas' understanding of the limits to our speaking about God, so that 'dealing with God is trying to talk of what we cannot talk of, trying to think what we cannot think'. We cannot know what God is but only what he is not, and we cannot know in what way he is, but only in what way he is not. The proofs for the existence of God do not represent an attempt to *understand* God therefore, but serve 'simply to prove the existence of a mystery'. Thomas seeks to show however that we can speak of God in a way that entails no contradictions, even if we cannot know the real meanings of the words that we use of him. Although we may not know in what way our words about God make sense, we can know that they are not nonsense. Our language about the Trinity is therefore highly provisional in that we are obliged to speak of God as both three Persons and one essence. Faith teaches us that there is no real contradiction here, although we cannot see how this is the case and must await a future resolution. Nor can we conceive of what it means for a relation not to be an accident but to be a subsistent relation within God, as Thomas proposes in his exposition of Trinitarian theology.

Bernard McGinn also finds influential elements of negativity as concealment in the theology of Martin Luther, as he draws out in his study '*Vere tu es Deus absconditus*: the hidden God in Luther and some mystics'. Here McGinn argues for two modalities of divine hiddenness in the thought of Luther, firstly in the incarnation itself and the *theologia crucis*, and secondly in the enigma of predestination. Using the work of Gerrish,

McGinn points out that the suffering and dereliction felt by Luther concerning his own sense of guilt and fear as to his ultimate destiny causes him to flee to the revelation of God *sub contrariis* in the person of Christ. Without seeking specifically to draw out points of influence, McGinn argues for significant medieval parallels to the dereliction and fear expressed by Luther in his experience of the second hiddenness of God, in predestination. His proof texts come from the writings principally of women mystics such as Angela of Foligno, Mechthild of Magdeburg and Marguerite Porete, as well as John Tauler. Here he argues that there is an experience of negativity, as alienation and abandonment, which resonates with Luther's *Anfechtungen*. In the medieval mystical paradigm of negativity however, abandonment and the experience of divine absence is understood to be the veiled presence of the divine fullness, in contrast to Luther's movement from the hiddenness of predestination to the divine concealment in the incarnation.

Rowan Williams points to the tendency in Christian tradition to attribute negativity to the divine essence, which is then set above or beyond the visibility of the Trinitarian relations. In his reading in particular of the *Romanzas*, Williams argues that the Trinitarian theology of St John of the Cross breaks with this tradition by taking negativity into the Trinitarian relations themselves. This is achieved by extending the filial relation between Son and Father beyond the range of a closed mutuality and of gender so that it becomes an infinite, erotic desire. Trinitarian or 'deflected' love transcends the mutual affirmations of an I–Thou relation, which fixes the other as object of desire, and realises desire as excess and movement within infinity. It is this that St John identifies with the *ser* or essence of God. The self which is caught up into this relation desires not the Son but the Son's own desire for the Father, opened up through the Spirit. The empirical self, which rests upon a subject–object relation mediated by self-referential desire, is now dissolved by the resolution of that desire into movement towards an infinite term, which is personal participation in the life of the Trinity. This is the 'dark night of the soul' and the dereliction of Jesus, for whom the Father 'has ceased to be in any way a graspable *other* for the subjectivity of the Son', before it becomes the divine freedom.

In his paper, 'The formation of mind: Trinity and understanding in Newman', Mark McIntosh argues for the view that apophasis plays a key role in Newman's theology, particularly in his critique of knowledge. The apophatic moment is intrinsic to the preservation of mystery, which guarantees against the reductionism and positivism of sciences which are no longer in touch with religion on the one hand, and superficial rationalist forms of religion on the other. Through a reading of Gregory of Nyssa, McIntosh proposes that a robustly Trinitarian theology always delivers an uncompromising apophasis, and thus confronts the mind with a reality that transcends its own terms. This leads to the *formation* of the mind not as instruction in propositional doctrines but as a life which is conformed in its essential rhythms to the Trinitarian reality. For Newman, it is this principle which becomes the base of all human knowing, for secular reason too must constantly confront its own limits, and refuse reduction, if it is to begin to grasp reality in its wholeness. Small-mindedness remains fixed and fragmentary. Formation, therefore, predicated upon an apophatic excess, is the principle which unites both the knowledge that is faith, leading to the lived experience of truth from within, and the operations of discernment and judgement that are integral to advances in human understanding.

In 'In the daylight forever?: language and silence', Graham Ward opposes two contemporary thinkers on silence, George Steiner and Jacques Derrida. He argues that Steiner's silence as the cessation of speech looks back to a binary opposition which dates from the Baroque period and which manifests as the sublime on the one hand and as kitsch on the other. The sublime seeks to transcend language, which is no longer adequate to its expressive tasks, while kitsch empties the sign of its meanings, trading signification for visibility and the banal multiplication of surfaces. Both are of ecclesial provenance, the former originating, according to Michel de Certeau, in the rhetorical excess of mystical writings and the latter in the triumphalistic theatricality of the Church as spectacle. But both are also predicated upon a corrupted correspondence view of language, whereby language fails adequately to refer. Against this, Ward advocates allegory, as a non-violent way of maintaining otherness 'within the familiar'. This is specifically to renounce the dualisms of a referential, denotative view of language, since otherness is now creatively contained within language itself as an unfolding of multiple meanings which do not cancel each other out. Ward understands Derrida's philosophy of *différance*, and the 'angelology' of Michel Serres, to be precisely an argument for allegory, offering a constructive, transformational, even Eucharistic view of language which, freed from any possible criterion of in/adequacy, now offers the possibility of creative transference as seeing 'as'. Within such an economy of language, silence ceases to be opposed to speech, and becomes – as communication – a rhythm in speech itself.

David Ford juxtaposes Anne Michaels' text 'Fugitive Pieces' with Dietrich Bonhoeffer's 'Christology' within the context of an attempt to answer the question: 'Apophasis and the Shoah: Where was Jesus Christ at Auschwitz?'. Ford compares the diverse images of silence that are scattered throughout Michaels' work of testimony, with the silence before the Word invoked by Bonhoeffer at the beginning of his 'Christology'. Ford sees the silence of the Church as grounded in the silence of Christ himself before Pilate, and defines the 'simultaneity of silence and word' as 'the simultaneity of the life, death and resurrection of Jesus Christ'. Ford sees a resonance between Michaels and Bonhoeffer to the extent that silence is constitutive of personhood, or the 'Who', in both, and believes that the imagery of affirmation and negation in Michaels is sufficiently analogous to Bonhoeffer's Christ to make a comparison of the two illuminating. Ford then poses difficult questions regarding Christian supersessionism, with its historical complicity in the Shoah, and argues that desire for the Kingdom of God is a common ground uniting Christians and Jews. Adopting Levinas' notion of 'face' and 'facing', Ford argues that Jesus Christ can be said to 'face' Auschwitz. Living before that face, Christians are therefore summoned to remember Auschwitz, to critique power in the interests of the weak, to pursue 'an ethic of gentleness and being for others', and 'forms of communication that have the crucifixion as their central criterion and dialogue as their central practice'.

In 'Soundings: towards a theological poetics of silence', Oliver Davies offers perspectives on the concept of silence which engage with some of the issues that surface in the volume as a whole. Here the focus is on silence in different textual environments, and – as a sign that is ultimately empty – its dependence on other signs for the inscription of its meanings. Davies points to two Russian words which express the distinction between the silence which speech interrupts and silence as suppressed speech: between 'natural' and personal silence. Old Testament texts relating to divine speech show an emphasis upon the latter rather than the former. The divine refusal of speech as *ḥārēš* is equivalent to the divine wrath and calls forth the parallel human response of *dāmam*, which expresses respectful awe at divine action. In contrast, the neoplatonic Greek tradition is interested in primal silence as divine and human transcendence (*sigē* and *hesychia*). Since apophasis in Christian speech about God is embedded in liturgical and devotional life, it therefore becomes expressive of a celebratory sense of presence and conforms to pragmatic as well as semiotic language use. Davies also briefly surveys the place of silence in modern Christian art (René Girard), deconstruction

(Jacques Derrida) and post-Holocaust poetry (Paul Celan), and concludes that as an empty sign silence lends itself as a resource for dialogue between Christianity and secularism, and between Christianity and other religious traditions.

The contributions to this volume reflect an engagement with negativity in each period of Christian history, from the Old Testament background to post-Holocaust debates. The subject matter found here also ranges over many of the significant expressions of theological life, from biblical texts, to the work of major medieval and reformation theologians, from the doctrines of Trinity and Incarnation, to Christian art and literature. Although diversely analysed and explicated, as silence, hiddenness, dereliction, difference and otherness, negation plays a central role in all the theological reflections and textual readings presented here. This is not to suggest that the reader will discover a unified programme of apophatic theology in these pages, although certain themes do reoccur, such as the thinking of negation *within* the Trinity and not in a divine essence beyond it (Fiddes, McCabe, Williams, McIntosh), dereliction as negation (Davies, McGinn, Ford), negative theology and dialectic (Turner, Soskice, Ward). But each contribution argues in its own way for the importance of silence for mainstream Christian theology. It is this recognition of the potential fertility and creativity of the apophatic moment for Christian thinking that constitutes the thematic unity of the volume and grounds its contribution to contemporary debate.

Apophaticism, idolatry and the claims of reason

Denys Turner

The revival of interest in our times, not alone within theology, but pursued with equal intensity within literary and cultural theory, in the ancient topic of the 'apophatic', no doubt has its explanations within the intellectual history of Western culture. But it is no purpose of this essay to explore them. My starting point is rather in one of the principal issues with which a number of those engaged in this rediscovery are explicitly preoccupied, whether or not they themselves avow consciously theological interests: and that issue is the question of what it is exactly that is being denied when it is said by the atheist that there is no God.

It is some time now since it could be supposed without challenge by the intellectual and cultural elites of Western society that there *is* no question of God, that nothing hangs on whether there is or is not a God, for nothing follows either way, though it is a fair guess that for very large sectors of the populations of Western countries, life is lived broadly in a mental condition of indifference to the matter. And it is true that, even among the intellectual elites, for many of whom it is fashionable to *permit* theism as an option within a generalised relativism of thought (for which there can be no grounds for ruling out any beliefs anyway) the licence granted to theism can seem to amount to no more than a higher indifferentism. Yet, such attitudes are not any longer unchallenged: nor does the challenge emerge only from the predictable sources of avowedly religious traditions, but immanently from within the most contemporary analyses of the predicaments of late twentieth-century Western culture. In much continental philosophy, from Heidegger to Levinas and Derrida, it is acknowledged, with varying degrees of unease at having to concede the point, that the predicaments of our culture have an ineradicably *theological* character. And I suggest that if that cultural diagnosis has identified any one indicator revealing the irreducibility of the theological more clearly than most, it will be the recognition that it is by no means as easy as it was once thought to deny the existence of God.

If once – perhaps at some point in the late nineteenth century – it was clear, and agreed, what it was to think the existence of God, then what was to count as atheism was relatively unproblematical. In those good old days atheists knew what they were denying. For, as Thomas Aquinas used to say, following Aristotle, *eadem est scientia oppositorum*[1] – affirmations and their corresponding negations are one and the same knowledge: clarity about the affirmation permitted clear-minded denials. But now that theologians once again make claims for an *apophatic* negativity, which in pre-atheistic cultures provoked no possibility of confusion with atheism, today there is an issue: what is it that the atheist denies which the apophatic theologian does not also deny? Just how are we to distinguish between the theologian who affirms that it is better to say that God does not exist than to say that God exists, and the atheist who simply says: 'There is no God'? Moreover, it is asked by some who had thought their position to be safely atheistical: What differentiates negative theology and deconstruction?[2] For sure a question is provoked concerning what exactly it is that the atheist denies that is not already denied in these powerfully deconstructive words of Meister Eckhart, who tells us:

God is nameless, because no one can say anything or understand anything about him. Therefore a pagan teacher says: 'Whatever we understand or say about the First Cause, that is far more ourselves than it is the First Cause, for it is beyond all saying and understanding.'[3] So if I say, 'God is good', that is not true. I am good, but God is not good. I can even say: 'I am better than God', for whatever is good can become better, and whatever can become better can become best of all. But since God is not good, he cannot become better. And since he cannot become better, he cannot be best of all. For these three degrees are alien to God: 'good', 'better' and 'best', for he is superior to them all . . . If I say 'God is a being', it is not true; he is a being transcending being and [he is] a transcending nothingness . . . [So] do not try to understand God, for God is beyond all understanding. One authority says: 'If I had a God whom I could understand, I should never consider him God.'[4] If you can understand anything about him, it in no way belongs to him, and insofar as you understand anything about him that brings you into incomprehension, and from incomprehension

[1] See Aristotle, *Peri Hermeneias*, 17a 31–3.
[2] For example, Jacques Derrida in 'How to Avoid Speaking: Denials', in Sanford Budick and Wolfgang Iser, eds., *Languages of the Unsayable – The Play of Negativity in Literature and Literary Theory* (New York: Columbia University Press, 1989), pp. 1–50; *On the Name*, Thomas Dutoit, ed., trans. David Wood, Thomas Leavey and Ian McLeod (Stanford: Stanford University Press, 1995).
[3] *Liber de Causis*, prop. 6.
[4] A rough paraphrase of a saying often attributed to Augustine, though he nowhere says anything exactly as Eckhart quotes him here.

you arrive at a brute's stupidity . . . So if you do not wish to be brutish, do not understand God who is beyond words.[5]

Of course the obvious response of a determined atheist to so radical a theological negativity, this denial of all nameable divine essentiality, used to be that it can be no more than a strategy of theological evasion, a death of God by endless qualification, and that you might just as well be an atheist as maintain so extreme an apophaticism.[6] But it is a matter of some interest that this is not the response found in some of our radical deconstructionists, who less complacently – indeed, with some considerable anxiety – have been caused by the encounter with a Meister Eckhart or a pseudo-Denys to question the ultimate radicalness of their own atheistic deconstruction. For those who, since Nietzsche, had supposed their deconstruction to be as radical as is possible in consequence of its *atheism*, might indeed wonder whether they have not been outflanked in point of radicalness by the theism of a fourteenth-century Dominican friar. In any case, what degree of negativity, it may be asked, is available to be called upon whereby to negate so wholesale a denial as is already contained in Eckhart's theology?

For sure, the denials of the apophatic theologian exceed the reach of any such atheistical negation as proposes merely to excise God without consequences, that atheism which thinks it can do without God while leaving everything else in place – an inference which inevitably follows from the denial of that God whose existence had in any case had no consequences, the God we know of – stereotypically, but emblematically – as the 'deist' God of 'enlightenment rationalism', the God of 'modernity'.[7] But what unnerves the contemporary mind, for it problematises the *post*-modern project, is the thought that an authentically apophatic theology destabilises more radically than *any* atheistic denial can, even Nietzsche's.

Therefore, one is inclined to say what Marx had already suggested as early as 1844, that the issue between theism and atheism is as such an

[5] Sermon 83, *Renovamini Spiritu*, in *Meister Eckhart: The Essential Sermons, Commentaries, Treatises and Defense* (trans. and introd. Edmund Colledge and Bernard McGinn, New York: Paulist Press, 1981), pp. 206–7.

[6] As, for example, famously by Anthony Flew in *New Essays in Philosophical Theology*, A. Flew and A. MacIntyre, eds, (London: SCM Press, 1963), p. 97.

[7] The reader will have to forgive this appeal to a stereotype, which ought not to be taken seriously as anything but such, short of detailed critique of particular 'Enlightenment' theisms, e.g., those of Locke, or of Leibniz. Here, what is relevant about that stereotype lies in what today is being *rejected* by post-modern atheism, whether or not it has genuine historical instantiation, for as I shall go on to explain below, much of this atheism is so parasitical upon the theism it abandons as to be intelligible only in terms of what it imagines itself to be rejecting.

issue characteristic of *modernity*, an *issue* which it is necessary to surpass and deconstruct if modernity itself is to be surpassed and deconstructed.[8] Our problem, therefore, cannot, as Feuerbach thought, any longer be restated in terms of the disjunction between the existence and the non-existence of God, for it is not *atheism* which retrieves our cultures from the grip of modernity. Atheism leaves us trapped within the constraints of the modernist disjunctions, since it explores only the more nihilistic of the options it makes available. Our problem, therefore, consists in identifying that negation which is the 'negation of the negation' between theism and atheism, in identifying that ground which is opened up upon emancipation from that disjunction which is, if anything is, definitive of 'modernity' as such: theism and its negation.

I do not find it to be in the least paradoxical if, in the search for the form of negation which dissolves the theism/atheism project, pre-modern theological sources seem profitably to be explored. For, after all, a contemporary interest, whether of theological or of non-theological inspiration, in the dissolution of modernist theological disjunctions is at one level at least the same interest as was consciously intended to be served by much late medieval theological apophaticism: the dethronement of theological idolatries. What we can see – and seeing it differentiates our reception of those medieval apophaticisms from their authors' conscious intentions – is that there is as much idolatrous potential in *merely atheist negativity* as there is in *merely theistical affirmativity*, for again *eadem est scientia oppositorum*. Hence, our problem – and I mean, it is *everyone's* problem and not that of the 'theologian' alone – is to know how to negate the disjunction between atheism and theism – which you cannot claim to have done if thereby you merely fall prey to the atheist disjunct. In short, our problem is to know how to construct an apophatic theology distinguishable from the mere denial of theism.

That this might be more easily said than done may be illustrated by the following anecdote. Some years ago, and in younger, more foolhardy, days, finding myself in a tight spot in a public debate with a philosopher atheist at Bristol University, I made a wager with my audience: I would give anyone present five minutes to explain his or her reasons for atheism and if, after that, I could not guess correctly the Christian denomination

---

[8] See, K. Marx, *Early Writings* (trans. R Livingstone and George Benton, London: Penguin Books, 1975), pp. 357–8, where he says, '...the question of an *alien* being, a being above nature and man...has become impossible in practice. *Atheism*, which is the denial of this unreality, no longer has any meaning, for atheism is a *negation of God*, through which negation it asserts the *existence of man*. But socialism as such no longer needs such mediation...' (p. 358).

in which that person had been brought up, I would buy her a pint of beer. As luck would have it I was not broke at the subsequent revels, though in taking the risk I was backing the mere hunch that most philosophical, principled, not merely casual atheisms are the mirror-images of a theism; that they are recognisable from one another, because atheisms fall roughly into the same categories as the theisms they deny; that they are about as interesting as each other; and that since narrowly Catholic or Methodist or Anglican atheisms are no more absorbing than narrowly Catholic, Methodist or Anglican theisms, they do not exactly amount to an over-rich diet for the theologian.

A second proposition is capable of being related to the first and is that most atheists are but apophatic theologians *manqué*. Like the first, this proposition is in part a generalisation from experience, the sort of experience this time being represented by the rather curious phenomenon of an Anthony Flew, for example; this is the type who is a militant atheist on the one hand but on the other a stout critic of movements of change and renewal within Christianity, and so of the adoption of inclusive language, of the ordination of women, of ecumenism or of revisions to the Prayer Book. One might even suggest that atheists of this species resist any such renewal of Christian faith and practice as would require the renewal of their rejection of it. Indeed, it must be upsetting for atheists when the target of their rejections moves; for insofar as a moving Christian target does upset the atheist, it reveals, depressingly, the parasitical character of the rejection. So a static atheism can have no wish for a moving theism.

Of course the contrary proposition is, in some periods of Christian history, equally plausible. There are Christian theisms which are parasitical upon forms of atheism, for they formulate a doctrine of God primarily in response to a certain kind of grounds for atheistic denial. It is a case worth considering that much eighteenth-century theodicy has this parasitical character, being a theism designed to respond primarily to the threat to it posed by the particular formulation of the problem of evil which prevailed in that century. In our time, the ill-named 'creationists' seem to offer but a craven reaction, trapped as they are into having to deny the very possibility of an evolutionary world, simply because they mistakenly suppose an evolutionary world could only be occupied by atheists. Thereby they play the atheist's game, on the undemanding condition that they play on the losing team.

It goes without saying that such parasitical forms of theism are idolatrously reactive. They need a space for God and, since evolutionary biology, or historical evidence, or cosmology, occupy the space where they think God ought to be, they propose to clear the space of whatever, on their account, excludes God from it. And it is enough to propose an apophatic remedy of theological dieting in face of such Christian theologies – fundamentalisms – which are fat on what they can tell you about God, as if language about God provided some kind of rival explanatory account of that which science or history explains – necessarily therefore on all epistemological fours with one another, since, again, *eadem est scientia oppositorum*.

But the connection of the phenomenon of parasitical atheism with theological apophasis is more problematical. Far from rejecting too much from the Christian point of view, most philosophical atheists reject all too little. That is why their atheisms are generally lacking in theological interest. Atheism is often limited in interest because it is limited in its rejections. It is, as it were, an arrested apophaticism: in the sense in which atheists of this sort say God 'does not exist', a pseudo-Denys, a Thomas Aquinas and a Meister Eckhart are happy to agree. And if that is so, and if I am right that most atheisms are mirror-images of the theisms they abandon, the converse ought to be true, namely, that most atheisms are too limited in their negativity because most Christian theisms are too limited in their affirmativeness.

That, of course, starts a lot of hares, too many to be pursued in this essay, so let me retreat with renewed resolution into further naive paraphrase. An adequately apophatic theology has to be unremitting in its denials of theological language, for all talk about God is tainted with ultimate failure.[9] But this is because an adequate cataphatic theology has to be unremitting in its affirmations of theological language, for everything about the world tells us something of its creator. You cannot understand the role of the apophatic, or the extent to which it is necessary to go in denying things of God, until you have understood the role of the cataphatic and the extent to which it is necessary to go in affirming things of God. And the reason for this, as I see it, logical interdependence of the negative and the affirmative ways is not the true but trivial reason that *logically* until you have something to affirm you have nothing to negate. The reason is the more dialectically interesting one that it is in and through the very excess, the proliferation, of discourse about God that we discover its failure as a whole.

---

[9] Please note – because some reviewers of my book *The Darkness of God* (Cambridge: Cambridge University Press, 1995) have failed to do so – that to say that all talk about God is 'tainted with failure' is not to say that we can make no true affirmative statements about God. We can. But ultimately they fail, not of truth, but of God.

It would be appropriate here, but impossible, to explore in detail the fourth and fifth chapters of the *Mystical Theology* of that shadowy sixth-century Syrian theologian known as 'the pseudo-Denys';[10] for these last few remarks were meant as a sort of potted summary of them. But the matter can be put briefly in this way: for the pseudo-Denys the way of negation is not a sort of po-faced, mechanical process, as it were, of serial negation, affirmation by affirmation, of each thing you can say about God, as if affirmative statements about God were all false; nor is it, as in some late medieval Dionysian theologies, the tedious pedantry of simply adding the prefix 'super' to already superlative Latin adjectives predicated of God – the *Deus superoptimus* of a Denys the Carthusian; nor yet is it adequately expressed in the somewhat more contemporary partiality for austere metaphors of spiritual deserts, silences or mystical 'dark nights'. Rather, for the pseudo-Denys, the way of negation demands prolixity; it demands the maximisation, not the minimisation of talk about God; it demands that we talk about God in as many ways as possible, even in as many conflicting ways as possible, that we use up the whole stock-in-trade of imagery and discourse in our possession, so as thereby to discover ultimately the inadequacy of all of it, deserts, silences, dark nights and all.

Now all that linguistic stock-in-trade is creaturely in its reference. And this is a point worth noting. For it is a common belief among Christian theologians today that there is, as it were, a domain of human discourse which is specifically and distinctively 'religious', religious positively in that it is somehow especially privileged to be expressive of the divine; and 'religious' also by contrast with other, secular, discourses, such as those, perhaps, of politics, or science, or sex. Now the pseudo-Denys will have none of this. It is doubtful if he could have made sense of the idea of a 'religious' language as distinct from any other. Indeed, if anything he is rather more inclined to the opposite view that, since all language has an intrinsic creaturely reference, the more obviously inappropriate our language about God is, the less likely it is to seduce us into supposing its adequacy:[11] high-sounding 'religious' language can, he says, more easily mislead us into idolatrous anthropomorphisms than does, say, the Psalmist's description of God's moods as like those of a soldier with a hangover.[12] So for the pseudo-Denys theological language is at its best, is

[10] In *Pseudo-Dionysius, The Complete Works*, trans. Colm Luibheid (New Jersey: Paulist Press, 1987).
[11] *Celestial Hierarchy* 141A–B, Luibheid, *Pseudo-Dionysius*, pp. 152–3.
[12] *Mystical Theology*, 1033B, Luibheid, *Pseudo-Dionysius*, p. 139.

least misleading, when it is most concrete, imaginative, and even carnal.[13]
But if that is so, it will be only when the range and density of imagery
is maximised, when all the resources of human language are deployed,
that it is possible to do justice to the language-defeating reality of the
divine. As I say to my students, if you want to do theology well, then, for
God's sake get your metaphors as thoroughly mixed as you can.

The apophatic therefore presupposes the cataphatic 'dialectically' in
the sense that the silence of the negative way is the silence achieved only at
the point at which talk about God has been exhausted. The theologian is,
as it were, embarrassed into silence by her very prolixity, as in a seminar
one can be embarrassed into silence in the shameful realisation that one
had hogged the conversation and begun to babble beyond one's power
of understanding. Theology, one might say, is an *excess* of babble.

The apophatic and the cataphatic are therefore not, for Denys, independent theological strategies; nor are they to be set in opposition to
one another; nor do they fall into some given order of succession to one
another, in *either* order of priority. So it is not that, first, we are permitted
the naive and unself-critical indulgence of affirmation, subsequently to
submit that affirmation to a separate critique of negation. Nor is the
'way of negation' the way of simply saying nothing about God, nor yet
is it the way simply of saying that God is 'nothing'; it is the encounter
with the failure of what we must say about God to represent God adequately. If talk about God is deficient, this is a discovery made within
the extending of it into superfluity, into that excess in which it simply
collapses under its own weight. In the anarchy of that linguistic excess
theological language is discovered to be, in a phrase of Nicholas Lash's,
a 'broken language';[14] and somewhere, within that anarchy, the silence
which falls in the embarrassment of prolixity is transformed into awe; the
via negativa, as later Thomas Aquinas might have put it, is transformed
into the *via eminentiae*.

Our routine principled atheist knows none of this. She has, as it were,
but tinkered with negation – perhaps, it might be said, because of a
Christian experience which, or an experience of Christians who, have
but tinkered with affirmation. When I said that most atheists deny too
little about God it was because I was thinking of the pseudo-Denys saying

---

[13] *Divine Names*, 709B–713A, Luibheid, *Pseudo-Dionysius*, pp. 81–3.
[14] Nicholas Lash, *A Matter of Hope* (London: Darton, Longman and Todd, 1981), p. 144 – a
Christological statement implicitly, though for Bonaventure it is so explicitly: for him the
'brokenness' of Jesus on the Cross is the brokenness of all human discourse, a *transitus* into
the unknowability of the *Deus absconditus*.

that God is to be found only on the other side of *every possible* assertion and denial; and because I was thinking that Christians themselves need to be every kind of atheist possible in order to deny every kind of idolatry possible: for much atheism, as one knows it today, is but the negation of the limited features of a particular idolatry. And so we return to the question of how this, as I think we may call it, 'apophatic critique of idolatry' is related to our question: 'How is apophatic theology to be distinguished from deconstruction?'.

In pursuit of an answer to this question, let us therefore return to the pseudo-Denys. In those final two chapters of his *Mystical Theology* the pseudo-Denys describes a hierarchy of denials, denials, that is, of all the names of God. Those names, he says, form a ladder, ascending from the lowest 'perceptual' names – 'God is a rock, is immense, is light, is darkness . . . ' – derived as metaphors from material objects – to the very highest, 'proper' or 'conceptual' names of God – 'God is wise and wisdom, good and goodness, beautiful and beauty, exists and existence' – and all these names the pseudo-Denys negates one by one as he progresses up the scale of language until at the end of the work the last word is that all words are left behind in the silence of the apophatic. This ascending hierarchy of negations is, however, systematic, not just a sort of gung-ho scatter of negative shot: it is governed by a general theological principle and is regulated by a mechanism.

As to the general theological principle, the pseudo-Denys has already said earlier in *Mystical Theology*[15] what he had emphasised in *Divine Names*,[16] that all these descriptions denied are legitimate names of God, they give some positive idea of God. For being the cause of all God may be described in consequence by the names of all the things he has caused. Theological language, for the pseudo-Denys, therefore consists in a clamour of metaphor and description and if we must also deny all that speech then we must remember that those denials are themselves forms of speech; hence, if the divine reality transcends all our speech, then, as he says in the concluding words of *Mystical Theology*, 'the cause of all . . . is both beyond every assertion and beyond every denial'.[17] The point of the serial negations of the last two chapters of that work, therefore, is not to demonstrate, as some have supposed, that negative language is somehow superior to affirmative in the mind's ascent to God; rather it is to demonstrate that our language leads us to the reality of God when,

---

[15] *Mystical Theology*, 1033B, Luibheid, *Pseudo-Dionysius*, p. 139.
[16] *Divine Names*, 593C–D, Luibheid, *Pseudo-Dionysius*, p. 54.
[17] *Mystical Theology* 1048B, Luibheid, *Pseudo-Dionysius*, p. 141.

by a process simultaneously of affirming and denying all things of God, by, as it were in one breath, both affirming what God is and denying, as he puts it, 'that there is any kind of thing that God is',[18] we step off the very boundary of language itself, beyond every assertion and every denial, into the 'negation of the negation' and the 'brilliant darkness'[19] of God.

So much for the general principle of his apophaticism. As for the mechanism which governs this stepwise ascent of affirmation and denial, we may observe how that mechanism is itself a paradoxical conjunction of opposites: the ascent is, as I have said, an ordered hierarchical progression from denials of the lower to denials of the higher names, and yet at every stage on this ascent we encounter the same phenomenon of language slipping and sliding unstably, as the signifying name first appears to get a purchase on and then loses grip of the signified it designates. We may say legitimately, because the Bible says it, that 'God is a rock' and as we say the words they appear to offer a stable hold on the signified, God: we have said, have we not, something true of God, albeit by metaphor, and something of the divine reality is thereby disclosed – for something of God's reliability and stability is affirmed which even higher metaphors of God's vigorous life fail to declare, given the fecklessness and unreliability of the living beings of our experience. But just as we have let some weight hang from the grip of this word 'rock' on the being of God, the grip slips: God is not, of course, 'lifeless', as rocks are and we also have to say, since the Bible tells us we must, that the divine power holds sway over all things and only the most vigorously alive of beings could exercise such power; or that God is love and so must be possessed of intellect and will, and so must enjoy the highest form of life that we know of. Hence, in order to retain its grip on the signified, the signifier has to shift a step up the ladder of ascent there itself to be further destabilised. For God is not 'intelligence' or 'will' either, and the signified again wriggles away from the hook of the signifier and shifts and slides away, never, as we know, to be impaled finally on any descriptive hook we can devise, even that of existence. For in affirming 'God exists', what we say of God differs infinitely more from what we affirm when we say that 'Peter exists' than does 'Peter exists' from 'Peter does not exist.' Thus, the difference between Peter's existing and Peter's not existing is a created difference, and so finite. Whereas the difference between God's existing and Peter's existing is uncreated, and

---

[18] *Divine Names*, 817D, Luibheid, *Pseudo-Dionysius*, p. 98.
[19] *Mystical Theology* 997B, Luibheid, *Pseudo-Dionysius*, p. 135.

so infinite. Hence, any understanding we have of the distinction between existence and non-existence fails of God, which is why the pseudo-Denys can say 'It falls neither within the predicate of nonbeing nor of being'.[20] Mysteriously, the pseudo-Denys insists that we must deny of God that she is 'divinity';[21] more mysteriously still the signified eludes the hold even, as he puts it, of 'similarity and difference';[22] mysteriously, that is, until we remind ourselves that of course God cannot be different from, nor therefore similar to anything at all, at any rate in any of the ways in which we can conceive of similarity and difference: or else God would be just another, different, thing. Just so, for the pseudo-Denys: for 'there is no kind of thing', he says, 'which God is'.[23] Therefore, there is nothing we can say which describes what God is.

That said, might it not seem necessary to conclude, not, now, that deconstruction is necessarily atheistical but, on the contrary, that deconstruction has been so reduced to theology that theology itself has simply disappeared into deconstruction, into a sort of meta-rhetoric of the ultimacy of postponement, the divine 'defined' by the impossibility of definition, destabilising therefore *all* possibility of definition; characterised as the one, as Eckhart was to put it in the fourteenth century, which alone is not countable, thereby subverting *all* ostension; as the 'other', as Nicholas of Cusa was to put it in the fifteenth century, which alone is not and cannot be contained by our categories of otherness and difference, *so* 'other' as to be *non-Aliud* – the one and only 'not-Other' – thereafter reducing *all* alterity to indeterminacy? It is not surprising that, having read such extremes of apophaticism into the pseudo-Denys, Eckhart and Nicholas of Cusa, Jacques Derrida was in the end prepared to accept a certain symmetry between negative theology and his deconstruction, but only on condition that negative theology was thus reduced to a post-metaphysical rhetoric of *différance* from which is excised any residue of 'hyperessentiality', any residual appeal to an *existent* 'other', held in reserve at the back of endless 'deferral', thus, surreptitiously to effect a secret, and metaphysically theistic, 'closure'. But this Derridean wholesale deconstruction of theological metaphysics, this concession to a 'theology' which *is* the ultimate agent deconstructive of metaphysical theism, is in fact unrecognisable in the mirror of medieval apophaticism, and I turn next to the negative theologies of two thirteenth-century

---

[20] *Mystical Theology*, 1048A, Luibheid, *Pseudo-Dionysius*, p. 141.
[21] *Mystical Theology* 1048A, Luibheid, *Pseudo-Dionysius*, p. 141.
[22] Ibid.   [23] *Divine Names*, 817D, Luibheid, *Pseudo-Dionysius*, p. 98.

contemporaries – indeed, two friends – the Franciscan Bonaventure and the Dominican Thomas Aquinas, to see why.

Bonaventure's *Itinerarium Mentis in Deum*[24] provides in the middle ages one of two conceptually and theologically complex models for construing the relationships between the apophatic and cataphatic moments in theological speech, and his is a distinctly incarnational, indeed, a distinctly Christological model. For in that work we find a complex interweaving of at least three strands of theological tradition. First, his own Franciscan piety and devotion, which places centrally within Christian thought and practice the human nature of Christ, but very particularly the passion of Christ. Secondly, a rampantly affirmative theology of exemplarism, in which, in classically medieval dionysian style, he constructs a hierarchy of 'contemplations' of God, beginning from the lowest *vestigia* in material objects, upwards and inwards to our perception of them, through the *imagines* of God in the human soul, especially in its highest powers, further 'upwards' and beyond them to 'contemplations' through the highest concepts of God, 'existence' and 'goodness'. In just such an ascending hierarchy constructed in the first six chapters of the *Itinerarium* does Bonaventure construe the whole universe as the 'book of creation' in which its author is spoken and revealed; all of which theological affirmativeness is resumed in the human nature of Christ, only there no longer is it merely the passive 'book of creation' in which the Godhead can be read, but now the 'Book of Life', who actively works our redemption and salvation.

But in the transition from the first six chapters of the *Itinerarium* to the seventh Bonaventure effects, thirdly, a powerfully subversive theological *transitus*, from all the affirmativeness with which creation in one way, and Christ in another, speak God, to a thoroughgoing negative theology. For beyond the knowing of God is the unknowing of God; nor is this 'unknowing' merely 'beyond': through the increasing intensity and complexity of its internal contradictoriness this knowing *leads to* the unknowing. As one might say, the very superfluity of the affirmativeness sustained by the books of creation and of Life collapses into the silence of the apophatic: and chapter 7 consists in little but a string of quotations from the more apophatic sayings of the *Mystical Theology* of the pseudo-Denys. But the organising symbolism of that theological *transitus* from the visibility of the Godhead in Christ to the unknowability

---

[24] In Philotheus Boehner and M. Frances Loughlin, eds., *The Works of St Bonaventure*, vol. II (New York: The Franciscan Institute, 1956).

of the Godhead brings Bonaventure back to his Franciscan starting point; for that *transitus* is also effected through Christ – more to the point, through the passion and death of Christ. For in that catastrophe of destruction, in which the humanity of Christ is brought low, is all the affirmative capacity of speech subverted: thus it is that through the drama of Christ's life on the one hand and death on the other, through the recapitulation of the symbolic weight and density of creation in his human nature on the one hand, and its destruction on the Cross on the other, is the complex interplay of affirmative and negative fused and concretely realised. In Christ, therefore, is there not only the visibility of the Godhead, but also the invisibility: if Christ is the Way, Christ is, in short, our access to the *un*knowability of God, not so as ultimately to know it, but so as to be brought into participation with the *Deus absconditus* precisely as *unknown*.

Thomas' theology is no less 'incarnational' than Bonaventure's, nor is this incarnational character of his theology combined with any less radical an apophaticism. Like Bonaventure, Thomas was deeply suspicious of over-zealous negativities, of theological negations unsecured in the affirmation of human, carnal, worldly experience. Moreover, like Bonaventure, Thomas was happy to anchor the negative, apophatic 'moment' of his theology in just the same secure bedrock in which is anchored the affirmative, incarnational moment: for both, what we *must* say about God and the fact that all that we say about God fails of God derive with equal force from the same necessities of thought, and converge in equal measures, in a sort of 'two-sidedness' of theological speech, speech which Michael Sells has so aptly described as a 'language of unsaying'.[25] Nonetheless, in this Bonaventure and Thomas also differ: for whereas for Bonaventure, this two-sidedeness of theological speech is rooted primordially in the unity of the two natures of Christ, and achieved concretely in the paradox of the passion and death of Jesus, for Thomas, the most primitive access of the human mind to this duality of affirmative and negative theologies is already given to us, in some inchoate sort, in our very created, rational power to know and experience our world. That world, which shows God to us, at the same time shows God to be beyond our comprehension.

Here, then, we turn to a question concerning that proposition which most sets Thomas' theology apart from the anti-metaphysical and anti-rational temper of our philosophical and theological times, the question

---

[25] Michael A. Sells, *Mystical Languages of Unsaying* (Chicago: University of Chicago Press, 1994).

of what those arguments for the existence of God are doing at the beginning of his *Summa Theologiae*, the so-called 'five ways'. They relate to our concerns, as I see it, because they are Thomas' account of the most *primitive* and rudimentary, the most *indirect* starting point of the human mind's route to God, and, at face value, the least obvious and promising of an apophatic theology. They are the least promising starting points because those proofs begin from what it would seem we are most likely to be distracted from God by, because it is what we would be most tempted to reduce God idolatrously to: the things of sense, bodily, material, worldly realities, the sphere of our human distinctiveness, which is the sphere of the *rational*. Nonetheless it is there, Thomas thinks, where all human knowledge begins anyway, so that there is, for him, a sense in which the possibility of deriving knowledge of God in any other way is dependent upon the possibility of deriving knowledge of God from this starting point.

But as everyone knows, the presence of these arguments at the outset of his massive theological construction so embarrasses contemporary theologians, even those otherwise glad to embrace Thomas' influence, that much energy and ingenuity gets spent in seeking to show that they are not, and are not intended as, formal *proofs* of the existence of God at all, not vehicles of a rational access to God achieved independently of faith, but are rather, as John Milbank has said recently, but 'weakly probable modes of argument and very "attenuated" showings',[26] which possess such power as they have to 'show' God only insofar as they already *presuppose* reason's participation by the gift of faith in the divine perfection. Contemporary friends of Thomas are embarrassed by these arguments if read as self-standing rational *proofs* because, so understood, they would indicate some sort of pre-critical commitment on Thomas' part to the possibility of a natural theology – to a purely 'rational' and pre-theological knowledge of God, such as are thought to be (since Kant we are all quite sure of it) a logical and epistemological impossibility. But worse than that, placed as they are at the very outset of Thomas' theological exposition, their presence would, it is thought, indicate a commitment by Thomas to an unacceptable form of theological 'foundationalism', which would place some metaphysical 'God of being', and therefore of ultimate 'oneness' – this, since Heidegger, has acquired the inelegant name of 'ontotheology' – in place of primacy before, and as underpinning to, the God of Jesus Christ, the Trinitarian God of Father, Son and

[26] John Milbank, 'Intensities' in *Modern Theology*, 15:4 (October, 1999), p. 455.

Holy Spirit. Thus, for example, Professor Colin Gunton[27] for the one part, and Professor Jean-Luc Marion[28] for the other. For both, Thomas' doctrine of God is ridden with monist and metaphysical infection, and the virus which carries it is natural theology.

It is possible that a Thomist camp-follower of a rather a prioristic cast of mind might offer a defence of a moderate form of rationalist foundationalism, thinking it reasonable to suppose that a Christian theology, whether properly focused on the Incarnation, or on the Trinity, or on creation, or on any other Christian doctrine, would still have to set out first *some* account of what God is, some conceptual presuppositions, some minimal regulative criteria governing what would count as talking about *God* when you are talking about the Incarnation, or the Trinity, or creation. You might particularly suppose this to be necessary if you reflect upon the naivety of the assumption which appears to underlie, for example, Gunton's polemic against Aquinas, who, Gunton supposes, *cannot* be talking about the Christian God when, in the *Summa Theologiae*, he prefaces his discussion of the Trinity and creation with a philosophically derived account of the existence and nature of God as 'one'; whereas he, Gunton, *can* be guaranteed to be talking about the Christian God *just because* he explains creation in trinitarian terms. In this theological naivety, Gunton appears not to be alone. Christians commonly tell us, rightly, that the God of Christian faith is the triune God; from which they appear to derive the complacent conclusion that *just because* they talk of the Trinity they could not be talking about anything other than God. But no such consequence follows, and if nothing else shows it, Feuerbach's *Essence of Christianity* ought to serve as a warning against such complacent assumptions, for there he demonstrates quite plausibly that it is possible to extend your 'theology' over the whole range of Christian doctrines and practices – the Trinity, the Incarnation, the Church, the sacraments, even devotion to the Virgin Mary – and to preserve every manner of Christian theological jot and tittle in the exposition of them, *but entirely as translated out in terms of the human,* by the simple device of inverting, as he puts it, subject and predicate.[29] Thereby he demonstrates, to put it in Christian terms, the possibility of a purely idolatrous theological exposition of the

---

[27] Colin Gunton, *The Triune Creator: A Historical and Systematic Study* (Edinburgh: Edinburgh University Press, 1998), pp. 99ff.

[28] Jean-Luc Marion, *God Without Being*, trans. Thomas A Carlson (Chicago and London: University of Chicago Press, 1991).

[29] Ludwig Feuerbach, *The Essence of Christianity* (trans. George Eliot, New York: Harper Torchbooks, 1957), pp. 17ff.

entire resource of Christian belief and practice, in which, in the guise of the soundest doctrinal orthodoxies, the Christian theologian but worships his own nature, in the reified form of 'God'. And if Feuerbach fails to persuade everyone of this possibility, Jesus might succeed with some: not everyone, he once said, who cries, 'Lord, Lord' is worthy of the kingdom of heaven (Matt. 7:21).

It might therefore be thought that it is in view of such considerations that Thomas, when asking what is the formal object of *sacra doctrina*, dismisses the obvious answer that it is the study of central Christian doctrines, such as the sacraments, or redemption of Christ as person and as Church, since those and other such doctrines give you the *material* object of *sacra doctrina* but not its *formal* object: that answer, he says, would be like trying to define sight in terms of the things that you can see – human beings, stones or whatever – instead of things *qua* visible, that is, *as coloured*. The *formal* object of *sacra doctrina* is rather, he says, all those things revealed to us through Jesus Christ, but specifically *sub ratione Dei*: either because they *are* about God, or because they have a relation to God as their origin and end: *unde sequitur quod Deus vere sit subiectum huius scientiae*.[30]

If that is so, then we need to know what would count as the consideration of the Christian revelation *sub ratione Dei* – as distinct, therefore, from a consideration of the same content of that revelation in the manner of a Feuerbach, *sub ratione hominis*; and, as I have said, a certain kind of aprioristic mentality might suppose that this is a conceptual matter which needs to be settled by a pre-theological definition, and, if pre-theological, then necessarily by a *philosophical* definition; and by a philosophical argument which establishes that the definition is instantiated – and thus proves the existence of the God so defined. This, if we could take it to be Thomas' opinion, would explain and lend credence to that account of his theological procedure which in different ways so worries the theological Guntons and Marions, and causes in them such suspicions of ontotheology, whereby after a preliminary discussion of theological method in the first question, Thomas engages in the *Summa Theologiae* in no less than twenty five questions – some 149 articles – in 'natural theology' *before* he gets round to even preliminary discussions of the Trinity. It is as if the necessity of establishing what would count as the *ratio Dei* before doing properly Christian theology, and as a regulative criterion of when we are doing it, requires proofs, as the first Vatican Council puts it, 'by the natural light of reason' of the existence of God, and then of

---

[30] *Summa Theologiae*, 1a q1 a7 *corp.*

his attributes.[31] Moreover, once you have supposed that that is Thomas' procedure, it would come naturally to mind that it is *that* 'necessity of faith' which the first Vatican council had in mind when it decreed it to be a dogma of faith that such proofs are naturally available to us.

But any reader of Thomas' *Summa Theologiae* who supposed that that was his procedure would be mightily puzzled by what she read in the course of the argument of those twenty five questions. First, because Thomas sets about demonstrating the existence of God without giving even preliminary thought – not to dignify what he omits with the denomination 'heuristic' – to the definition of God. In fact, the reader will be at a loss to find *any* 'definition' of God anywhere at all, even were he to read right through to the end of the *Summa*. All he appears to say on this matter, at any point, is immediately at the end of each of the five ways, when he says, with demotic optimism (and to the dissatisfaction of most readers today) that the prime mover, the first efficient cause and the necessary being and the rest, are 'what all people call God'[32] – exactly the proposition which Gunton is pleased to contest in the name of his Trinitarian priorities. Secondly, because when, immediately after his discussion of whether God exists, Thomas does appear to set about the more formal discussion of what it is that he might have proved the existence of, he tells us flatly that there is no definition to be had, for *there can be no answer to the question of what God is*, but only of what God is not. 'Once you know whether something exists', he says,

it remains to consider how it exists, so that we may know of it what it is. But since we cannot know of God what he is, but [only] what he is not, we cannot inquire into the how of God ['s existence], but only into how he is not. So, first we must consider this 'how God is not', secondly, how he is known by us, thirdly, how he is spoken of.[33]

That said, the reader will be further puzzled by the fact that, nonetheless, Thomas then proceeds for a further nine questions to discuss what, on

---

[31] 'If anyone says that the one, true God, our creator and lord, cannot be known with certainty from the things that have been made, by the natural light of reason: let him be anathema', *Dogmatic Constitution on the Catholic Faith*, canon 2.1 *On Revelation*, in Norman P. Tanner, *Decrees of the Ecumenical Councils*, vol. 2, *Trent to Vatican II* (London: Sheed and Ward, 1990), p. 810.

[32] *ST*, 1a q2 a3, *corp*. By the way: 'et hoc omnes dicunt Deum' is probably best translated as 'and this is what all people refer to by the name "God"' – which does not necessarily entail, still less does it necessarily mean, 'this is *how* all people refer to God'. So it is rather beside the point to observe that hardly anyone ever refers to God by the names 'prime mover', 'necessary being' and so forth. It is perfectly obvious that Thomas knew *that*. What he means is: 'this is what people are talking about when they talk about the Trinity, or the Incarnate Word or anything else theological'; in short, 'this is what it means to talk of these things *sub ratione Dei*'.

[33] *Summa Theologiae*, 1a q3 prol.

most accounts, will be considered classical attributes of God – his simplicity, perfection, goodness, infinity, ubiquity, immutability and unity – as if thereby ignoring what he has just said and supplying us with what to many will appear to be a quite unproblematised account of God's multiple 'whatnesses'. And as if that were not bad enough, after first telling us that we can only know what God is not, he then says that, once he has shown that, he will go on to tell us how God is, after all, known and spoken of – a case, we might imagine, of knowing the unknowable, of describing the indescribable, or perhaps of throwing your cake away in order to eat it. Something is badly wrong here: either, on this way of reading what Thomas' theological method is, he is plainly muddled and unredeemably inconsistent, or, if consistent, then some other way of reading his method will have to be found.

It is charitable at least to *try* for a consistent Thomas. Nor is it difficult. Nothing is easier, to begin with, than to see that, in his discussion of the divine simplicity in question three, what is demonstrated is not some comprehensible divine attribute, some *affirmation* which marks out God from everything else, but some marker of what constitutes the divine *in*comprehensibility, as distinct from the incomprehensibility of everything else. For what Thomas recognises to be in need of determination about the *ratio Dei* – that which in some way is criterial for speaking of God's otherness as distinct from all secondary, created othernesses – is the precise nature of *God's* incomprehensibility, lest it be mistaken for that more diffused and general sense of the mysteriousness with which we are in any case confronted within and by our own created universe – for there is puzzlement enough in creatures. 'You do not know the nature of God', he seems to say. 'You know only the divine unknowability.' But all the same, there is a job to be done of determining that the 'unknowability' you may have got to in your contemplation of the world is in truth the *divine* unknowability – as distinct, for example, from simply giving up on seeking to know at some lesser point of ultimacy. For *penultimate* unknowability is always idolatrous. 'Giving up' at the point of penultimate unknowability is exactly what Bertrand Russell once recommended when, confronted by Frederick Copleston with the question 'Why is there something rather than nothing?' he urged us to be content with no answer at all, to be satisfied that the world is 'just there', and to deny that the question can make sense.[34] For Thomas, on the contrary, we are constrained to acknowledge that, in the very form of that question, 'Why is there something rather

[34] See *The Existence of God* (ed. John Hick, London: Macmillan, 1964), p. 175.

than nothing?', we are confronted not with a mere passive ignorance of an inert facticity, but with the divine creative causality which *must* be incomprehensible to us. The question 'Why is there something rather than nothing?' is after all intelligible enough to us, for we can *ask* it out of our own native resources of creaturely cognitive capacity. As Geach points out, 'cause of . . . ' has an earthly sense, comprehensible to us; so does ' . . . every mutable thing'. But the question which conjoins them: 'What is the cause of every mutable thing?', must bear an answer, but one which, demonstrably, is incomprehensible to us: we know that we *could not know* the nature of what it refers to.[35] So what the five ways prove – I will allow that you can doubt if they succeed, but not that they are intended as anything less than proofs – is *simultaneously* the existence of and the unknowability of God. But only such demonstrated unknowability deserves the name 'God'; which is why Thomas says that what is thus shown is what all people call by that name.

Now the argument for the divine simplicity in *Prima pars*, question three, is designed to demonstrate the precise 'how' of that ultimate divine 'otherness' so that we could not confuse that divine otherness with any lesser, created form of otherness. In fact, of course, in thus demonstrating God's otherness to be ultimate he thereby demonstrates that otherness itself to be the source of that *divine* unknowability which surpasses all other unknowability: not only can we not know the how of God's existence, so other is it; so 'other' is God, that the very concept of otherness has, in respect of God, itself lost its threads of straightforward continuity with any conception of created otherness which we do know the how of. We do not know, therefore, how 'other' God is: which is why Thomas is at one with the pseudo-Denys when he says that, at the climax of ascending scales of God's differences from all else, God must be thought of as off *every* scale of sameness and difference and thus to be beyond 'every assertion . . . beyond every denial'.[36] So it follows: if you want to know what the *ratio Dei* is, that standpoint from which your speech about God is marked out as properly *theological*, then the answer is: you know you are talking about God when all your theological talk – whether it is *materially* about the Trinity, or the Incarnation, or the presence of Christ within Church or sacrament, or about grace, or the Spirit in history, or the manner of our redemption – is demonstrably ultimate, when, through the grace of revelation, we are led *deeper* than we otherwise might be, into

[35] P. T. Geach, 'Causality and Creation' in *God and the Soul* (London: Routledge and Kegan Paul, 1969), p. 81.
[36] Pseudo-Denys, *Mystical Theology* 5, 1048A.

the unknowability of the Godhead. We might not have supposed this. We might have supposed, as many late medieval opponents of Thomas clearly did, that reason's 'failure' lies not in its encounter with the divine unknowability itself, but derives rather from the impossibility in principle of unaided human reason's reaching out as far as the divine unknowability at all. The pagan philosophers, Jean Gerson thought, knew not the true apophatic unknowing of the Christian; they espoused Socratic ignorance out of the mere frustrations of an exhausted natural intellect.[37] Some Christians today, however, can imagine the opposite: that apophatic theology is a pagan, neoplatonic, merely philosophical thing and that they are better informed than the natural philosophers are about God, for Christians have been given the revelation of the Trinity in Jesus Christ. But not so, either way, for Thomas, his thought here converging on Bonaventure's: indeed Christians *do* know better by grace and revelation, but only so as to be inserted participatively into a darkness of God which is deeper than it could possibly be for the pagan, who can only *think* this unknowability, as it were, from outside it and cannot be drawn into a sharing in its nature as love, so as to share it in friendship with God. It is a darkness, therefore, which for the Christian is deepened, not relieved by the Trinity, intensified by the Incarnation, not dispelled. For which reason, he says:

> ... in this life we do not know what God is [*even*] *through the revelation of grace*, and so [by grace] we are made one with him as to something unknown.[38]

It is just because Thomas can see no conflict between the defence in principle of a rational demonstration of the existence of God and a through-going incarnational apophaticism – what shows God to exist is not other than what shows that existence to be unknowable – that he can resist with equanimity on the one hand any temptation to reduce his apophaticism to a mere meta-rhetoric while, on the other, eschewing any such rationalistic foundationalism as would reduce faith to the status of a mere adjunct to a rational theism. His position appears to be that, broadly, of the Fathers of the first Vatican Council, who maintained that

---

[37] 'I am much mistaken if it is not an obvious truth about the greatest philosophers, that, after all their enquiries, they declared in weariness of spirit, their labours having done nothing to refresh them, that the one thing they knew was that they did not know' [Fallor si non apparuit in maximis philosophis, qui post omnes inquisitiones suos tedio affecti, quia non refecti, dixerunt hoc unum se scire quod nichil scirent], Jean Gerson, *De mystica theologia, Tractatus Speculativus*, 1.34, 15–17.

[38] '... per revelationem gratiae in hac vita non cognoscamus de Deo quid est, et sic ei quasi ignoto coniungamur...' *ST*, 1a q12 a13 ad1.

it is a matter of *faith* that the existence of God is demonstrable 'by the natural light of reason'; for if that were not so, if there were no native human capacity to recognise when human talk is talk about *God*, then there could be no explanation of how what is revealed could be intelligible to us at all. This is no place to defend the validity of Thomas' 'five ways' as proofs. But it is worth noting that when contemporary deconstructionists observe themselves in the mirror of medieval apophaticism, it is, paradoxically, in the neo-platonic mirrors of a pseudo-Denys or an Eckhart or a Nicholas of Cusa, not as reflected in Thomas Aquinas, that they see some reflection of themselves; and it is worth asking why this is so.

For there is one major difference, instantly observable, between Eckhart and Thomas, which we could very well put down simply to a difference of *style and imagery*, were it not for the fact that that difference of style and imagery derives from a difference of another kind, much more fundamental than the first, which indicates what is very nearly – or perhaps it is – a conflict of theological truth-claims.

The difference of style and imagery is obvious: years ago Oliver Davies pointed to the significance of rhetorical features of Eckhart's theology, features which are, of course, more prominent in the vernacular sermons – naturally enough, since they *are* sermons, but by no means absent from his more technical, Latin treatises. As Davies says, Eckhart's theology is a sort of 'poetic metaphysics', in which, as in all poetry, there is a certain 'foregrounding' of the language itself, of the signifier;[39] and, one might add, this 'poeticisation' of theological discourse goes along with a certain rhetorical 'performativeness', or, as one might say, a quasi-sacramental character. For it is a characteristic of Eckhart's language that it does not merely *say* something: it is intended to *do* something by means of *saying*, in fact to do precisely what it says; and on the classical medieval account, that is exactly the nature of a sacrament: it is 'a sacred sign which effects what it signifies'.

When, therefore, we note the obvious, but otherwise apparently incidental, fact of the extreme negativity of Eckhart's theological language – saturated as it is with images of nothingnesses and abysses, by the featurelessness of deserts and ground, and by nakedness and emptiness – we can begin to see what is going on in a passage such as this:

Then how should I love God? You should love God unspiritually, that is, your soul should be unspiritual and stripped of all spirituality, for so long as your soul has a spirit's form, it has images, and so long as it has images, it has a medium,

39 Oliver Davies, *Meister Eckhart: Mystical Theologian* (London: SPCK, 1991), p. 180.

and so long as it has a medium, it is not unity or simplicity. Therefore your soul must be unspiritual, free of all spirit, and must remain spiritless; for if you love God as he is God, as he is spirit, as he is person and as he is image – all this must go! 'Then how should I love him?' You should love him as he is nonGod, a nonspirit, a nonperson, a nonimage, but as he is pure, unmixed, bright 'One', separated from all duality; and in that One we should eternally sink down, out of 'something' into 'nothing'.[40]

Here, the apophaticism of his theology is no mere formal, second-order, epistemological principle policing the boundaries of the sayable, it is a living, organising feature of the language itself, a *praxis* of negativity which is intrinsic at once to its compositional style and to his theological purposes. It is as if Eckhart were trying to pack the whole paradox-ical nature of the medieval apophatic project as such (it is at once a *language*, but 'a language *of unsaying*') into the language itself, so that it both directly says and as directly unsays in the one act of saying. Thereby the language *performs rhetorically* what it says technically. Or, to put it rather more crudely, it is as if he were trying to bully the apophatic into the picture by means of trope alone. And this rhetorical strategy, as it were of forcing into the sensuous, material sign the character of its own self-transcendence-in-failure as signifier, is what accounts for that most characteristic feature of Eckhart's language: its strained and strenuous, hyperactively apophatic nimiety. The language, naturally, bursts at the seams under the pressure of the excessive forces it is made to contain: it cracks open in order never again to 'close' on anything. For God is not a thing.

The contrast with the sobriety of Aquinas' theological discourse could not be more marked. If Thomas can understate the case, he will seize the opportunity to do so. If a thought can be got, as it were, to speak for itself he will do as little as necessary to supplement it. But this economy of speech accompanies, and probably derives from, a fundamental con-fidence in theological speech, a trust that our ordinary ways of talking about God are fundamentally *in order*, needing only to be subordinated to a governing apophaticism, expressed as an epistemological principle. Once we know that the very materiality and carnality of our speech about God is that which reveals itself to *our created and carnal rationality* as *created*, then we know both that that speech of creatures is predicable of the creator and that all such speech about God fails anyway; hence we can freely indulge the materiality of those metaphors, the carnality

---

[40] *Sermon 83, Renovamini Spiritu*, in *Meister Eckhart* (trans. and ed. Colledge and McGinn), p. 208.

of that imagery, calmly exploit all those possibilities of formal inference and logic, which appear so to unnerve the anxious Eckhart. Why this difference in theological temperament and style?

I think for this reason. Eckhart, as I have said, wants to constrain all the paradoxical tensions of the theological project into each and every theological speech-act, so that it is *the language itself* which is the bearer of those contrary forces of saying and unsaying, of affirmativeness and negativity, and so his discourse must be got endlessly to destabilise itself in paradox piled upon oxymoron. And Eckhart must in this way compel the rhetorical dimension of his discourse to do all the work of theology, because he has, in effect, abandoned that theological task which to Thomas seemed so fundamental to theological construction, that of *demonstrating* that our creaturely discourse about God can name God by all the names by which we name creatures, so that, as long as we know what we are doing, rooted as we are in our creatureliness, we can safely do theology *sub ratione Dei*. And we know what we are doing when we speak thus confidently of God, because that same theological act by which theological speech is shown to be *justified*, also shows that the God thus demonstrated lies, in unutterable otherness, beyond the reach of absolutely everything we can say. So, unlike Eckhart, there is in Thomas no need to try to say it, no overburdened, overcompensating negativity, no theologically motivated *fear of the sign*. For Thomas, theological speech is at once incarnated and apophatic speech, speech rooted in our common material condition and yet revelatory of that utterly unknowable reality which sustains that condition *as created*. To put it in yet other words, you reach down into the depths of creaturely reality precisely insofar as that reality reveals itself to us as *created*. Indeed, for Thomas, those ultimate, and ultimately mysterious, depths of creaturely reality – what he calls its *esse* – consists in its being created: as we might say, *esse creaturae est creari*, and knowledge of *that* is our knowledge of God.

I hesitate to conclude, as it occurred to me I might, that, by contrast, Eckhart's theology is 'all rhetoric', postmodern. But if it is possible to be misled about his purposes, as not only some of his contemporaries were, into suspecting a certain, paradoxical, 'hypostatisation' of the negative, a certain reduction of theology to a rhetoric of postponement, it is at least partly his own fault – but, if a fault, then it is precisely in that deficiency that he reflects the image most appealing to the anti-metaphysical instinct of our contemporary deconstructions. Thomas, by contrast, sits ill to our contemporary debates, since he is a metaphysician, but not one as offering what Heidegger rejects, a defender of natural theology, but not of 'theodicy', a theist who knows nothing of 'deism', an apophaticist whose negativity is rooted in rational foundations, and a rationalist whose conception of reason is as distanced from that of the Enlightenment as it is possible to be. As such, perhaps his position has the potential to loosen the grip of those antinomies of rationalism and irrationalism, modernity and post-modernity, foundationalism and anti-foundationalism, perhaps even of theism and atheism, which so constrain the philosophies and theologies of our day. In any case, what can be said is that if you want to be an Eckhartian, and say, as he does, that 'you should love God as he is nonGod', then you had better be a Thomist first, lest it be said of you with justice, as Scotus said of other over-enthusiastic apophaticists of his time, *negationes . . . non summe amamus*,[41] which, roughly paraphrased, means: you cannot love a mere postponement.

[41] *Ordinatio*, 1 d3 q2, *Doctoris subtilis et mariani Ioannis Duns Scoti Opera Omnia* III, ed. P. Carolus Balic, Vatican: Typis Polyglottis Vaticanis, 1954, p. 5. At least I suppose Scotus had others in mind, and certainly he cannot have been responding to Eckhart's sermon, which long post-dates Scotus' death. It is quite possible, however, that Scotus attended, or if not, read, Eckhart's disputations in Paris (known as the 'Parisian Questions') for both were in Paris in 1302 when they were conducted.

2

The quest for a place which is 'not-a-place': the hiddenness of God and the presence of God

Paul S. Fiddes

THE HIDDENNESS OF WISDOM

'But where shall wisdom be found?
And where is the place of understanding?'

This question, placed in the mouth of the unfortunate Job (Job 28:12), appears to be an enquiry about a particular place where wisdom might be located. Likewise the answer, 'Mortals do not know the way to it (v. 13)', appears on first sight to be a denial of entrance to this mysterious place, and since it is divine wisdom which is in view the questioner is also apparently faced by the remoteness of God. Human beings are, it seems, confronted by an absolute transcendence excluding them from the dwelling-place of God's wisdom, which is nothing less than a dimension of the divine personality. Only 'God understands the way to it' (v. 23). However, we shall see that the question 'where shall wisdom be found?' is in fact a riddle, and the answer is both surprising and playful as all riddles are. It is not a mere piece of rhetoric, expecting the answer 'nowhere by human beings' or 'in heaven with God'. Wisdom is certainly hidden, but the solution to the riddle is more positive, though cautionary, pointing us towards a 'place' which is not literally a place at all.[1]

In this essay I want to show that this quest for a 'not-a-place'[2] offers an important clue to the nature of the presence of a God who is hidden, but

---

[1] For this idea in more detail, see my essay '"Where Shall Wisdom be Found?" Job 28 as a Riddle for Ancient and Modern Readers', in John Barton and David Reimer (eds.), *After the Exile. Essays in Honour of Rex Mason* (Macon: Mercer University Press, 1996), pp. 171–90; also see my unpublished D.Phil. thesis, 'The Hiddenness of Wisdom in the Old Testament and Later Judaism' (University of Oxford, 1976).

[2] This is a literal translation of 'Utopia', and the human quest for a Utopia has in fact some affinities with the quest I am examining here. In the play of words first made by Sir Thomas More in his seminal account of the imaginary island of Utopia (1515), the *Utopia* (no-place) is also a *Eutopia* (good place). I work out further the concept of 'place' with regard to utopias and eschatology in my book, *The Promised End. Eschatology in Theology and Literature* (Oxford: Blackwell, 2000), chs. 8–9.

not absent and inaccessible. Moreover, since the Christology of the New Testament is quite largely based on Old Testament wisdom material, I believe that the reason why wisdom is thought to be hidden in this literature throws a good deal of light on the way that Jesus Christ is thought to incarnate and disclose the nature of the invisible God (John 1:18).

First we should observe, however, that the perplexity of the wisdom scribes of Ancient Israel, as expressed in Job's question, has some affinity with the 'postmodern' mood of today. 'Wisdom' in Job 28 stands both for the divine wisdom with which God created the cosmos (vv. 25–7) and for the human wisdom with which created beings explore and master it, opening up paths of discovery above and below the earth (vv. 1–11). The question 'where shall wisdom be found?' thus expresses a sense of elusiveness about naming the world, about the self as subject over against the world, and about God as the foundation for this sapiential activity. Correspondingly, the background to this mood of uncertainty has some similarity with the project of the Enlightenment against which the postmodern mood is reacting.

In the wisdom enterprise of the Ancient Near East, including Israel, the wise observe the events and objects of the world in order to find patterns of meaning, to establish regularities that can offer guidance to those who are willing to listen to their teaching. They make lists of phenomena, find analogies between things (A is like B), and especially note sequences of cause and effect so that they can 'steer' their way through the maze of life with the confidence that 'if you do A then B usually follows'. There are obvious affinities here with the approach to the world of modernity, promoted by Enlightenment confidence about the thinking human subject and its ability to control a world treated as an object of observation. However, there was a critical difference between the ancient and modern eras, in that from the beginning the wisdom movement seems to have recognised limits to human skills, often associated with the phrase 'the fear of the Lord'.

The wisdom sayings in the Book of Proverbs show us, I suggest, that this sense of limit is rooted in the complexity of the phenomena confronting the wise.[3] Their caution does not derive, as has often been proposed, from any anxiety about divine intervention or unpredictable divine activity in the world.[4] Rather, the wise are aware of the incalculabilities that arise out of the very material they are dealing with.

---

[3] See further, Fiddes, '"Where Shall Wisdom be Found"?', pp. 183–8.
[4] Against e.g. J. L. Crenshaw, *Old Testament Wisdom: An Introduction* (London: SCM Press, 1982), pp. 197ff.

The multiplicity and variety of the world order can never be completely mastered, and always has the capacity to surprise. The wise man is fairly confident that he can cope with situations through careful observation of how things are, fixing his conclusions in proverbs, riddles and lists of natural phenomena. These guidelines represent order won from the chaos of life (Prov. 1:1–6). But for all this hard discipline, the teacher of wisdom in Ancient Israel was prepared to recognise an element of the unpredictable in all calculations, whether it is in achieving speech which accurately reflects thought (Prov. 16:1), happiness (16:20), victory in battle (21:31) or the choice of a right wife (19:14). Because of the complexity of the world there are unknown factors that the wise man must reckon with in all these areas, and so the proper approach is humility. In making analogies between nature and human life, for instance, the wise man is always ready to admit that, 'there are things too wonderful for me':

> Three things are too wonderful for me;
> four I do not understand:
> the way of an eagle in the sky,
> the way of a serpent on the rock,
> the way of a ship on the high seas,
> and the way of a man with a maiden
> (Prov. 30:18–19)

In the roots of the wisdom movement, this humility is associated with the 'fear of the Lord' (e.g. Prov. 16:6), because only God's vision of the world is perfect. The point is not that God will suddenly intervene to trip the wise man up, but that only God has the perfect wisdom to operate successfully in areas where human wisdom falters through a lack of grasp on the situation. Only God sees all the factors involved in the vast extent of the world. There was a particular temptation in Israel to forget this 'fear of the Lord' in employing guidelines which reflect cause–effect linkages ('if you do A, B will usually follow'). The observation that the righteous will be rewarded and the wicked punished, for example, has a certain truth in particular circumstances, but the wise should be humble enough to make ship-wreck of this rule when confronted by events that fail to fit it. Faced by the complexities of experience, however, there was a tendency for these empirical statements to rigidify into an inflexible 'principle' of retribution. It is this hardening into dogma that the Book of Job protests against, attempting to return the flow of wisdom to its original well-springs. It recalls the early openness of wisdom to the shock of new experience.

This brings us to the riddle of Job 28, 'where shall wisdom be found?' The solution to the riddle is that unlike precious stones and ores buried in the earth (vv. 1–2, 6), there is no single place in which wisdom is located, and no path that can be followed to find it. Wisdom, understood objectively as a body of knowledge corresponding to the world, can only be observed by observing the whole world. God knows where wisdom can be found because in the act of creation he surveyed it and searched it out (vv. 25–7). There is no literal place where wisdom is buried and no path to it. *Wisdom can only be found in exercising it.* God knows its 'place' and the 'way' to it, because he has total knowledge of all places in the world and sees the paths for all the elements in the world, such as the wind, the waters, the rain and the thunderbolt.

> God understands the way to it,
> and he knows its place.
> for he looks to the ends of the earth
> and sees everything under the heavens . . .
> when he made a way for the lightning of the thunder,
> then he saw it and declared it;
> he established it and searched it out.

The phrase 'he looks to the end of the earth' cannot mean that God literally sees a place on the earth where wisdom is located, since the poet has already told us that it has no dwelling place in the land of the living or the depths of the sea. The phrase celebrates the perfect grasp of the world by God, as is made clear by the occurrence of the idea in other texts (Ps. 19:6, Ps. 33:13–14, Isa. 40:27–8). Wisdom cannot be found somewhere, because it is the comprehending of everywhere. Wisdom cannot be possessed objectively, but only known through exercising it.

The poem therefore does not deny any grasp of wisdom whatever to human beings, as is often asserted. The point is that there is no short cut to wisdom, as if it could be simply mined out of the earth like a precious stone or purchased like a commodity. In the context of the whole book of Job the intermezzo of the wisdom poem in chapter 28 acts as a riposte to those who have been trying to find a single place where wisdom dwells, such as in the dogma of retribution applied inflexibly to Job's case. Chapters 38–41 achieve the same effect by listing scores of items in the world that the wise can never grasp ('were you there when . . . ?'). Job 28 offers an apophatic approach to the divine wisdom, but not one based on an absolute transcendence. Wisdom is hidden, it defeats encapsulation in the linguistic devices of the wise (lists, proverbs, analogies), not because it is a reality beyond the being of the world, but because of its extent and complexity. It is not situated beyond finite bounds, but is boundless.

The riddle of a search for a 'place' which is not-a-place thus presents a certain sort of transcendence of wisdom. Wisdom 'goes beyond' the grasp of the human mind in its inexhaustible extent, and divine wisdom transcends human wisdom because God alone comprehends all. This can be expressed poetically by affirming that 'God knows the place of wisdom' (v. 23). But divine wisdom is not characterised by an exclusive and absolute transcendence, as would be the case if wisdom were depicted here as a figure who dwells remotely in a place in heaven. Bultmann, for instance, regarded the phrase 'mortals do not know the way to wisdom' as the remnant of a Jewish myth in which wisdom supposedly descends from heaven, searches for a home on earth, is rejected by all and so returns to heaven where she lives at the side of God hidden from human beings.[5] But the hidden wisdom of Job 28 is not personified like this, and no distinction in *kind* is being made between divine wisdom and human wisdom; both the wisdom with which Yahweh orders the world (vv. 24–7) and the skills employed by human beings in exploration and mining (vv. 1–11) are of a practical kind. Wisdom is thus immanent as well as being transcendent, open to some extent at least to its exercise by human beings.

THE QUEST FOR A PLACE

The affinity between the postmodern mood and the sense of hiddenness of wisdom in ancient Israel is especially close in the function of language. The wisdom scribes reminded themselves that there was no simple correspondence between verbal signs and the multiplicity of objects in the world to which they referred; although they worked hard at making the links, analogies could always break down, and truth might not always be deducible from observation. In our age there is an even greater crisis of representation. There is a sense that the reader of a text is caught within an endless chain of verbal signs; the meaning of a sign is to be found only in its 'difference' from others, and as what is signified becomes a signifier in its turn, final meaning is perpetually postponed. In fact, this lack of final closure in the written text is a significant reason for the reaction of such critical theorists as Jacques Derrida against the attempt of Enlightenment thinking simply to equate 'being' with 'presence'.

---

[5] Rudolph Bultmann, 'Der Religionsgeschichtliche Hintergrund des Prologs zum Johannes-Evangelium', in *Gunkel-Festschrift* 2 (1923) repr: *Exegetica* (Tübingen: J. C. B. Mohr, 1967), p. 16.

If the conscious human subject is conceived as mastering the world as an object and subduing the world to its control, then 'beingfulness' is understood as the capacity to be present to oneself (in self-awareness) and to be immediately present to others. God is then the great controller who is omnipresent, grounding and validating human subjectivity by communion with the eternal mind. On this reckoning, as Derrida puts it, 'God is the name and the element of that which makes possible an absolutely pure and absolutely self-present self-knowledge.'[6] It is this simple equation of being and presence that the 'postmodern' mood challenges, replacing immediate and self-contained presence with 'traces' of presence, whether of the self or the world. The phenomenon of the written word is of key importance in this shift of thinking. For if the being of something consists essentially in its *presence* to others, then the voice or the *spoken* word will be the original, immediate presence from which written words are merely derivative. But as Derrida insists,[7] all objects in the world can be inscribed in some kind of mark or sign (not necessarily a literal written text), and this mark can always be repeated in other contexts, with the promise that meaning may change and develop.

Openness of meaning, secured by the written sign and representing a protest against all oppressive ideology, places a question against absolute presence. But it is important to notice that the key proponents of this deconstruction of full presence are not denying presence altogether, whether of the self or the world (or indeed, of God). As Terry Eagleton summarises it, they find 'a kind of constant flickering of presence and absence together',[8] or as Derrida himself expresses it, 'Nothing is . . . anywhere either simply present or absent. There are only, everywhere, differences and traces of traces.'[9] Indeed, in this deconstructive mood, there is also an orientation towards a nameless 'place' that is a non-foundational origin of this flickering presence. As Graham Ward discerns in the work of Derrida, Julia Kristeva, Luce Irigaray and others, there is 'an unstable, mysterious, ungrounding origin'.[10] This place which is not-a-place represents an 'otherness' that disturbs all attempts

[6] Jacques Derrida, *Of Grammatology*, trans. G. C. Spivak, corrected edition (Baltimore: Johns Hopkins University Press, 1998), p. 98.
[7] Derrida, *Of Grammatology*, pp. 8–10, 20–5.
[8] Terry Eagleton, *Literary Theory. An Introduction* (Oxford: Blackwell, 1983), p. 128.
[9] Jacques Derrida, *Positions*, trans. A. Bass (Chicago: University of Chicago Press, 1981), p. 26.
[10] Graham Ward, *The Postmodern God. A Theological Reader* (Oxford: Blackwell, 1997), p. xxxiii. To some extent this essay takes up Ward's challenge to articulate theologically 'the living in and journeying towards another city' which he also describes as 'a new spacing in which the other is housed': ibid. pp. xlii, xli.

to establish either full presence or full absence; it is a critique of immanence as well as transcendence, constantly breaking open boundaries
and upsetting rigid ideas as to what is 'inside' or 'outside' the reality
established by language.

This no-place is named by several 'postmodern' philosophers as the
khora, following Heidegger's borrowing of the term from Plato's *Timaeus*
where it denotes the 'space' which is neither being nor non-being, but
a kind of 'interval' between.[11] According to Derrida, it is impossible to
speak about this 'place', but it 'dictates an obligation by its very impossibility; it is necessary to speak of it'.[12] As John Caputo aptly comments,
talk about the *khora* is 'discourse about a desert, about a barren and naked
place, a pure taking place, an empty place . . . [a] no-place'.[13] In his essay,
'How to Avoid Speaking; Denials', Derrida denies that the *khora* is equivalent to the God of negative theology, despite apparent similarities; one
reason is that the *khora* is not 'the giver of good gifts'.[14] According to
Derrida, one must avoid saying that the *khora* gives anything at all, since
while giving a gift initially breaks open the power-games of commer-
cial exchange, the gift is soon entrapped within that same process, and
with it the giver as well. Yet 'although it is nothing, this referent appears
irreducible and irreducibly other'.

So the Totally Other is there (*il y a*), and it is necessary to speak about
this 'place' of the Other in order to keep the chain of verbal signifiers open
to the promise and the desire which is at the heart of difference. This is not
only a promise that any piece of writing can be repeated in new contexts
with increased meaning and that this will have performative power to
shape the lives of its readers. It is also an open-ended desire that cannot
be confined within the network of linguistic signs; it is open beyond
the web of language, reaching after a 'primordial yes' which Derrida
finds reflected in the final 'yes' of Molly Bloom's soliloquy at the end of
James Joyce's *Ulysses*.[15] Feminist post-modern thinkers such as Irigaray
and Kristeva have further developed the concept of *khora* to stress the
element of non-violent desire (against the will to power of Nietzsche)

---

[11] Martin Heidegger, *What is Called Thinking?* trans. J. Gray (New York: Harper and Row, 1968),
pp. 245ff.
[12] Jacques Derrida, 'How to Avoid Speaking: Denials', trans. K. Frieden, in H. Coward and
T. Foshay (eds.), *Derrida and Negative Theology* (New York: State University of New York Press,
1992), p. 107.
[13] John D. Caputo, *The Prayers and Tears of Jacques Derrida. Religion without Religion* (Bloomington:
Indiana University Press, 1997), p. 37.
[14] Derrida, 'How to Avoid Speaking', pp. 106–8.
[15] Jacques Derrida, 'Ulysse Gramaphone: Deux Mots pour Joyce', repr. in Peggy Kamuf (ed.),
Derrida Reader (Hemel Hempstead: Harvester Wheatsheaf, 1991), p. 596.

and the effect of the traces of the *khora* in opening language towards the transcendent. In Kristeva's thought the *chora* is a womb-like, nurturing place of origin, a space which contains the archetypal impressions of love and relationships which precede language and sexual experience;[16] traces of the *chora* in the consciousness can break through verbal signifiers, subverting the usual order of symbols and reaching towards something altogether 'Other'.

The *khora* is thus both absent and present; it is a place and yet not a place. There is a complexity about the relation of this space to the space or 'void' that has appeared in human experience with the loss of the centred self and the difficulty of naming the world. This elusive relationship has, by contrast, been short-circuited in some postmodern a-theologies, which have confined themselves to the immanent 'void' that has opened up within the self, asserting the pure absence of any transcendent reality: as Mark Taylor states, 'The very search for presence testifies to the absence of presence and the "presence" of absence.'[17] The *khora*, by contrast, represents an 'outside' to the web of human linguistic signs which is 'inside' at the same time, without being an area that can be actually reached. What worries Derrida about giving it a theological description is that this might well lead to a totalitarian concept of Presence which would undermine the mediation of language, close down the expansion of meaning, and produce an oppressive ideology. The challenge posed by the concept of the non-theological *khora* is thus whether we can maintain its disturbing effect in a theological form. That is, can we speak of a presence of God which is not oppressive, and which does not foster the split between subject (the thinking mind) and object (the world)?

The 'no-place' of Job 28 similarly acts as a symbol of transcendence, breaking open the confidence of the wise that they have complete control of the world through their linguistic codes and meta-narratives (for example, the dogma of retribution), and affirming a hiddenness at the heart of reality. Yet for all this, wisdom – both human and divine – is, unlike the *khora*, accessible; hiddenness and silence is accompanied by real presence, expressed finally in the theophany of chapter 38:1, when God speaks to Job out of the whirlwind. To meet the challenge set by the no-place of the *khora* we should, I suggest, follow up the clue of the wisdom poem and abandon talk of a dialectic of 'absence' and 'presence'. The task is to clarify the nature of a 'hidden presence'.

[16] Julia Kristeva, *Revolution in Poetic Language* (1974); extracts repr. in Toril Moi (ed.), *The Kristeva Reader* (Oxford: Blackwell, 1986), pp. 93–8.

[17] Mark Taylor, *Erring. A Postmodern A/theology* (Chicago: University of Chicago Press, 1984), p. 72.

THE HIDDENNESS OF A NON-ABSENT GOD

To speak of hiddenness is to indicate presence and not absence. The metaphor of a 'place' which is not a place has in fact proved helpful to a range of theological thought in attempting to speak of the hidden presence of a God who does not legitimate the subjective project of the human self. These pictures of a 'place' are not literally locations *in which* God is hidden, but which *accord* (like Job 28) with a sense of the hiddenness of God. They express a transcendence, breaking open the circle of human immanence, but a transcendence which is not absolute but an accessible Otherness.

The first, and most comprehensive, idea is that there is a place *in God*. In creation, it may be affirmed, God has opened up a kind of space within God's own being for created beings to dwell. This 'making room' within God fits well with a triune model of God, as the place that God opens can be envisaged as being within the interweaving and interpenetrating fellowship (*perichoresis*) of Father, Son and Spirit. Through creation we participate in the relationships of ecstatic love, of mutual giving and receiving, within God. Jürgen Moltmann has aligned this picture with the Jewish kabbalistic tradition of *zimsum*, according to which God 'withdraws' from the fullness of the divine being in order to make a space of nothingness from which creation can emerge *ex nihilo*.[18] Although there are some conceptual problems with the way that Moltmann uses this image,[19] it has the advantage of associating the presence of God with the humility of God. In voluntary self-humiliation, God limits God's self in bringing into being a world of created beings within the divine life.

The logic of this image of dwelling in God is that God in turn dwells in the space opened up for created reality, unless God is to be excluded from a space which is within God's own life. It is also consistent that this dwelling in the world will take the form of a hidden, patient and suffering presence, persisting with created persons in their growth and development, and acting in persuasive and sacrificial love rather than coercion. If God has created a living-space for creation through humble self-limitation, then God's presence in the world will have the same

[18] Jürgen Moltmann, *God in Creation*, trans. M. Kohl (London: SCM Press, 1985), pp. 86–9; Moltmann, *The Coming of God*, trans. M. Kohl (London: SCM Press, 1996), pp. 297–302. Moltmann discovered the Kabbalistic idea of *zimsum* as formulated by Isaac Luria in the modern presentation by G. Scholem.

[19] See further below; for a different kind of critique, see Alan Torrance, '*Creatio ex nihilo* and the spatio-temporal dimensions', in Colin E. Gunton (ed.), *The Doctrine of Creation* (Edinburgh: T. and T. Clark, 1997), pp. 88–93.

character; the Christian story finds this focused in the final presence of
God in the life and death of Jesus Christ. I want later to suggest a further reason why the presence of God will take the form of hiddenness,
rooted in the nature of Trinity itself. We must, however, take issue with
a reason offered by Moltmann for the 'hiding of the face of God'; he
maintains that while creation is 'in' God, God is not 'in' creation but
remains 'over against it' until the moment of future new creation when
the universe will be filled with the presence of God. Until the eschaton,
he asserts, 'Only God can be the space of the world, and the world cannot be God's space.'[20] Moltmann cannot, of course, deny indwellings of
God in the world during the course of history altogether, but describes
them as 'special presences', temporary acts of self-humiliation, rather
than a 'general presence'.[21] He conceives them as transient hidden presences in which the Shekinah of God is 'homeless' in the world, awaiting
redemption; the pre-eminent instance of this presence, anticipating the
eschaton, is Christ himself.

As well as being out of kilter with the image of *zimsum* which Moltmann
adopts, this view of hidden presence as a temporary stop-gap for the
absent God comes ironically from one of the group of theologians who
opposed the 'death of God' movement in the 1960s. This movement,
observing a loss of awareness of God within cultural consciousness in
the West, proposed various forms of absence of God from the world.
One version, advocated for example by Dorothee Sölle, suggested that
the suffering Christ 'represents the absent God by giving him time to
appear . . . Because God does not intervene to establish his cause, Christ
appears in his place.'[22] We can keep a sort of doubting faith in the absent
God whom we no longer experience, because Christ the representative
stands in for him in the world. At the same time, however, 'death of God'
theologians like Sölle and William Hamilton wanted to rebut the image
of a dictatorial God and found the idea of a suffering God to be a powerful symbol for this; Hamilton, for example, affirms that 'humiliation,
patience and suffering are the ways God has dealt with man [sic] in
the world'.[23] This was strictly inconsistent with divine absence, as an
absent God cannot suffer with the world. Indeed, it was the German
'theologians of the cross' (especially Jürgen Moltmann, Eberhard Jüngel,
Hans Urs Von Balthasar) who insisted that God was not dead – that

[20] Moltmann, *The Coming of God*, p. 302.   [21] Ibid., p. 303.
[22] Dorothee Sölle, *Christ the Representative. An Essay in Theology after the 'Death of God'*, trans. D. Lewis
(London: SCM Press, 1967), p. 137.
[23] William Hamilton, *The New Essence of Christianity* (New York: Association Press, 1961), pp. 102–3.

is, not irrelevant to the world – precisely because God suffered death. Sharing empathetically in the human condition of alienation, oppression and death, this was a God who was alive to a world where human suffering had become an overwhelming problem for belief in God.

Summed up in Jüngel's phrase 'the death of the living God',[24] this is an insight which I suggest is undermined if the suffering of God with the world is restricted to fragmentary moments of presence amid intervals of absence, rather than a universal and continuous hidden presence. We should clarify our language, as I have already suggested, and dispense with talk of divine 'absence' altogether. Transcendence and 'otherness' of God from the world is not about absence, but about a mode of presence in which God cannot be confused with the world. Presence might of course be envisaged in such a way that all otherness is lost in a merging of God with the world, in a dying into the material cosmos in a brilliant moment of self-immolation, as with Thomas Altizer's concept of an apocalyptic 'total presence'.[25] But this kind of Hegelian self-negation and self-embodiment of God without a return ticket is really another form of absence. As Altizer puts it, 'the absence of all nameability whatsoever [is] an absence that is a necessary and inevitable absence for a full and total apocalyptic enactment.'[26] By contrast, we may say that the 'hiddenness' of God requires both the presence and otherness of God, but is not a totalitarian presence suppressing the otherness of created beings.

The quest for a 'place' which disturbs the self-enclosure of human life is thus fulfilled, from one aspect, in the place opened up within God. It is *consistent* for this to entail a hidden presence of God in the living-space of creation, although it remains to establish more clearly the *reason* why this should be so.

A second approach to this 'place' which is not-a-place moves the focus from the mutual indwelling of God and the whole cosmos to the individual person. It has been a part of the apophatic 'mystical' tradition in Christianity to find an overlap between a hidden ground of the self and the God who is hidden in light which is so bright it causes a sense of profound darkness. There is a 'place' in which it is not possible to articulate in words the difference between God and the soul. So, for

[24] Eberhard Jüngel, 'Vom Tod des lebendigen Gottes. Ein Plakat' (1968), repr. in Jüngel, *Unterwegs zur Sache* (Münich: Chr. Kaiser, 1972), pp. 105–25.
[25] Thomas J. J. Altizer, *Genesis and Apocalypse. A Theological Voyage Toward Authentic Christianity* (Louisville: Westminster/John Knox Press, 1990), pp. 117–19, 179–85.
[26] Ibid., p. 182.

example, the Lady Julian of Norwich in an apophatic mood declares that 'I saw no difference between God and our essential being, it seemed to be all God . . .'[27] As Denys Turner has pointed out, this is not a simple affirmation that the soul *is* God or that the soul has been totally absorbed into God, but that it is not possible to 'see' or 'name' the difference with our resources of language.[28] Using spatial imagery, the journey of 'descent' into this inward place in the soul is at the same time an 'ascent' to God,[29] so that both the divine nature and the innermost 'refuge' of the self can be named as an 'emptiness' or 'silence' or a 'desert place'.[30]

The breakdown in language at this place of union with God is naturally understood by such mystical writers as Denys the Areopagite, Meister Eckhart and the author of 'The Cloud of Unknowing' in terms of the neo-Platonist tradition within which they stand. First of all, the inability to 'see' the difference between God and the 'empty place' in the soul stems from the incomparability of God with all beings, so that there is no point of comparison from which a distinction can be observed. Second, in contrast but not inconsistently, there is often thought to be a divine 'spark' in the human person, the uncreated mind, which is inseparable from God as uncreated mind. Third, it is not possible to 'see' anything cognitively because God as pure intellect will be apprehended as totally 'simple' essence and so as formless, featureless, a desert place, and 'nothingness'. As Turner exegetes Eckhart's thought, this is the divine *esse indistinctum*, and insofar as we are intellect, we are also *esse indistinctum*.[31]

While I would wish to take issue with the second two factors, on behalf of an idea of God as a complex interaction of relationships, it is important to listen to the witness of the apophatic theologians about a 'place' of encounter with God in the self in which God is so near to us that we cannot distance God as an 'object' over against us.[32] This 'no-place' where both God and the self are hidden and which can therefore be metaphorically designated as an 'empty place' can, I aim to show, be rooted in a

[27] Julian of Norwich, *Revelations of Divine Love*, trans. E. Spearing (Harmondsworth: Penguin Books, 1998), ch. 54, p. 130. While Julian is usually classified as a 'cataphatic' mystic, it is better to regard all medieval Christian mysticism as an integration of apophatic and cataphatic aspects.
[28] Denys Turner, *The Darkness of God. Negativity in Christian Mysticism* (Cambridge: Cambridge University Press, 1995), pp. 160–3.
[29] Turner explores the influential merging of these two spatial images in Augustine's thought: ibid., pp. 74–81, 92–101.
[30] For this terminology see Sermon 9 in Meister Eckhart, *The Essential Sermons, Commentaries, Treatises and Defence*, trans. and ed. E. Colledge and B. McGinn (London: SPCK, 1981).
[31] See Turner, *The Darkness of God*, pp. 164–5.
[32] Cf. Julian of Norwich: 'God is nearer to us than our own soul, for he is the ground on which our soul stands', *Revelations*, ch. 56, p. 133.

trinitarian theology of relationships rather than in a concept of purely intellectual essence. This may also help to avoid the tendency of apophatic theology to focus on the individual self – although the self is certainly negated in the process – rather than the self in relationship.

A third kind of 'no-place' through which the hidden presence of God can be known is thus the space opened up between the self and other selves, or between ourselves and our neighbours. There is a place created 'between' persons when we allow others to enter our world and challenge us to recognise their particular identity and needs. This is a theme central to the thought of Emmanuel Levinas, who finds that the infinite Other – God – turns our world upside down by inserting a 'space' in time and materiality,[33] setting the stage for our encounter with other persons and so calling us to limitless responsibility for our neighbour. For Levinas, and significantly for our own theme, we can find traces of the infinitely Other in the 'face' of our neighbour, not because the face is a static model of God, but because it becomes a means by which we can 'find ourselves in his trace'.[34] That is, Levinas is concerned with *participation in* the transcendent and not observation or objectification of it. However, for Levinas the space between persons, the 'stage' set by the irruption of the infinite, is not a place where God is now present; what is present is a trace of the God who has always 'passed by'. Here Levinas employs the imagery of Exodus 33:22–3, understanding Moses' vision of the back of God to mean that 'Someone has already passed.' But rather than speaking – as Levinas does – of an 'absent infinite', we must, I suggest, try to speak of the God who is hidden and so present in the 'between' of relations.

A fourth and final kind of 'no-place' comes rather close to the Job poet, who finds divine wisdom not in one literal place but as exercised in all places. We may say that God is present in a hidden way because God takes the many places of the world as a place for encounter and self-revelation. As Karl Barth points out, created objects are totally unsuitable means for the communication of the divine glory because of the finitude and sinfulness of the world, and so 'the veil is thick';[35] in the very moment of self-unveiling God will be veiled, and God is hidden precisely

---

33 Emmanuel Levinas, 'Meaning and Sense', in *Emmanuel Levinas, Basic Philosophical Writings*, ed. A. Peperzak, S. Critchley and R. Bernasconi (Bloomington: Indiana University Press, 1996), p. 62; cf. Levinas, 'God and Philosophy', in *Of God who Comes to Mind*, trans. B. Bergo (Stanford: Stanford University Press, 1998), pp. 67–70.
34 Levinas, 'Meaning and Sense', p. 65.
35 Karl Barth, *Church Dogmatics*, English translation, ed. G. W. Bromiley and T. F. Torrance (Edinburgh: T. and T. Clark, 1936–77), I/1, p. 165.

because God is revealed. We may also learn from Barth that the meeting with God through secular objects is only made possible through God's self-identification with the worldly object of Christ's humanity, so that all other places in the world point to Christ as the 'primary sacrament'.[36] This is a clue to which I intend to return. However, Barth is less helpful when he proposes that in encountering God in this mediated immediacy we are really sharing in the 'primary objectivity' of the divine self-knowledge, that we participate in God's own knowledge of himself as an object.[37] If we are ever to escape from a dualism of subject and object in our knowledge of God we must think more radically about the nature of participation than this.

The 'place' which is not literally a place, but which evokes the hidden presence of God may thus be understood as (a) a place in God, (b) a place in the self which is inseparable from (but not identical with) the being of God, (c) a place between persons and (d) a place concurrent with many objects in the world which mediate the immediacy of God. As I have already indicated, these aspects of the place which is 'not-a-place' may all best be understood in terms of participation in the triune God, but before examining this claim further we should step back for a moment and consider how the wise of Ancient Israel coped with the limits that they faced.

WISDOM: PARTICIPATION AND CONTRACTION

Confronted by the hiddenness of wisdom, in both its divine and human practices, the wise men of Israel came to two conclusions which we may describe in shorthand as 'participation' and 'contraction'. The first seems to be the older strategy, and is focused upon the female figure of personified Wisdom who appears explicitly in Proverbs 1–9 (and later in Ben Sirach 1:1–10, 24:1–12). In contrast to the supposed myth of a rejected and hidden wisdom figure which is claimed to underly such passages as Job 28, wherever wisdom *does* actually appear as personified she presents herself as someone who is available to human beings. Indeed, the whole point of personification seems to be to invite human beings into a personal relationship with her; according to Proverbs 8:22–31 the wisdom which was at the side of God in creation 'delights' in the human race.

---

[36] Barth, *Church Dogmatics*, II/1, pp. 54–55. Cf. IV/3, Part 1, pp. 116–23.
[37] Barth, *Church Dogmatics*, II/1, pp. 49–50.

On the one hand, the personification of wisdom as a beautiful woman bidding pupils to receive her instruction and so receive life (Prov. 9:1–6) is a device by which the wise, as envoys of wisdom, seek to advertise their curriculum and attract pupils to *their* schools. But on the other hand, the image surely points to a discovery made by the wise, that there is something *participatory* about knowledge. Faced by the complexity of the world and the limits of their instructions, the wise seek to align themselves to what would later be called 'the Spirit of Wisdom'.[38] However elusive it might be, it was possible to have a relationship with wisdom, expressed in the image of 'walking in the paths of wisdom' (Prov 8:22). While there is no path *to* wisdom as an object that can be simply found in a particular place (Job 28), whether mined or purchased there, there are paths *of* wisdom; there are tracks through the complexity of life which wisdom treads, and it is possible to develop an approach to the world in sympathy with her movements. The author of the later Wisdom of Solomon picks up a much earlier sense of the nature of wisdom when he says of wisdom:

She herself ranges in search of those who are worthy of her; on their daily path she appears to them with kindly intent, and in all their purposes meets them half-way (6:16, NEB translation).

The idea of participation in the movements of Wisdom has something open-ended about it, inviting a never-completed process of interpretation of the world. Personified wisdom is evidently 'not-a-place'. However, the other strategy of the wise for coping with the hiddenness of wisdom had the potential for an abrupt closure. This was to contract the span of wisdom to a smaller body of knowledge which could be mastered, namely the Torah. In the later wisdom material in the Old Testament, the 'fear of the Lord' which earlier on denoted a basic attitude of humility in investigation, became an expression for the observation of Torah, the written law-codes of Israel. It is not clear when wisdom began to be identified with Torah, but references can probably be discerned behind the admonitions to 'fear of the Lord' in the later sentence material of Proverbs 1–9 (e.g. 1:7, 2:5–8) and the phrase certainly refers to Torah in Ben Sirach 1:1–20.

It is commonly argued that true wisdom comes to be equated with Torah as a way of solving the problem of the transcendent 'absence' of wisdom in heaven, perhaps in a period of crisis of faith induced by

[38] e.g. Wisdom of Solomon 7:22–30.

the exile.[39] Torah is then to be seen as an intermediary, making wisdom present on earth. However, our discussion so far has highlighted the problem as a different kind of transcendence, not absence but complexity. Wisdom is hidden, as we have seen, because of its multiplicity and *extent*, and so I suggest that the Torah is seized upon as a convenient contraction of knowledge to a manageable span. When the wise man responsible for the 'Sayings of Agur' in Proverbs 30 complains that he is 'weary and worn out' by trying to explore the heights and depths of the cosmos (30:1–4), another scribe appends his solution: 'every word of God stands true', and 'we must add nothing to his words' (30:6). The fixed text of the Torah is to stand over against a world where boundaries cannot be measured.[40]

I suggest that this desire to contract the vast expanse of wisdom to a limited scope of reliable words is also expressed at the end of Koheleth, in two consecutive postscripts. The first (12:9–12) appears to be from an editor standing within the School of Koheleth, who has taken to heart his master's weariness at the baffling complexity of the world (1:5–7). His solution is therefore to urge scribes to concentrate on the limited number of tried and tested sayings ('nails firmly fixed') which have been collected by Koheleth himself ('given by one shepherd') and not to seek to multiply them (v. 12). A second editor (12:13–14) has a different view of the restricted material in which wisdom is available; it is the Torah. 'Fear God', he urges, 'and keep his commandments'. Picking up Koheleth's favourite phrase 'the all is futility', he defines the 'all' or the 'sum' of the multiplicity of life as keeping the commandments:

This is the conclusion of the matter: let us hear the whole [the 'all']. Fear God and keep his commandments, for this is the 'all' for humanity.

In the light of the editorial postscripts in Proverbs 30:5–6 and Koheleth 12:13–14, it seems likely that there is a similar addition referring to the Torah in Job 28:28. A Torah scribe has offered his own solution to the question, 'Where shall wisdom be found?', contracting the measureless extent of wisdom to a measurable span:

And [God] said to humankind,
'Truly, the fear of the Lord, that is wisdom . . . '

[39] Notably in the influential account by J. C. Rylaarsdam, *Revelation in Jewish Wisdom Literature* (Chicago: University of Chicago Press, 1946), chs. 2–4.
[40] Cf. M. Weinfeld, *Deuteronomy and the Deuteronomic Tradition* (Oxford: Clarendon Press, 1972), pp. 258–60; but Weinfeld misses the contrast between the vast and the comprehensive.

Although it is not impossible that the phrase 'the fear of the Lord' bears its earlier sense of exercising humility in observing the world, the abruptness of its appearance in verse 28 spoils the sequence of the unfolding of the riddle, and the Baruch poet is probably right to interpret it as meaning the study of Torah (Baruch 3:36–4:1) when he comes to make his commentary on Job 28.

In intertestamental Judaism the two strategies of participation in wisdom and contraction of the scope of wisdom interact in various ways. There is the obvious danger that the identification of wisdom with Torah will close down the endless process of enquiry, by replacing the 'not-a-place' of personified wisdom with a single place that can be possessed. But the association of Torah with the personification of wisdom led to at least one kind of open-ended exploration, namely a world of boundless interpretations of the Torah text itself. In the 'wisdom Christology' of the New Testament we shall see that there is a heritage of both participation and contraction.

PARTICIPATING IN TRIUNE SPACES

Earlier I suggested that the presence of the hidden God, associated with various kinds of places that are 'not-places', was best understood in terms of our participation in the triune life of God. Now I want to propose that this makes most sense if we understand the 'Persons' of the Trinity *as relationships*. This proposal is ostensibly often made in current discussion of the doctrine of the Trinity, but usually what the writer means is that the persons of Father, Son and Spirit are wholly *constituted* by their relationships with each other.[41] It is rightly being asserted that relationship is not something merely added on to a person, as if a core of *hypostasis* could exist without or before the relationships in which a person is engaged.[42] The being of God is communion, and the persons can only be understood in terms of their sharing in *perichoresis*, or mutual indwelling. This follows the thought of the Cappadocian Fathers, who found the relations to be those of paternity, filiation and spiration (begetting, being begotten and being breathed out). These are relationships of ecstatic, outward-going love, giving and receiving.

However, I suggest that we should go further in the direction of a relational understanding of God than this, and think of the 'persons'

---

[41] We can observe this conflation happening in e.g. T. F. Torrance, *Trinitarian Perspectives* (Edinburgh: T. and T. Clark, 1994), pp. 33, 49; Leonardo Boff, *Trinity and Society* (London: Burns and Oates, 1988), pp. 88, 92.

[42] See John Zizioulas, *Being as Communion* (London: Darton, Longman and Todd, 1985), pp. 27–41.

in God as not simply formed by their relations, but as being the relations themselves.[43] The relations do not simply *make* the hypostases what they are, but *are* themselves hypostatic. The term 'hypostasis' as used by the Church fathers indicates distinct identity and particularity of being, and so to equate relationships with hypostases is to affirm that the relationships are three identities in God and are more being-full than anything in created reality. This idea was already hinted at by Augustine when he declared that 'the names, Father and Son do not refer to the substance but to the relation, and the relation is no accident'.[44] Aquinas then gave formality to the notion with the term 'subsistent relations', stating that 'divine person signifies relation as something subsisting . . . relation is signified . . . as hypostasis'.[45] While Augustine's approach was experimental[46] – even playful – Aquinas unfortunately based the subsistent relations in the simplicity of divine substance, thus giving grounds for the suspicion that such talk is simply in aid of the typical Western stress on the unity of divine essence with the loss of real three-ness and 'otherness' in God.

We can, however, free the idea of subsistent relations from its Neoplatonic and Aristotelian settings in Augustine and Aquinas. Taking a clue from Barth's insistence that 'with regard to the being of God, the word "event" or "act" is final',[47] we may speak of God as an event of relationships, or three *movements* of relationship subsisting in one event. Focusing on relations rather than personal agents who *have* relations takes us from an ontology of substance to one of event. Correspondingly, talk of the triune God changes from being a language of observation to one of participation, helping us to overcome the split between subject and object that has been a regrettable inheritance of Enlightenment rationalism. For of course it is not possible to visualise, paint or etch in glass three interweaving 'relationships' without any personal agents who exercise them. We cannot 'see', even in our mind's eye, three movements of being which are characterised by relationship. This kind of talk only

[43] A similar case for taking subsistent relations seriously is made by David Cunningham, *These Three are One. The Practice of Trinitarian Theology* (Oxford: Blackwell, 1998), pp. 59–71; cf. pp. 168–9, and his phrase 'relation without remainder'. But in developing substantive expressions (Source, Wellspring and Living Water) to name the three subsistent relations (which he identifies as initiation, fruition and emergence) Cunningham still refers to 'addressing' or 'speaking to' the relations (p. 72) rather than 'speaking in' the flow of relations.

[44] Augustine, *De Trinitate*, 5.6.   [45] Aquinas, *Summa Theologiae*, 1a.29.4.

[46] He was grappling with the alternatives presented to him by the Arians that the persons of the Trinity must be distinguished either by substance (hence tritheism) or accident (so lacking the enduring nature of divinity).

[47] Barth, *Church Dogmatics*, II/1, p. 263.

makes sense in terms of our *involvement* in the network of relationships in which God happens.

To refer to God as 'Father' thus does not mean to represent or objectify God as a father-figure, but to *address* God as Father, and so enter into the movement of a son–father relationship that is already there ahead of us. For instance, when we say 'Abba, Father' in prayer this fits into a movement of speech like that between a son and a father; our response of 'yes' ('Amen') leans upon a filial 'yes' of humble obedience,[48] glorifying the Father, a response which is already there. We find a 'place' which is there for us. At the same time, we find ourselves involved in a movement of self-giving like that of a Father sending forth a Son, a movement which the early theologians called 'eternal generation' and which has its outworking in the mission ('sending') of God in history. So we take our part in the mission of God. These two directions of movement are interwoven by a third, as we find that they are continually opened up to new depths of relationship and to the new possibilities of the future by a movement for which scripture gives us impressionistic images – a wind blowing, breath stirring, wings beating, oil trickling, water flowing, fire burning. We can only say that this is like a movement of Spirit coming from a Father and breathed out into us through the Son. In the language of the New Testament, we are praying to the Father, through the Son and in the Spirit.

Thus, through our participation, we can identify three distinct movements of speech, empathy and action which are *like relationships* of 'Father to Son' and 'Son to Father' and which are continually being opened up by a movement like a Spirit of newness. In their flow and direction they are quite different from each other,[49] although we can of course only speak of their particular identity through analogies ('like a Father–Son relationship') which are created in our language by God's own self-opening of communion. Two aspects of these analogies should not be misunderstood. First, I have followed the form of address that Jesus himself taught his disciples – 'Abba, Father' – but it should be clear that these movements of giving and receiving can also, in appropriate circumstances, give rise to feminine images; for instance, we may need to say that we are engaged in a flow of relationships like those originating in and responding to a

[48] 2 Cor. 1:19–21; cf. Heb. 5:7–10.
[49] Against the often-repeated criticism that identifying the person with relationship absorbs the divine persons into one undifferentiated divine substance: so Jürgen Moltmann, *The Trinity and the Kingdom of God*, trans. M. Kohl (London: SCM Press, 1981), p. 172; Colin Gunton, *The Promise of Trinitarian Theology* (Edinburgh: T. and T. Clark, 1991), pp. 39–41; Miroslav Volf, *After Our Likeness. The Church as the Image of the Trinity* (Grand Rapids: Eerdmans, 1998), pp. 204–6.

mother (cf. Isa. 49:14–15). Second, the analogy is between *relationships* in human experience on the one hand and divine movements of relationship on the other, not between human and divine *persons*. However deep and empathetic the communion is in human relationships, however much it releases the participants from self-sufficiency and isolation, since they are finite relationships there will still be 'persons' who are individual agents exercising the relationships. The appropriateness of such terms as 'King, Shepherd, Friend' and especially 'Father, Son, Spirit' when speaking of the divine communion is in pointing us, not to agents at the 'ends' of the relationships, but to the direction and flow of the relationships in which we participate. The transcendent reality to which the analogies point, without exactly describing it,[50] is the movement of relationship. To speak of the 'mission of the Father' for instance, enables us to participate in a movement of sending like that of a Father sending forth a Son.

The place which is 'not-a-place', yet for which we long, is thus best understood as the space between the movements of relationship in God. We dwell and dance in triune spaces. The room that God makes for us within God's own self is not a widening of the gap between individual subjects, but the opening up of intervals within the interweaving movements of giving and receiving. Understanding the triune persons as relations thus has noetic implications; the presence of God will always be hidden in the sense that it cannot be observed or known as an object of perception, but can only be participated in.

Indeed, all the aspects of the hidden presence of God that we have explored above are illuminated by the notion that we share in the movements of the divine relationships. The 'place' opened up for created beings in God by the divine humility is felt to be the 'nothing' or 'empty place' of apophatic theology or the nameless *khora* of Kristeva and Derrida, because there are no 'infinite subjects' present making the relations and dominating the finite participants. Yet at the same time this emptiness is an absolute fullness, because the space is embraced and inter-penetrated by movements of giving and receiving in love. While remaining opaque to the glory of God in their secularity, objects in the world become places for drawing us into this encounter with a self-relating and other-relating God (so Barth), and the ethical demand

---

[50] Here I adopt the 'cautious theological realism' of Janet Martin Soskice, *Metaphor and Religious Language* (Oxford: Clarendon Press, 1985), pp. 133–41. But, unlike Soskice, I am only taking a 'critically realistic' view of personal *relations* in God, not of personal *subjects* in God.

of our neighbour makes a place between us (so Levinas) which is a 'trace' of the space opened for us in the infinitely Other.[51] Moreover, in the moment of being aligned with divine movements of relationship we cannot 'observe a difference' between the self and God (though of course one remains); as the negative theologians point out, God is not the *object* of desire but the one *in whom* we desire the good.[52] God offers a movement of desire in which we can share, and in leaning upon this movement it can be hard to disentangle created from uncreated desire.

When we talk of participating in an event of relationships in God, this is therefore both a saying and an unsaying, both cataphatic and apophatic, both word and silence. In speaking of the relationships, much is being affirmed in an analogical way; revelation and experience both lead us to characterise these relationships as, for instance, 'sending', 'obeying' and 'glorifying'. But since we cannot observe these relations, not even as an object of conception in the mind and imagination, we are also plunged into silence.

HIDDENNESS AND INCARNATION

The doctrine of the Trinity fills out what it means to 'participate' in the divine wisdom, an experience which the wise of Ancient Israel found to be the 'place' (which was not-a-place) in which hidden wisdom could be found. However, we also saw that the wise had a view of the 'contraction' of wisdom, and both ideas flow together into the Christology of the opening poem on the Logos in the Fourth Gospel (John 1:1–18).

We may take for granted, in view of the vast literature of commentary on this passage, that in depicting the becoming flesh of 'the Word' the author has drawn upon two basic traditions, those of Wisdom and the Logos. We may also accept that while wisdom is explicable against an Old Testament and intertestamental background, Logos cannot be fully explained by reference to the Old Testament 'Word of God', and reflects some Hellenistic speculation. It is further clear that the author is familiar with the magnifying of Torah by its being identified both with wisdom and the Old Testament divine word (*dabar*). Accepting this context for the poem, our interest here is in the light that the Israelite wisdom tradition

---

[51] Here I differ from Levinas, in proposing that the trace actually gives us access to the presence of God, whereas for Levinas God is always absent, as having 'just passed by'.
[52] Turner, *The Darkness of God*, pp. 183–5.

throws upon John's declaration that the incarnate word makes visible the hidden God:

No one has ever seen God. It is God the only Son, who is close to the Father's heart, who has made him known.

When John writes that 'the Word became flesh and dwelt (or "pitched his tent") among us', he is recalling the Exodus story of making a tent or tabernacle for God to dwell among the people of Israel (Ex. 25:8–9), which had become an eschatological image for God's final dwelling on earth (e.g. Joel 3:17, Zech. 2:10). At the same time the Greek verb *skenoun*, 'to pitch a tent' or 'to dwell', has an assonance with the Hebrew root *skn*, used in the Old Testament for the 'dwelling' of God among his people, and from which was later derived the term *shekinah* in Rabbinic theology as a reverent periphrasis for the divine presence. Thus, as Raymond Brown summarises it, 'we are being told that the flesh of Jesus Christ is the new localization of God's presence on earth, and that Jesus is the replacement of the ancient tabernacle'.[53] However, it is clear that language is being stretched here, as it is when Christ is pictured later in the Gospel as the replacement of the Temple (2:19–22). For Christ to be a tabernacle and a temple is to be a place which is not-a-place, for there is something elusive about a person (and especially about the person of Christ as depicted in the Gospels) which resists being treated as a mere object.

Now, there are also echoes here of passages in the wisdom writings about the dwelling of personified Wisdom among human beings, and notably the song of Wisdom in Ben Sirach 24:8–10:

> 'He that created me decreed where my tent should be.
> He said, "Let your tent be in Jacob
> and your inheritance in Israel"
> ... In the sacred tent I ministered in his presence,
> and so I came to be established in Zion.'

The fact that wisdom is accessible and available in these passages stands against Bultmann's theory that they reflect a widespread Jewish 'myth of hidden wisdom' in which Wisdom descends to earth, is rejected and returns to be hidden in heaven.[54] There is in fact no account of such a

---

[53] R. E. Brown, *The Gospel According to John, I–XII*. Anchor Bible (London: Geoffrey Chapman, 1971), p. 33.

[54] See above. This has been followed by a number of recent scholars, e.g. R. G. Hamerton-Kelly, *Pre-Existence, Wisdom and the Son of God*. SNTS Monograph Series 21 (Cambridge: Cambridge University Press, 1973), pp. 215ff.

complete sequence until 1 Enoch 42:2. Nor do I believe that Bultmann is right to detect the same myth as being visible in John 1:1–18, where the Logos is said to be rejected by those to whom he came in an apparently pre-incarnate form (vv. 10–11). While it is not impossible that the author has drawn upon 1 Enoch, it is more likely that the rejection of the Logos in the period prior to incarnation is a portrayal of the rejection of the *envoys* in whom wisdom/Logos has come to Israel over the years, namely in prophets and wise men.[55] Logos is described as 'the true light that enlightens everyone', just as Wisdom is a light 'more radiant than the sun' which 'enters into holy souls and makes them God's friends and prophets' (Wisdom of Solomon 7:27–9); Wisdom/Logos has been rejected insofar as those she indwells have not found acceptance.

This reading of John 1:9–11 is in accord with the view of the 'Q' material in the Synoptic Gospels about the 'children of wisdom' whose message is ignored.[56] 'Q' itself seems to regard not only John the Baptist (cf. John 1:6–8) but Jesus as the last of the envoys of Wisdom.[57] In his handling of the 'Q' source Matthew goes a step further and *identifies* Jesus with Wisdom,[58] and it is this same contrast between wisdom's envoys and wisdom/Logos itself that we find in the poem of John 1. John the Baptist and the earlier envoys are said to be *witnesses* to the light of wisdom, but not *the light itself* (v. 7). Christ however is the word and light of wisdom become flesh (v. 14), so that we have seen his glory.

But what is the real substance of this contrast? How is the incarnation of wisdom different from its 'entering in' to its friends and envoys? This is where the reason for the hiddenness of wisdom that we explored earlier becomes so significant. Wisdom is not hidden – *pace* Bultmann – because it has disappeared to heaven, but because of its inexhaustible scope; it is too extensive for comprehension, because the God to whom wisdom belongs has an infinite capacity for life and creative action. The word/wisdom is incarnate in Christ because this Son comprehends in himself the multiplicity of God's works and attributes. In 'one' Son (v. 18) there is the 'fullness' of the many (vv. 14, 16), just as Wisdom is 'unique'

---

[55] This is the view of C. H. Dodd, *The Interpretation of the Fourth Gospel* (Cambridge: Cambridge University Press, 1953), p. 270. However, the evangelist may have inserted vv. 12c–13 into the original hymn, thus giving this activity of Logos/Wisdom a secondary application to the ministry of Jesus.

[56] Luke 7:34–5 = Matt. 11:18–19; Matt. 12:38–42 = Luke 11:29–32; Matt. 23:34–6 = Luke 11:49–51.

[57] So M. J. Suggs, *Wisdom, Christology and Law in Matthew's Gospel* (Harvard: Harvard University Press, 1970), pp. 26–36.

[58] So Suggs, *Wisdom*, pp. 57–61.

yet also 'multiple' (Wisdom 7:22). In case we miss this idea that the complexity of divine wisdom has been 'contracted to a span/ incomprehensibly made man',[59] the author makes reference immediately to Torah: 'the law indeed was given through Moses; grace and truth came through Jesus Christ'. As we have seen, wisdom was thought to be made accessible by being contracted into the narrow bounds of the Torah; so Morna Hooker has argued, though from a different standpoint, that the Torah was celebrated as comprehending the many attributes of God.[60] The song in Ben Sirach 24 about Wisdom 'tenting' in Zion and its temple, which is echoed in John 1:14, goes on to affirm that wisdom dwells in 'the covenant-book of God most High'; although wisdom's thoughts are 'vaster than the ocean', and 'from first to last no one has fathomed her', the Torah 'pours forth wisdom in full flood' (Sirach 24:23–9).

The *pleroma* which is in Christ (v. 16) is therefore not an early reference to the Gnostic cosmos, but to the way that one human son makes known the many aspects of God. God, like the divine attribute of wisdom, is hidden because human minds cannot get a grasp on the complexity and inexhaustibility of the divine life, love and creativity through which 'all things came into being' (v. 3) and which fills all things. We can only know this God through participation, as we have seen, and also through 'contraction', the focusing of the many in the one person. The envoys mentioned in verses 6–11 (including John the Baptist) knew the divine wisdom through participation, but in Christ this wisdom has been compressed into a place which is not-a-place. Wisdom has 'tented', not in a city, or a temple, or even in a book (the Torah), but in a person.

Origen rather later was to say that 'in so far as Christ is the wisdom of God, he is a multiplicity'[61] and that 'Jesus is many in accordance with the *epinoiai* [aspects]'. For Origen, the eternal Son makes visible in his aspects and titles (*epinoiai*) all the many transcendent perfections of the Father, enabling us to grasp the God who would otherwise be ineffable. He takes the illustration of a statue which is so large that it fills the whole universe, and which we cannot 'see' because its immensity blocks our view; we could only see the characteristics of the statue if they were manifested in a smaller copy, precisely reproducing all the detail. So the Son is the 'exact image' of the Father.[62] While this image illustrates the compression of

---

[59] Charles Wesley, Hymn 'Let heaven and earth combine', in *Hymns for the Nativity of our Lord*, V, verse 1.

[60] Morna D. Hooker, 'The Johannine Prologue and the Messianic Secret', *New Testament Studies* 21, pp. 40–58.

[61] Origen, *In Lib. Iesu Nave (On the Book of Joshua)*, Homily VII.7.

[62] Origen, *De Principiis* I.2.8.

infinite complexity into an accessible span, it has the defect of objectifying God. It is also set in the context of Origen's Neo-Platonism, since the reason for Origen *why* God is beyond comprehension is because the many divine perfections and attributes are absolutely unified in the One and in this bare unity there is nothing for the human mind to grasp. We should put Origen's insight, developed from John, in the context of the relational ontology we have been developing: that is, Christ as the true Son makes manifest the many aspects of the relationships of love within God.

The comprehensiveness of Christ as incarnate wisdom consists therefore in his relationship as Son to Father. This relationship in which Christ participates within the communion of God's life comprehends the infinite aspects of all relations of giving and receiving in God. The filial relationship of this particular human son to God exactly corresponds to the movement of relationship within God which is like that between a son and a father; thus, in Christ, human sonship is the same as divine sonship not only in function but in being, since relations in God are more being-full than anything else. This means that the pattern of son-to-father relationship made visible in the life, death and resurrection of Christ becomes the key to our own participation in God. It is this flow of relationship upon which we are dependent as we engage in the complex and inexhaustible communion of God's life. As a person who is the tent and temple of divine wisdom, Christ is the place which is not-a-place which draws us into the place opened up for us within God.

In his reflections on Christology, John Milbank comments on the elusiveness of the person of Jesus in the Gospel records, and the multiple metaphors to which the narratives resort in order to identify him: 'Jesus is the way, the word, the truth, life, water, bread, the seed of a tree and the fully grown tree, the foundation stone of a new temple and at the same time the whole edifice.' Milbank notes that these metaphors are essentially spatial:

They suggest that Jesus is the most comprehensive possible context: not just the space within which all transactions between time and eternity transpire, but also the beginning of all this space, the culmination of this space, the growth of this space and all the comings out and in within this space.[63]

Milbank's own conclusion is that Jesus is the 'comprehensive space' and 'our total situation' in the sense that the total shape of his actions and words can be realised again and again in new situations.[64] Divine

[63] John Milbank, *The Word Made Strange. Theology. Language, Culture* (Oxford: Blackwell, 1997), pp. 149–50.
[64] Ibid., p. 156f.

personhood is 'an instruction to go on re-narrating and re-realizing Christ'.

Although Milbank does not notice it, this perception is in accord with the writer of the poem in John 1 and with Origen's Christology. Learning from ideas of the hiddenness of wisdom they reflect, we must add that it is only possible to 're-realise Christ' in ever new situations because Christ is the 'comprehensive space' where we have access to the inexhaustible depths and multiplicity of the divine wisdom, and so of the personal being of God. Christ is the 'place' which enables participation in God, and which includes within its span all the complexities of loving relationships in God and all the variety of finite relationships which are in the image of God.

Standing in the place, and moving in the space which is Christ, we are drawn into those places where we know the hidden presence of God. This is why the writer of the poem in John 1:1–18 can say *both* that God remains unseen, *and* that Christ has made God known (v. 18). The Word does not cancel the silence. For the incarnation of the Word does not invite us to observe God, but to enter the tent of meeting and participate in relationships which are there ahead of us.

3

The gift of the Name: Moses and the burning bush

Janet Martin Soskice

You are great, Lord, and highly to be praised (Ps. 47:2): great is your power and your wisdom is immeasurable.

(Ps. 146:5)

Man, a little piece of your creations, desires to praise you, a human being 'bearing his mortality with him' (2 Cor.4:10), carrying with him the witness of his sin and the witness that you 'resist the proud' (1 Pet. 5:5). Nevertheless, to praise you is the desire of man, a little piece of your creation . . . Have mercy so that I may find words.

(From the opening lines of St Augustine's *Confessions*)[1]

I have become worried lately about the God of the attributes – the God of omnipotence, eternity, wisdom, immutability and unity – the God of these divine names.[2] Reflection on this God, whether of a philosophical or a more contemplative nature, has been a uniting practice for Christians, Jews and Muslims. Yet lately this God, or this manner of speaking of God, has come under attack and it is not secular critics who are voicing criticisms but Christian preachers and theologians. 'This God', we hear, 'is remote and unfeeling.' . . . 'This powerful, impassable and eternal God is far from us. This is a God "over and against" us', and so on. Jürgen Moltmann (no mean critic) puts it this way:

If, in the manner of Greek philosophy, we ask what characteristics are 'appropriate' to the deity, then we have to exclude difference, diversity, movement and suffering from the divine nature . . . Impassable, immovable, united and self-sufficient, the deity confronts a moved, suffering and divided world that is never sufficient for itself.[3]

---

[1] All excerpts from the *Confessions* are from the translation by Henry Chadwick, *Confessions* (Oxford: Oxford University Press, 1992).

[2] This article was originally published in *Gregorianum* 79, 2 (1998), pp. 231–46. It is here slightly modified.

[3] Jürgen Moltmann, *The Trinity and the Kingdom of God* (London: SCM Press, 1982), p. 20.

Such a view, Moltman suggests, may have sufficed in a pre-Enlightenment theology where the ruling concept was 'God as supreme substance but will not do for a post-Enlightenment (and especially post-Enlightenment Protestant) view which begins from "God as Absolute Subject"'. In the latter the emphasis must be on our experience and how, Moltmann asks, does God experience me? Focusing his criticisms on impassability he suggest that Christianity may never have developed 'a consistent Christian concept of God', but rather adopted 'the metaphysical tradition of Greek philosophy, which it understood as "natural theology" and saw as its own foundation'.[4]

A number of other theologians have written that we can no longer relate with any sympathy to the God of the attributes.[5] Although Catholic theologians seem less likely to voice these complaints nonetheless the tendency to downplay, or at least to sideline, the God of the attributes is tangible in Catholic worship. In popular hymn books (at least, in the English language ones) hymns that praise the

> Immortal, invisible, God only wise
> In light inaccessible hid from our eyes . . .

are now far less common than tunes which exhort us to

> Follow me, follow me,
> Leave your home and family,
> Leave your fishing nets and boats upon the shore.

An element of this may be a laudable preference for hymns based on the gospels; nonetheless an overall impression is given that the fusty old God of the attributes is (or was) the God of Empire and Colony, a powerful God for the era of powerful nation states: ruling, judging, lording, 'nor wanting, nor hasting', and so on. In preference to a sagacious emperor, it seems we prefer a 'biblical' God. And yet a biblical god, in the words of the Bible is the inspiration of the more 'philosophical' hymn 'Immortal, invisible', which is based on I Timothy 1.17: 'To the eternal King, the undying, invisible and only God, be honour and glory for ever and ever.'

Why then, is the God of the attributes suffering liturgical and, in some cases, theological 'neglect'? One theologian who is an admittedly rather extreme case of the tendency to deplore the God of power and might

[4] Ibid., p. 22.
[5] Amongst whom are Maurice Wiles, Jon Sobrino, David Jenkins, Don Cupitt, Mary Daly and Gordon Kaufman.

is Gordon Kaufman of Harvard Divinity School. While few wish to go as far as Kaufman, his views represent a consistent extreme of positions enunciated by many others.

Kaufman sees a clear development of religious thought whose culmination in modernity will be that all but the most idolatrous will discard a God conceived as infinite and almighty. He is clearly exasperated by theologians and especially by Christian philosophers who defend a God whom he thinks no longer deserves defending. The God who is 'an arbitrary, imperial potentate, a solitary eminence existing in glorious transcendence of all else' is, he tells us, a thing of the past. We can no longer think of God as 'an objectively existing powerful agent-self'.[6] We should no longer speak of God as 'creator/lord' or 'father' either for these terms cannot be purged of the anthropomorphism responsible for the oppression (of the weak, of women, of the poor) in the past. Now if this is simply a warning against idolatrous reification then many might wish to agree with Kaufman. But he is not simply reminding us, as has almost every theologian before him, of the dangers of anthropomorphic language. He is clear that we should move beyond belief in a God altogether. His is then a thoroughgoing theological anti-realism – we once needed what he calls this 'God symbol', but we do not need it now. In fact its retention keeps us in a state of moral immaturity, for ever waiting for a powerful deity to pick up the pieces of our fractured world. In the end there is little to distinguish Kaufman's position from atheism, deploying the rhetoric of religion where it suits our moral and social aspirations, but without 'God' except as a pious turn of phrase.

Atheism, as Michael Buckley has reminded us, is not a uniform state – there are as many atheisms as there are 'Gods' which are rejected – a particular atheism is usually a rejection of a particular conception of God.[7] The first question to put to any atheistic strategy is, then, which 'God' does it reject? In Kaufman's case (and not his alone) it is a God who is solitary, arbitrary and imperial – a God 'over and against us' whose very majesty deprives us of the power or the will to think and act for ourselves. The questions to ask is whether we recognise this God? Is it really, as Kaufman assures us, the Christian God? It seems to me that we might recognise in his description a version of Newton's God,

---

[6] Gordon D. Kaufman, 'Reconstructing the Concept of God: De-reifying the Anthropomorphisms', in eds., Sarah Coakley and David A. Pailin, *The Making and Remaking of Christian Doctrine* (Oxford: Clarendon Press, 1993), p. 104.

[7] Michael Buckley, S. J., *At the Origins of Modern Atheism* (New Haven and London: Yale University Press, 1987), see his Introduction.

an eighteenth-century deity who occupies his everlasting day in making adjustments to the cosmic frame. But is that God the God whom Christians pray to as infinite, almighty and wise?[8] It is frankly hard to believe that the God Kaufman sketches for us in such lurid and oppressive colours could be the God who excited the love and devotion of Anselm or Aquinas, Augustine or Julian of Norwich or, for that matter, that this could be the God of the Bible itself.

Kaufman for his part is not in doubt that his 'imperial potentate' is the God of the Bible. He says this,

In the Bible God stands behind and governs all that exists. In this picture it was apparently the autonomous, free agent, the 'I' (ego) existing alone in its solitude, that was the core model on the basis of which the image/concept of God was constructed. When Moses, in a very early story, asks the voice from the burning bush, 'Who are you? What is your name?', the answer that comes back to him is 'I AM; I AM WHO I AM' (Exod. 3:13–14, paraphrased). God is identified here as the great 'I AM', the ego-agent par excellence, sheer unrestricted agential power. Given this model, it is not surprising that God has often been conceived of as an all-powerful tyrant, a terrifying arbitrary force before whom women and men can only bow in awe and fear.[9]

We have now reached the focal text from which this chapter takes its title; Exodus 3 with its famous account of Moses' encounter with God in the burning bush. Let us consider the God who Kaufman finds there – *ego-agent par excellence* – this terrifying force before whom we tremble in awe and fear. Is not this alien and alienating 'agent' strangely familiar? Is it not indeed remarkably like the picture of God which David Hume demolished in the eighteenth century? Is this 'ego-agent' not remarkably similar to the God which Feuerbach lauded as 'man made ideal' in the nineteenth, and to the picture of God from which Freud has tried to wean us in the twentieth century? Is this not a picture of the God whom Freud regards as a hangover from the childhood of the human race – the product of our stubborn delusion that an omnipotent father can protect us from all harm? What is surprising in our own time is that we find, not the Freuds, Feuerbachs and Humes, but professors of theology like Kaufman engaged in this naturalising, atheistic exegesis of Christian texts. It seems Kaufman is singing a familiar song of modern atheism, but we dismiss him (and others like him) at our peril, for we cannot,

[8] Walter Kasper in *The God of Jesus Christ* makes a useful distinction between 'atheism' and a/theism', the latter being a quite proper rejection of Enlightenment theism (and not the God of Jesus Christ).

[9] Kaufman, 'Reconstructing the Concept of God', p. 104.

without wilful blindness, ignore the fact that this picture of the deity as a powerful, fearful tyrant is one which many atheistic and agnostic modern people take to be an accurate picture of the God in whom Christians believe – and in all honesty we may have to admit that some Christians think so, too.[10]

It is well known that David Hume, especially in his *Dialogues Concerning Natural Religion*, effectively demolished the anthropomorphic picture of God as divine designer so favoured by eighteenth-century British religious apologetics. But Hume also goes out of his way to discredit the God of the classical attributes as well – the God of omniscience, omnipotence, eternity and so on. He does this in his essay on the *Natural History of Religion*, a natural companion piece to the *Dialogues*. In the *Natural History* Hume explains or, we may say, invents a history of religion from its origins which sees it as driven always by the emotions of craven fear and blind hope. Since human society improves 'from rude beginnings to a state of greater perfection', Hume concludes that 'polytheism or idolatry was, and necessarily must have been, the first and most ancient religion of mankind'.[11] Indeed, says Hume, (showing little sensitivity for Jewish feelings) until about '1700 years ago' (roughly 50 CE) 'all mankind were idolators'. A 'barbarous and necessitous animal' such as human beings were at the first origin of society, must necessarily have had a grovelling and familiar notion of superior powers. Primitive man, concerned with the terrors which threatened his life, conceived of a multitude of deities to invoke for protection, and since 'there is a universal tendency amongst mankind to conceive all beings like themselves', human beings attributed human characteristics to these gods. Even monotheism, according to Hume, although 'ancient and widespread' owes little of its success to reason, but is simply a more refined polytheism. People (the simple and barbaric) will naturally choose a particular god as their patron and, having done so, will endeavour by every act

to insinuate themselves into his favour; and supposing him to be pleased, like themselves, with praise and flattery, there is no eulogy or exaggeration which will be spared in their address to him.[12]

---

[10] While writing this, I heard an interview with a film producer who said that, since he wanted to create an atmosphere of darkness, power and fear in a particular scene, he set it in a church! I rest my case.

[11] David Hume, 'The Natural History of Religion', in *Four Dissertations (1757)* (Bristol: Thoemmes Press, 1995), p. 3.

[12] Ibid., p. 45.

Praise of their 'god' as the greatest god soon leads to praise of him as the 'only god' and,

elevating their deities to the utmost bounds of perfection, at last beget the attributes of unity and infinity, simplicity and spirituality.[13]

Monotheism, in sum, is only the highest (and therefore most con-cealed) form of idolatry and the attributes, far from being the reasonable results of philosophical or spiritual reflection, are nothing but metaphys-ical grovellings. The servile and fear-driven believer, anxious to please a capricious deity, will invoke his 'god' as not only 'good' but 'very good' – in fact the greatest of all gods; as not only old, but eternal; not only powerful but omnipotent, and so we go on. Where God is so elevated, says Hume (anticipating Kaufman, or for that matter Nietzsche and Freud), the hu-man mind is abased. Monotheism is furthermore not morally preferable to polytheism – rather the reverse. Polytheism, while untidy and prim-itive, at least is tolerant, but those religions which maintain 'the unity of god' are intolerant, implacable and narrow. A refined and reasonable religion, Hume concludes, would be quite acceptable to him – but as to religions as they are actually found,

You will scarcely be persuaded, that they are other than sick men's dreams.[14]

Hume's would-be historical account of religions, then, in fact contains an only thinly concealed attack on that tradition of philosophical and spiritual theology sometimes called negative theology. This kind of the-ology, far from being a saving moment in which the believer attempts to purge her thought of anthropomorphism is, according to Hume, no more reasonable a practice than the base idolatry of which it is a sophisticated derivative.

It should be noted that this puncturing of the pretensions of negative theology is of utmost importance to Hume's case, since his overall attack on the coherence of religious belief depends upon showing that reli-gious language is either vapid or grossly anthropomorphic. On Hume's account even the predicates of negation turn out to be anthropomor-phisms; even that kind of cautious and qualified apophatic language by which Christian theologians have warned of the dangers of presuming we know and name God directly is no more than servile toadying after all.

Part of Freud's anti-religious genius was to conflate his own antipa-thetic picture of God's fatherhood with the distant and powerful God

---

[13] Ibid., p. 55.   [14] Ibid., p. 115.

of the attributes already familiar to European critics of religion. The God of Exodus becomes, in Freud's terms, the murdered primal father who is behind every divine figure, and the father who is giver of the law. While echoing in *The Future of an Illusion* the Humean contention that religion for the most part was little more than sick men's dreams, Freud goes beyond both Hume and Feuerbach in his willingness to borrow, or perhaps to 'recycle', the religious language of both Judaism and Christianity to suit his own theoretical needs. His talking cure revolved around 'our God, the word' and his late work, *Moses and Monotheism*, can be read as an extended and eccentric modern midrash on the Exodus story, in which Freud himself appears at times to be Moses, leading the people from pre-scientific slavery to the promised land of psychoanalysis. This borrowing of overtly religious terminology is even more apparent in Freud's famous French interpreter, Jacques Lacan. Lacan's essay, 'The Function of Language in Psychoanalysis', for instance, is filled will reference to 'the Word' of the patient, with quotes from scripture (sometimes in Greek), and with theological terminology such as anamnesis, 'nature and grace' and so on.[15] Neither does Lacan neglect to provide his own psychoanalytic gloss on Exodus, providing his own reading of the famous Exodus 3 passage. Moses at the burning bush, according to Lacan, meets the Symbolic father who is literally capable of laying down the law – of saying 'I AM WHO AM'. Here, analytically, is the fixed point of the law to which all who wish to enter psychic maturity must relate.

Since almost everyone who has ever written a book has said something about Moses and the burning bush, it might seem only fair that Freud and Lacan be allowed their analytic allegories of the text as well. The problem is that many modern Westerners have been brought up on a (largely unnoticed) diet of psychoanalytic terminology, and take Freud's reading not as *a* reading of Exodus, but as *the* reading: gospel truth. In a new kind of gnosis, the 'real meaning' of the God of Jewish and Christian origins is taken to be this Oedipal father, standing over and against us at the gates of psychic pre-history. Many who would shudder at fundamentalist exegesis by Christian theologians swallow uncritically those of a Freud or a Lacan. Perhaps indeed Freud's God is the real intellectual ancestor of Kaufmann's ego-agent par excellence, before whom we can only cower and tremble. But is it the God who Moses meets

---

[15] Jacques Lacan, *Speech and Language in Psychoanalysis*, trans. Anthony Wilden (Baltimore: John Hopkins University Press, 1968).

on Sinai, and who Jews and Christian subsequently have associated with the burning bush? I quote the relevant passage in full:

Moses was looking after the flock of Jethro, his father-in-law priest of Midian. He lead his flock to the far side of the wilderness and came to Horeb, the mountain of God. There the angel of Yahweh appeared to him in the shape of a flame of fire, coming from the middle of a bush. Moses looked; there was the bush blazing but it was not being burnt up. 'I must go and look at this strange sight,' Moses said 'and see why the bush is not burnt.' Now Yahweh saw him go forward to look, and God called to him from the middle of the bush. 'Moses, Moses' he said, 'Here I am' he answered 'Come no nearer' he said. 'Take off your shoes, for the place on which you stand is holy ground. I am the God of your father,' he said, 'the God of Abraham, the God of Isaac and the God of Jacob.' At this Moses covered his face, afraid to look at God . . . (Exod. 3:1–6)

Then Moses said to God, 'I am to go, then, to the sons of Israel and say to them, "The God of your fathers has sent me to you". But if they ask me what his name is, what am I to tell them?' And God said to Moses, 'I Am who I Am. This' he added 'is what you must say to the sons of Israel: "I Am has sent me to you"'. And God also said to Moses, 'You are to say to the sons of Israel: "Yahweh, the God of your fathers, the God of Abraham, the God of Isaac, and the God of Jacob, has sent me to you". This is my name for all time; by this name I shall be invoked for all generations to come.' (Exod. 3:13–15)

Moses, whose very name (in popular Hebrew etymology) meant 'drawn out' had been 'drawn out' of the Nile, miraculously saved by Pharaoh's daughter. The next we hear of him is as a grown man – educated as an Egyptian, but apparently with some social conscience about the conditions of his fellow Israelites. He is unfortunately over-zealous and kills an Egyptian who he sees striking a Hebrew, an act unlikely to impress the Egyptians and which does little for his reputation with the Hebrews either. Moses feels it wise to remove himself to Midian where he finds employment as a shepherd and marries the non-Jewish Zipporah. Following the narrative line as it is given us, we might imagine that tending of his father-in law's sheep was to be the only steady and relaxing job Moses ever had.

Seeking new grazing land in 'the far side of the desert', Moses comes to Horeb – a place of double isolation, a mountain in a desert – and his life is changed once and for all.

Moses looked, we are told, and there was the bush blazing but it was not being burnt up. 'I must go and look at this strange sight', Moses said, 'and see why the bush is not burnt.' Then Yahweh called,
'Moses, Moses'.
'Here I am' he answered.

'Come no nearer. Take off your shoes, for the place on which you stand is holy ground. I am the God of your father – the God of Abraham, the God of Isaac, the God of Jacob.'

Let us consider this, not in terms of a source-critical analysis, but at the level of a narrative reading,[16] for if Freud, Lacan and Kaufman are to be allowed this licence why should we not claim it, too? Notice then that Moses does not appear from the narrative to be particularly impressed by the initial *sight* of the burning bush. Rather he is curious. His response seems more, 'Odd, a bush which is burning and not consumed . . . I must have a closer look.' It is when God speaks to him from the bush that Moses appears truly awed. This is not, then, in its first moments an 'awe-inspiring theophany'. Lacan, for all the idiosyncrasies of his reading of Exodus, has at least noticed that this decisive revelation of God to Moses is in the medium of speech, *in words.*[17]

God calls Moses *by name* – 'the drawn out one', first from the water and now from the desert – and tells him to take off his shoes. And then, importantly, God gives Moses His name. This is not yet 'I AM WHO I AM'. Rather God says, 'I am the God of Abraham, Isaac and Jacob', the God, that is, of Moses' ancestors. This name is repeated at least five times over the next few chapters of the book, by God, and finally by Moses. God tells Moses that he has seen the misery of his people, Israel, in Egypt and that he means to deliver them. Furthermore he, Moses, is to be the agent of this delivery. Moses is to go to Pharaoh and bring the sons of Israel out of bondage.[18]

Far from crumbling in front of this 'all-powerful tyrant before whom we can only bow in awe and fear', Moses at this stage clearly wonders whether God has really thought about what he is suggesting. Moses has all kinds of objections – he can't speak well, Pharaoh won't listen to him, and so on.[19]

Moses begins to haggle . . . 'Who am I to go before Pharaoh' . . . 'I shall be with you' is God's reply. This promise, 'I shall be with you' from God, one might think, would be good enough for most people – but

---

[16] We will not, for instance, consider suggestions that the three names belong to different traditions brought together in one text – 'Elohistic', 'Priestly', etc.

[17] Walter Brueggemann notes that this is not so much a 'theophany' as a 'voice to voice encounter'. 'Exodus 3: Summons to Holy Transformation', in Stephen E. Fowl, *The Theological Interpretation of Scripture* (Oxford: Blackwell, 1997), p. 157.

[18] I confess to unhappiness in using the male personal pronoun for God in discussing this most cautious and numinous locus of biblical naming.

[19] Brevard Childs speaks of the prophet's resistance to his inclusion in the divine plan. See Brevard S. Childs, *Exodus: A Commentary* (London: SCM Press, 1974).

Moses is even less certain about his reception from the Israelites than by Pharaoh.

'What' he says 'if the sons of Israel ask me what your name is – what am I to tell them?' At this stage God gives a second name.
And God said to Moses 'I AM WHO I AM' – you must say to the sons of Israel 'I AM has sent me to you'. (Exod. 3:13–14)

Then follows a third name, the Tetragrammaton,

You are to say to the sons of Israel: Yahweh, the God of your fathers, the God of Abraham, Isaac and Jacob, has sent me to you. This is my name for all time; by this name I shall be invoked for all generations to come. (Exod. 3:15)

So then, three names are given in this sequence of text, names whose origins are perhaps lost in the overlapping layers of originating textual traditions, but names whose significance in this final canonical form have been meditated upon for generations by Jews and subsequently by Christians.

Of these three it cannot be doubted that it is 'I AM WHO I AM' as a gloss on the Tetragrammaton which has exercised the most fascination for Christian theologians, especially those whom we associate with 'negative' or mystical theology. Its suggestion of metaphysical ultimacy, of God as 'Being Itself', was attractive to Platonically formed theologians of the early church. The Septuagint translation of the Hebrew (*ehyeh asher ehyeh*) as *Egō eimi ho ōn* acted as an encouragement to just such a metaphysical reading. Nor were Christians alone in this.[20] Today most scholars emphasise that such a reading does not do justice to the Hebrew text with its double future of the verb 'to be'. Metaphysical ultimacy – pure – was not of much concern to those who wrote the Pentateuch. Walter Kasper suggests that the verb *hāyāh* here means not so much 'to be' as 'to effect' or 'to be effective'. The name is a promise that God will be with Israel in an effective way. Brevard Childs similarly says the name emphasises the actuality of God – so we might right it as 'I am there, wherever it may be – I am really there'.

The Tetragrammaton and its gloss can be seen a high point in a series of names of God which begins in Genesis, with Abraham, and ends with the first of the Ten Commandments in Exodus 20, 'I am YHWH your God who brought you out of the land of Egypt, out of the house of slavery.'

[20] Maimonides and Moses Mendelssohn took a similar direction. See Stéphane Moses, '"Je serai qui je serai". La révélation des noms dans le récit biblique', in ed., M. M. Olivetti, *Filosofia della Rivelazione* (Rome: Cedam, 1994), pp. 572 3.

And it is not only God who is the subject of naming. Abram is renamed 'Abraham' for he will be the father of nations; Isaac is given his name from Sarah's 'laugh'. Naming in these texts is not simply a matter of tagging or simple denomination – it is rather a practice, a practice which locates a certain individual or place within the emergent, symbolic, remembered history of Israel. In the divine self-designation to Moses in Exodus 3, God is placed as the God of Israel's history. Moses is to know that what he meets is the God of Israel's past (of Abraham, Isaac and Jacob), of its present (who sees its suffering) and of its future (the God who will lead them from slavery to the promised land).

Contemporary Jewish writers emphasise the specificity of this disclosure on Sinai – this God speaks at this moment of Israel's history, and for this specific purpose. I AM WHO I AM is not an eternal, philosophical abstraction but the God whom Israel has met in her historical actuality. Jon Levenson is at pains to argue that the religion of Israel is not a philosophical system. Israel's origins, as recounted in her sacred texts, are not cosmic and primordial (as is the creation of the world) but in a named place with a named man. Truth comes to Israel through the medium of history, and not despite it, and Israel knows her God through her history.[21]

Wed as we Christians may be to readings of Exodus 3 in terms of metaphysical ultimacy, these better (and Jewish) readings of the Hebrew text add richly to our understanding of Moses and the Burning Bush. It is a God of presence and action, and not of stasis, who addresses himself to Moses from the bush – a God who has acted, acts, and will act.

In his *Mystical Theology*, and in direct allusion to Moses' ascent of Sinai, Pseudo-Dionysius prays that we will be led,

> up beyond unknowing and light,
> up to the farthest, highest peak of mystic scripture
> where the mysteries of god's word
> lie simple, absolute and unchangeable
> in the brilliant darkness of a hidden silence.[22]

---

[21] Jonathan Sacks, the Chief Rabbi, makes a similar point in saying Jewish thought is not so much logical as chronological – a lived history. See his *Faith in the Future* (London: Darton, Longman and Todd, 1995). See also Peter Ochs, 'Three Postcritical Encounters with the Burning Bush', in ed., Fowl, *Theological Interpretation*, on the specificity of the divine disclosure.

[22] In ed., Colm Luibheid, *Pseudo-Dionysius: Complete Works* (Mahwah, New York: Paulist Press, 1987), p. 135.

This would seem to be exactly the kind of abstracting and allegorising treatment of Exodus 3 that Jews find so annoying in Christian texts. What then are Christians to do with their inheritance of Platonised readings of the Exodus texts, readings dear to the mystical tradition? Certainly Christians should be careful not to render the story of the burning bush metaphysical and only that. We must take to heart the Jewish insistence on the specificity of that particular word at that particular moment in Israel's history. But we can, I believe, defend the integrity of Christian negative theology too, with its meditations on God's eternity, impassibility and unity, since in the hands of great theologians like Gregory of Nyssa, or Dionysius, this unknowable God who dwells in 'brilliant darkness' and hidden silence is also and always the God of intimate presence.

Perhaps the most powerful Western meditation on the God of the attributes (the God who Kaufman finds so difficult and remote) is to be found in Augustine's _Confessions_. Here God's omniscience and omnipresence, his unity and impassibility need scarcely to be discussed – and are not discussed in philosophical terms – since the text simply displays them. Augustine's God is 'omnipresent' because God is, simply, always present to Augustine – and was so even when Augustine was not aware of it. How do we know God is always there for Augustine? Because Augustine talks to his God, in any place, at any time – 'this, O Lord, you knew'. Augustine displays the presence of his God by his literary (and doxological) practice. There is no time at which God is not, no place in which God is not, no secret centre to the soul where God is not. The God of the attributes is not far away but near, very near – and so Augustine is able to mix, willy nilly, and without embarrassment, the language of divine perfection with the language of the Psalms and gospels, because all are terms of God's intimacy with us.

Who then are you, my God? What, I ask, but God who is Lord? For 'who is the Lord but the Lord', or 'who is God but our God?' (Ps. 17:32). Most high, utterly good, utterly powerful, most omnipotent, most merciful and most just, deeply hidden yet most intimately present, perfection of both beauty and strength, stable and incomprehensible, immutable and yet changing all things, never new, never old . . . you love without burning, you are jealous in a way that is free of anxiety . . . You recover what you find, yet have never lost.[23]

The recognition that 'I AM WHO I AM' is 'God with us', that the God of the philosophers is the God of Jesus Christ, is one Augustine makes

---

[23] _Confessions_, pp. 4–5.

when he moves from Neoplatonism to full Christian commitment. With the acceptance of the startling claim of the Jews that God has acted in their human history, and of the even more startling Christian claim that the Word became flesh and dwelt among us, living a human history, Augustine comes to the recognition that history, human temporality, lives as lived, far from being a distraction from things eternal is precisely the only place where we can meet and know that God who is eternal Lord.[24] Israel's God is known not by speculation but by inference from her history. Similarly Augustine comes to know God's omniscience not as the final deduction of some Neoplatonic theorem (however helpful he continues to find neoplatonism as a staging post) but because standing where he now stands he can see that God always knew and always knows his (Augustine's) ways. God is powerful because he has acted powerfully in Augustine's life, changeless because always present to him. It is precisely in human history that 'I AM WHO I AM' has disclosed himself to us. With this insight Augustine can begin to write his own human history, which is his *Confessions*. The metaphysical attributes are not discarded, rather their meanings are only given in fullness through God's self-disclosure – through revelation. For this God who acts in lived lives, whether that of the cosmos, of Israel, or Augustine, ultimacy and intimacy are one.

We are brought back to the words with which this essay begins, words of prayer with which the *Confessions* open. It is often remarked that Augustine begins this book with an epistemological quandary – how can he search for God if he does not yet know who or what it is he is searching for?[25] Yet Augustine puts a prior question in the very first sentences of the book – how, he wonders, can he praise God? 'How shall I call upon my God, my God and Lord?' How can he praise God if he does not know how to call upon him? How can he 'name' God without misnaming God? Here the former professor of rhetoric agonises over how he *can speak at all* about the God who is beyond all naming. This is not just an epistemological and metaphysical question – it is a spiritual and a doxological one – for to name God is to risk making God into an object or an idol, and this is as true of the most seemingly non-idolatrous names he may use of God, such as eternal, immutable, omniscient as it is of the more obviously metaphorical names like rock, shield and fortress.[26]

---

[24] Augustine himself, though coming to many insights I would deem to be fundamentally 'Jewish', was far from gracious in his stated attitude towards the Jews and Judaism.

[25] See for example Denys Turner's discussion in *The Darkness of God: Negativity in Christian Mysticism* (Cambridge: Cambridge University Press, 1995).

[26] Gordon Kaufman's God, or the one he credits to historical theology, would be just such a philosophical idol.

Augustine, we may be so bold as to say, has already anticipated the dangers Freud and Kaufman feel they have discovered in the twentieth century – that our speaking of God may be a false speaking, simply exalted and disguised ways of speaking once more about ourselves. This, for someone setting out to write a spiritual autobiography, must be an ever-present danger. At one level Augustine faces the problem of any of the prophets (whose language he echoes) – how can a man of unclean lips speak of God? But for Augustine the problem is even more acute since he has been in the past a rented 'mouth', speaking false words for payment and selling his skills to students whose object in acquiring them were avarice and self-aggrandisement. Augustine has been then, linguistic tart and pimp in one, words not too strong for the loathing Augustine feels for his past life – not of sexual concupiscence, but as a rhetorician. How can he, Augustine, speak truly of God?

The answer is that he cannot speak if God does not first call, and so Augustine beseeches his Lord, repeatedly, in this first chapter that he may find words, that God will *give* him words – 'Speak to me so that I may hear.' 'Allow me to speak.' The answer to his quandary is given in a practice, not a proposition – in the practice of prayer. God cannot be called down by human naming, however philosophically exalted this may be (here Hume is right) but surely, as Augustine says, 'you may be called upon in prayer that you may be known'. This prayer is, as he points out, itself already a gift.

My faith, Lord, calls upon you. It is your gift to me. You breathed it into me by the humanity of your Son, by the ministry of your preachers. (Book I. i (I))

God has given himself to be named. What Kaufman neglects to note of the fearful encounter in Exodus 3 is the remarkable fact that when Moses asks a name of his God, he is given one. God is established as the God who gives his name to Israel, and as the God who is named by his acts for Israel. That is the final sense of 'I AM WHO I AM'. Augustine's recognition is that we can speak of God only because, as to Moses and Israel, God has first spoken to us.

For 'those who have nothing to say or don't want to know anything', says Jacques Derrida, 'it is always easy to mimic the technique of negative theology'.[27] The language of the divine attributes is readily conceived, now as in the past, as either a language of an 'over and against God'

[27] 'How to Avoid Speaking: Denials', in ed., Harold Coward and Toby Forshay, *Derrida and Negative Theology* (Albany: SUNY Press, 1992), p. 75.

(Kaufman and Freud) or, alternatively, as vacuous (Feuerbach). Yet despite its cautions and qualifications this 'rhetoric of negative determination' is by no means vacuous and not, in the hands of theologians like Augustine or Dionysius a technique for 'those who have nothing to say'.[28]

Derrida, agnostic, here proves an unexpected ally for in contrast with Feuerbach, he does not seem to find theological apophaticism to be trapped in a circle of empty negation. The reason for this is the place it gives to prayer. Why do these texts, like that of Augustine, or Aquinas, or Gertrude of Helfta, or any number of others, begin with prayer? The prayer which precedes these apophatic utterances is, as 'the address to the other', a moment which is more than a pious preamble. One *must* begin with supplication, for the power of speaking and of speaking well comes from God – Derrida quotes Dionysius, 'to That One who is the Cause of all good, to Him who has first given us the gift to speak and then, to speak well'. And Derrida continues, 'This is why apophatic discourse must also open with a prayer that recognizes, assigns, or ensures its destination: the Other as Referent of a *legein* which is none other than its Cause.'[29] Far from condemning the theological enterprise, there is in Derrida's essay the wistful implication that only the language of true theology, language whose destination is assured not by verbal domination but by grace, is truly language at all. To be a theologian, we might say, is always to stand under the primacy of the signified over the signifier (an exact reversal of what Derrida thinks to be the case for language in general) but at the same time to know the signified can only be named through gift. The problem with which Derrida's reader is left is not one for theological language, but for any speaking or theory of speech which is atheistic. How, indeed, can Derrida speak if he cannot first pray?

Above all this is true of course when speaking of God. The naming of God can never be, without risk of idolatry a matter of simple denomination. Its foundation is gift – the gift of God's self-disclosure in history (both Israel's and our own) – and practice, the practice of prayer which is itself a gift. Our faith, as Augustine says, is God's gift, through his son, through his preachers. This speaking of God, made possible because God first speaks to us, opens for us not only the possibility of praise but of our true sociality, our true and truthful use of the shared possession that is speech. Augustine's search for self-knowledge and true speaking finds its conclusions not with a *cogito ergo sum* but in 'only say the word, Lord, and I shall be healed'.

---

[28] Ibid., p. 74.   [29] Ibid., p. 98.

4

Aquinas on the Trinity

Herbert McCabe

That God is one and three is, of course, for Aquinas a profound mystery which we could not hope to know apart from divine revelation, but we can only begin to understand what he has to say about it if we recognise that for him God is a profound mystery anyway. There are people who think that the notion of God is a relatively clear one; you know where you are when you are simply talking about God whereas when it comes to the Trinity we move into the incomprehensible where our reason breaks down. To understand Aquinas it is essential to see that for him our reason has already broken down when we talk of God at all – at least it has broken down in the sense of recognising what is beyond it. Dealing with God is trying to talk of what we cannot talk of, trying to think of what we cannot think. Which is not to say that it involves nonsense or contradiction.

This similarity is sometimes obscured for us by the fact that Aquinas thinks we can prove the existence of God by natural reason whereas such unaided natural reason could tell us nothing of the Trinity. This, however, does not, for him, make the latter a mystery where the former is not, for he thought that to prove the existence of God was not to understand God but simply to prove the existence of a mystery. His arguments for the existence of God are arguments to show that there are real questions to which we do not and cannot know the answer. He seeks to show that it is proper to ask: 'Why is there anything at all instead of nothing at all?'; he seeks, that is, to show that it is not an idle question like 'How thick is the equator?' or 'What is the weight of Thursday week?' It is a question with an answer but one that we cannot know, and this answer all men, he says, call 'God'. He is never tired of repeating that we do not know what God is, we know only *that* God is and what he is *not* and everything we come to say of him, whether expressed in positive or negative statements, is based on this.

After his arguments for the existence of God, for the validity of our unanswerable question, he says

> When we know that something is it remains to enquire in what *way* it is, so that we may know *what* it is. But since concerning God we cannot know what he is but only what he is not, we cannot consider in what way God is but only in what way he is not. So first we must ask in what way he is not, secondly how he may be known to us and thirdly how we may speak of him.[1]

This, at the opening of question 3, is his programme for the next ten questions and beyond. And none of the hundreds of questions that follow in the four volumes of the *Summa* mark a conscious departure from this austere principle. Indeed he constantly comes back to it explicitly or implicitly.

God must be incomprehensible to us precisely because he is creator of all that is and, as Aquinas puts it: outside the order of all beings. God therefore cannot be classified as any kind of being. God cannot be compared or contrasted with other things in respect of what they are like, as dogs can be compared and contrasted with cats and both of them with stones or stars. God is not an inhabitant of the universe, he is the reason why there *is* a universe at all. God is in everything holding it constantly in existence, but he is not located anywhere, nor is what it is to be God located anywhere in logical space. When you have finished classifying and counting all the things in the universe you cannot add: And also there is God. When you have finished classifying and counting everything in the universe you have finished, period. There is no God in the world.

Given this extreme view of the mysteriousness and incomprehensibility of God we may well ask Aquinas how he thinks we have any meaning at all for the word 'God'. Surely if we do not know what God is we do not know what 'God' means and theology must be a whole lot of codology. To know what a daisy is and to know the meaning of the word 'daisy' come to much the same thing. Aquinas replies that even amongst ordinary things we can sometimes know how to use a name without knowing anything much about the nature of the thing named. Thus the businessman may quite rationally order a computer system to deal with his office work without having the faintest idea of how a computer works. His meaning for the word 'computer' is not derived precisely from

---

[1] *Summa Theologiae* 1 a q. 3, *prologue.*

knowing what a computer *is*, it is derived from the effect that it has on his business. Now Aquinas says that with God it is like this but more so. We have our meaning for the word 'God', we know how to use it, not because of anything at all that we know about God, but simply from the effects of God, creatures. Principally that they *are* instead of there being nothing. But the businessman is better off because knowing what a computer is for is a very large part of knowing what it is. Whereas God does not exist in order to make creatures. So the meaning of 'God' is not the same as the meaning of 'the existence of things instead of there not being anything'; we have the word 'God' because the existence of things instead of there not being anything is *mysterious* to us (and, Aquinas argues in the five ways, *ought* to be mysterious to us).

What we say of the word 'God' had also to be said of every other word we use of God; if we speak of God as good or wise it is not because we understand what it is for God to be good or wise, we are wholly in the dark about this; we use these and similar words because of certain things we know about creatures. When we do this we take words which have at least a fairly clear sense in a context of creatures and seek to use them in a different context. This, in Aquinas' terminology, is to use them *analogically*. Certain words, of course, simply cannot be taken out of their creaturely context because this context is *part* of their meaning. Thus we could not, even speaking analogically, say that a mighty fortress is our God, because mighty fortresses are essentially material things and God could not be a material thing. We could only say that metaphorically not analogically. Thus when we say that God is maker or cause of the world we are using 'maker' and 'cause' outside their familiar contexts in senses which we do not understand.

So it should be clear that for Aquinas the existence of God at all is as mysterious as you can get. The Trinity for him is no less and no more mysterious. To say that there is Father, Son and Holy Spirit who are God is for him no more mysterious than to say there is God at all. In neither case do we know what we are saying, but in neither case are we talking nonsense by contradicting ourselves. This latter is, of course, the next point to consider.

Aquinas holds that although we do not know what it is for God to be maker of the world it is not *nonsense* to say this of God in the way that it would be nonsense to say literally that God is a mighty fortress or a cup of tea. It is frequently the case that we find we have to apply several predicates to God and because we do not understand them in this context we cannot see *how* they can be compatible with each other;

but this is very different from saying that they are incompatible. It is one thing not to know how something makes sense and quite another to know that it does *not* make sense. Aquinas' task is to show that while we do not see *how* there can be Father, Son and Spirit who are all one God, we can show that it is not nonsense.

The thought may (at least at first) appear to be simpler if we look at the mystery of the incarnation. Here Aquinas holds that we do not understand how anyone could be simultaneously divine and human in the way that, for example, we *can* understand how someone could be simultaneously Russian and human. But he holds that we can understand that for someone to be both divine and human does *not* involve a contradiction in the sense that for something to be both a square and circle *would* involve a contradiction.

Now similarly he holds that we cannot understand how God could be both Father, Son and Spirit as well as utterly one and simple, but we do understand that this does not involve the kind of contradiction that would be involved in saying, say, that God is three Fathers as well as being one Father, or three Gods as well as being one God. What we have to do in this case is to see how we are compelled to say each of the things but not to try to imagine them being simultaneously true or even try to *conceive* of them being simultaneously true; we should not expect to form a concept of the triune God, or indeed of God at all, we must rest content with establishing that we are not breaking any rules of logic, in other words that we are not being intellectually dishonest.

There is nothing especially odd or irrational about this. It only seems shocking to those who expect the study of God to be easy and obvious, a less demanding discipline than, say, the study of nuclear physics. In physics we are quite accustomed to the idea that there are two ways of talking about the ultimate constituents of matter, both of them necessary and both of them internally coherent, and yet we do not know how to reconcile them: one in terms of waves and the other in terms of particles. It is not a question of choosing between them; we have to accept them both. We do not, however, *need* to conceive of how anything could be both wave and particle; we simply accept that, at least for the moment, we have these two languages and that the use of them does not involve a contradiction although we cannot see *how* it avoids contradiction. It is true that most physicists would look forward to some future theoretical development in which we will devise a single language for expressing these matters but they do not see themselves as talking nonsense in the meantime. This too is rather similar to Aquinas' position, for he too looks forward to a theoretical development by which we will come to see, to understand, how God is both one and three, but this he thinks can only come by sharing God's own self-understanding in the beatific vision. But meanwhile we are not talking nonsense.

To take another parallel: the square root of a number is that which when multiplied by itself yields that number. Since any number whether positive or negative when multiplied by itself yields a positive number, what could be made of a notion like the square root of a *negative* number, the square root of minus 2 for example? There is plainly no way in which we could conceive of the square root of minus 2 but this does not faze mathematicians; they are content to use it in a rule-governed way and find it a very useful device.

Aquinas, then, is faced with a situation similar to the physicist's. We have on the grounds of revelation to say two quite different kinds of things about God, that God is altogether one and there are three who are God. We cannot *see* how they can both be true but that need not faze us; what we have to do is show that there are no good grounds for saying that they are incompatible. We have to show in fact that the conditions which would make them incompatible in other cases do not and cannot apply to God – remember that all we know of God is what he is not, what he cannot be if he is to be God, the reason why there is anything instead of nothing.

One of the basic principles which Aquinas employs in considering the Trinity is the principle that *everything that is in God is God*. This is again something we cannot understand, we cannot see *how* it could be true but we are forced to assert that it is true. It follows, in Aquinas' view, from the fact that there can be no passive potentiality in God. This means that there is nothing in God which might not have been in him; there is never anything which he might be but is not or that he is but might not have been. This in its turn follows from the fact that God cannot be changed by anything. If God were the patient or subject or victim of some other agent he could not be the source of the existence, the reality of everything that is. Rather, there would be something (this other agent) who would be a source of something in God. If God were not the source of the existence of all that is he would not be what we use the word 'God' for. Now Aquinas holds, surely reasonably, that it makes no sense to speak of what does not exist as acting or doing anything or bringing anything about. Hence what is merely potential – what might exist but does not – cannot act to bring itself about nor can it bring anything else about. What is potential can only be brought into existence by something that is actual. We must not confuse potentiality in this sense with power, an active capacity to do something; we mean simply what might be but is not. Thus if there were any potentiality in God in this passive sense, he would need to be acted on by some other agent and thus, as we have seen, would not be God. God is thus, in Aquinas' phrase, *actus purus*, sheer actuality. He does not become, he just is. He cannot become because then there would be something he might be but is not. It is for these reasons that Aquinas says that God is totally unchanging and timeless.

Because of this, Aquinas argues that there can be no 'accidents' in God. Let me explain that. It is accidental to me that I am writing this paper. This means that I would still be me if I were not writing it. Similarly it is accidental to me that I am wearing these clothes and that I am 6 feet high. I am still *me* in bed and I was the same me when I was 4 feet high. What is accidental is opposed to what is essential. Thus it is not accidental but essential to me that I am an animal or that I am a human being. If I ceased to be an animal I would cease to exist, I would turn into something else – a corpse. By what is essential to a thing we mean what it takes for it to exist. What it take for me to be is my being human, what is takes for Fido to be is being a dog, but both Fido and I have many other things about us which are not essential in his sense, many things which we could lose or gain without ceasing to be. This is what 'accidents' means.

Now it is clear that if writing this paper is accidental to me I might not have been writing it – I mean I would still have been me if I had gone down with flu or simply been too lazy. To have accidental features then is to be potential in some respect. Fido is eating a bone but he might not have been, he is not barking but he might be. To have accidental features as distinct from essential ones is to have some potentiality. Hence a being, God, with no potentiality can have no accidents. Every feature of God must be of his essence, essential to him.

Now please notice that all this argument is based not on any knowledge or understanding that we have of God; it is simply what we are compelled to say if we are to use the word 'God' correctly, i.e. to mean whatever unknown mystery is the source of the being of all that is. Whatever would answer the question: 'Why is there anything rather than nothing at all?' Whatever 'God' refers to, it could not be anything with potentiality and hence it could not be anything with accidental features. This means that whatever is in God *is* God. My writing this paper is not my being me, it is accidental to me, whereas my being human *is* my being me. Now with God *everything* he is is just his being God. So if we say that God is wise or omnipotent we cannot be referring to two different features that God *happens* to have over and above being God. This wisdom of God just is his being God; so are his omnipotence and his goodness and whatever else we attribute to him. Now of course we cannot understand what it would be like for something to be its own wisdom. The wisdom we understand is always an accidental feature of persons, and so is power or goodness. When we use such words as God we must be using them analogically, outside the context of their first use, and we do not understand what we mean by them. We have no concept of the wisdom of God; for that matter we have no concept of God.

So every feature we attribute to God just is God, it is the divine essence or nature. But now we come to a complication because not everything we *say* of God attributes in this sense a feature of him. I mean not every sentence beginning 'God is . . .' or 'God has . . .' is intended to attribute some real feature to him. This is because some of the things we say about God are relational.

Suppose that next week I shall become a great-uncle. At the moment it is, we shall say, not true that I am a great-uncle; next week it will become true. Are we then to say that a potentiality in me to become a great-uncle has been fulfilled? Not so, because my becoming a great-uncle involves no change in me at all; it is entirely a matter of a change in my niece Kate and what is in her womb. So although a sentence like 'Herbert is becoming a great-uncle' sounds just like 'Herbert is becoming wise' or 'Herbert is becoming a Dominican', we should not be misled by the grammar into thinking we are talking about a change in what is named by the subject term. The fact that there really is a new thing to say of me does not have to mean to say there is a new reality in me. Relational expressions are quite often like this. For example: 'You are on my left but you used to be on my right' doesn't have to imply any change in you; I may simply have turned round. You have not fulfilled any potentiality in yourself to become on my left. There would be only a *verbal* change – something new to say about you. Similarly 'you are farther away' or 'you have become richer than I' may or may not be true because of changes in you; they may be, for you, merely verbal changes.

Now consider the profoundly mysterious truth that God sustains Mr Pinochet in existence. This was not true of God in, say, 1900 because in those far off happy times Mr Pinochet did not exist and so God could not have been sustaining him in existence. So God began to sustain him, he *became* the sustainer of Mr Pinochet. But, Aquinas says, this does not entail any change in God any more than becoming a great-uncle entails any change in me. Thus becoming the sustainer of Mr Pinochet is not a real happening to God, in our sense, although it becomes true of him. It is true of him not because of some new reality in him but because of some reality in Mr Pinochet – that he began to be alive. Of course that he is alive is *due to* a reality in God; his profoundly mysterious eternal will that he should come to exist at a certain date. But this eternal will is not something that comes about at a date so this does not imply any real change in God. So when Mr Pinochet was conceived there was something going on in him, but on God's side the change is merely verbal; we have a new thing to say about God, it is not a new thing about God that we are saying.

There is therefore a great deal of logical difference between saying God is *wise* and saying that God is the sustainer of Mr Pinochet, or in general saying that he is creator. In the first case we attribute a real feature of God, wisdom, which (because there can be no accidents in God) must therefore be identical with being God. In the second case the reality is in the creature, there is merely a verbal change in God – a change in what has to be said of him. For this reason we are rescued from the appalling fate of suggesting that being creator and sustainer of Pinochet is essential to God, that he would not be God had he not created Pinochet.

So being creator of the world is not part of what it is to be God. God did not become God when in, say, 4005 BC he created the world. Indeed he did not change at all. Although saying he became creator sounds like attributing an accident to God it is not in fact attributing any new feature to him at all; we say it in order to say something new about the world.[2] We should remember, of course, that when we say God does not change, we do not mean God stays the same all the time. God is not 'all the time'. God is eternal. To attribute stasis to God is as mistaken as to attribute change to him. The main point is this: that what we say of God because of his creative relationships to creatures does not attribute any new reality to God and thus does not speak of God's essence.

James Mackey in his interesting book *The Christian Experience of God as Trinity* (the title ought to be enough to warn you) has a generally hostile account of Aquinas' treatment of the Trinity; and he finds the notion I am trying to explain especially unlovable. He says,

(Aquinas) is quite clear in his insistence that the Trinity cannot be known from creation – the principle *opera ad extra sunt indivisa* is by now sacrosanct and he

---

[2] Strictly speaking of course even the world itself did not *change* when it was created because until it was created it was not there to change. But that is another question.

further distances from our world all discussion of real divine relation by stating quite baldly 'there is no real relation in God to the creature'. Creatures, that is, may experience a real relationship of dependence upon and need of God, but God experiences no such real relationship to creatures.[3]

I am afraid this is a dreadful muddle. Whether a relationship in me is real or merely verbal has nothing whatever to do with experience. The fact that the relationship of being a great-uncle is not a real one in me in no way makes it something I do not experience; it in no way makes me less aware of my great-niece nor less concerned about her. God, of course, for Aquinas does not experience anything in the world. He has no need to. He does not, as I do, have to learn about the world from outside. He is at the heart of absolutely everything in the world, holding it in existence and bringing about everything it does.

The principle that whatever is in God is God, then, does not apply to such relational predicates as being creator or being sustainer of Pinochet. It *does* apply to non-relational predicates like 'is wise' and 'is good' and 'is merciful'. God's wisdom, goodness and mercy are all identical with his essence and there is no real distinction in God between his goodness and his wisdom. On the other hand there *is* a real distinction between God sustaining Pinochet and God sustaining me but it is not a real distinction in God but a very fundamental one between myself and Pinochet.

It is indeed a great mystery that the wisdom of God is God, and the power of God is God, and the goodness of God is God, and all three are the same God – we cannot understand how this can be, but it is not like the mystery of the Trinity because we cheerfully admit that (in some way we do not understand) all three are in fact identical, there is no distinction between the goodness and the power and the wisdom of God. In the case of the Trinity, however, we want to say that the Father is God and the Son is God and the Spirit is God and all three are the same God but nevertheless they are not identical. There is distinction between Father, Son and Spirit.

What we have got to so far is that when we are speaking of *what is real in God* we are speaking of what is God's essence and all our predicates refer to one and the same identical essence of divinity, not to a number of accidents; our different predicates do not mark real distinctions in God. When, however, we are speaking of God's *relationship to creatures*, our different predicates *do* mark real distinctions but not in God because they entail no reality in God.

---

[3] James Mackey, *The Christian Experience of God as Trinity* (London: SCM Press, 1983), p. 182.

Aquinas' next move is to speak not of God's activity with regard to creatures, his creative act, but of God's activity within himself. And here we have to notice a difference between transitive and intransitive verbs. Aquinas points out that not all our acts are actions upon something else, acts which make a difference to something else. Carving and writing and teaching are all acts whose reality consists in what happens to some subject, and so is creating. Carving can only be going on if some stuff is being carved, writing can only be going on if some words are being written; but what about the act, of say, growing? You can of course grow in a transitive sense, as when a gardener grows begonias, but growing in the intransitive sense is not an activity that does something to something else, nor is boiling or collapsing. To use Aquinas' phrase, it remains within the agent. Still more clearly the act of understanding is not an act which does anything or makes any difference to anything else. It is a kind of growing or development of the mind itself; not an operation on what is understood or on anything else. Of course there are philosophers who, partly for this reason, think it a mistake to talk of understanding as an *act*, but we cannot pause here to argue with them. For Aquinas, at any rate, it was an act performed by the agent but not passing outside the agent or one altering or influencing or changing anything else. Aquinas occasionally calls such actions 'immanent' acts as opposed to 'transient' ones.

Now can we speak of *God's* act of understanding? It would take much too long to give an account of Aquinas' general theology of understanding. You will just have to take it from me that for him both understanding and being intelligible have to do with not being *material*. To understand a nature is just to possess the nature immaterially. To possess the nature of a dog materially is to *be* a dog; to possess the nature of a dog immaterially (to have it in mind) is to *understand* a dog; to know what a dog is, or what the word 'dog' means. For Aquinas, you might say, the *norm* for being is that it should be intelligent, understanding, *immaterial* being; the exceptional ones are those whose being is curbed and restricted by matter; matter not thought of as some special kind of stuff but as the limitedness and potentiality of things. For Aquinas *we* can understand because we are just about able to transcend our materiality. While almost all our vital operations of the body are circumscribed by matter, in the act of understanding we have an act which, although it is heavily involved with bodily activity and cannot ordinarily take place without concomitant bodily working, is not of itself an act of the body, a bodily process. Beings which are not material at all, quite unlimited by matter, angels for example, would understand much better than we do, without the tedious need for bodily experience, for what he calls the sense power of the *imaginatio* or *phantasmata* and for the use of material symbols and words. For Aquinas, then, it follows simply from the fact that God cannot be material that he cannot be non-intellectual, he cannot fail to be understanding. This is part of our negative knowledge of God, our knowledge of what God is not.

We should, however, be quite clear that in saying that we know that God is not impersonal, not lacking in understanding and knowledge, we are laying no claim to knowing what it means for God to understand. Aquinas will go on to speak of God having an understanding of himself or forming a concept of himself but it is clear that we have so far no warrant for saying this. There is no reason to suppose that God's act of understanding is so much like ours. But on the other hand we have equally no warrant for saying that it is not. I mean we do have warrant for saying that God does not *hear* or *see* anything just as he does not chop down trees, for all these are operations of a material body; the idea of God forming a concept of himself is not excluded in *that* way. It is simply that other things being equal we would have no reason to assert it. Aquinas, however, thinks other things are not equal for he interprets the Logos theology of John as suggesting just this.

When we understand a nature – say, what an apple is – we form a concept of what an apple is and this concept is the meaning we have for the word 'apple'. (When I speak of understanding the nature of an apple I do not mean some profound grasp of the essence of apples; I just mean the situation of someone who knows what apples are as distinct from someone who has never come across them or heard of them.) The concept is not precisely *what* we understand; what we understand is what apples are, *the nature of apples*, but the concept is what we have in mind in understanding this nature. It is the meaning for us of apples, the meaning expressed in the word 'apple'. So when you learn, say, what peevishness is, you do so by forming a concept which is the meaning of the word 'peevish' or 'peevishness'. It is not exactly that you learn the word itself, for you may not know that useful word and you may express the meaning you understand by some complicated circumlocution, and again a Frenchman who comes to the same understanding of what peevishness is will form the same concept which for him will be the meaning of the word 'maussaderie'. The concept, then, is what is conceived in the mind in the act of understanding and because it is the meaning of a word it was called by the medievals the *verbum mentis*, the word of the mind. This does not commit them to any doctrine that we can have concepts before we have any words in which we express them; indeed Aquinas clearly thought we could not, but it is plain that many different words or signs may express the same concept; that is what we mean when we say that this word or phrase means the same as that one.

Now let us return to the understanding of God. God's understanding of me or of any of his creatures is not something other than his creating and sustaining of them. God, you may say, knows what he is doing and what he is doing is keeping these things in their being and everything about them. God's knowledge of me, then, like his creating of me is a relational predicate true of God because of a reality in me, just as I will be a great-uncle because of the reality of my great-niece. God knows me not by having a concept of me distinct from a concept he has of you, he knows me by knowing himself and thus knowing himself as creator of me and you. Thus that God knows me and also knows you does not imply that there are two different concepts, two different realities in God, any more than when I become a great-uncle three times over there will be three different realities in me.

But what, asks Aquinas, about God's understanding of *himself*? He forms a concept of himself. The concept, remember, is not *what* is understood but *how* something is understood, what is produced, brought forth, conceived, in the understanding of something. *What* God understands is himself, identical with himself, but *in* understanding he conceives the concept, the *verbum mentis*, and this because *produced*, brought forth by him, is not him. Let us remind ourselves again that there is no 'must' about it. Aquinas is not trying to deduce the Trinity from God's intellectuality. We do not understand God's understanding, and apart from the revelation about God's Word we should not be talking about God forming a concept.

Notice the importance of the switch from looking at God's activity that *passes outside him* to creatures, to looking at this *immanent* activity of self-understanding. In the former case there is no reality in God on which the relationship of being created or being understood is based; it is a reality in the creature and a merely verbal thing in God, a change in what is to be said of him. In the latter case, however, there is a reality, a concept, in God himself. A reality distinct from God in God.

But what about the Aquinas' principle mentioned and agreed earlier: 'everything that is real in God is God'? We cannot see the concept in God (as we can see our own concepts) as an accident distinct from the essence. In us our concept is a reality distinct from us in us. It is an accident. Our concepts come and go, and we remain what we are; this cannot be true of God. If God has formed a concept it is not an accident of God, it is God. This is quite beyond our understanding, we are merely forced to it by our reasoning. We are not, of course, forced by our reasoning to say that God forms a concept of himself, but we are forced to say that *if* he does so it cannot be merely accidental, it must be God.

The act of creating brings about a relationship between God and his creature. They are *distinct* but *related* to each other as creator and creature. But the basis of this relation is real only in the creature, just as the basis of the relationship of being a great-uncle is real only on one side. The act of God's self-understanding which involves the bringing forth of a concept, a *verbum mentis*, also brings about a relationship between God and the concept. They are *distinct* but related to each other as conceiver and what is conceived, meaner and meaning. But the basis of this relationship, unlike the relationship of creation, is real at *both* ends. The mind and the *verbum* it produces are really distinct as the opposite ends of a relationship. And whatever is real in God is God.

St Thomas shifts, as does St John himself, from Logos language – 'In the beginning was the word and the word was with God and the word was God' (Jn 1:1) – to the language of Father and Son. He argues that these come to the same thing: there are two essential requirements for the act of generation – first that A should have been *brought forth* by B and secondly that it should have the *same nature* as B. I did not generate *you* because although you have the same nature as I, I did not bring you forth. On the other hand, I did not generate my nail clippings or my thoughts, although I brought them forth, because they are not themselves human beings. I would generate only my children which are both brought forth and of the same nature. The *verbum mentis* of God, however, is *both* brought forth by him, conceived by him, and *also* is of the same nature, for, being real in God, it is God. Thus the language of generation, of Son and Father, is here applicable.

It does not in any case seem fortuitous that the language of mental activity should parallel that of sexual generation. The word 'concept' itself belongs primarily to the context of generation. Of course all this fits much more easily into an Aristotelian and biblical biology according to which fathers generate their sons merely in the environment of women. Nothing was then known of the splitting of chromosomes and sharing of genes, women were not thought to contribute actively to the generative process. From our more knowledgeable point of view it would make more sense to speak of God the Parents rather than God the Father.

(The plural of 'parents' would be no more misleading than is the sexual connotation of 'Father'.) However, that of course is not in Aquinas.

So for Aquinas, as indeed for the Catholic faith, Father and Son do not differ in any way (*homo-ousion*). In each case what they are is God and they are nothing except that they are God. The Father has no features or properties which the Son has not. The only thing that distinguishes them is that they are at opposite ends of a relationship. The Father generates the Son, the Son *is generated* by the Father. Being the Father just is standing in that relationship to the Son; being the Son just is standing in that relationship to the Father. The Father *is a relation*. It is not that he *has* a relation. Just as in creatures wisdom is always an accident, the wisdom of some subject, so in creatures 'a relation to . . .' is always an accident supervening on some already existing subject. But of course, as we have seen, nothing supervenes on God. In him there are no accidents. Whatever really is in God is the essence of God. So the Father does not *have* a relationship of Fatherhood to the Son; he *is* that relationship subsisting as God. And the Son *is* the relation of being generated by the Father, subsisting as God. Need I say that the notion of subsisting relation is mysterious to us, we do not know what it would mean or what it would be like, but (to repeat) we do not know what subsisting wisdom would mean or what God would mean or what God would be like.

We see then that the only distinction in God is that of being at opposite ends of a relationship due to an act or 'process' within the Godhead. Nothing that is said non-relationally about God makes any distinction between Father and Son, and nothing that is said even relationally about God in virtue of his dealings with creatures refers to any real distinction in God at all. God turns to creatures, *as his creatures*, the single unified face of the one God, the unchanging, the eternal, the single source of all that is. It is only with God's own interior life, his own self-understanding, that there is a basis for distinction. And of course that interior life is of vast interest to us because we are called on to share it. God does not look upon us human creatures simply as creatures; he has invited us by our unity in Christ to share in Christ's divine life within the Trinity, to share in his Sonship. And this of course brings us, perhaps a little belatedly, to the Holy Spirit, for it is by receiving the Spirit through faith in baptism that we share in the interior life of the Godhead.

The main principles for Aquinas' treatment of the Spirit are already laid down in his discussion of the Father and the Son. This indeed is one of the major difficulties with his treatment. He is, however, quite

conscious and explicit about what he is doing. He says that it is necessary
to consider the Holy Spirit on the same lines as we consider the Son. His
reason for this is that the only possible distinction in the Godhead is the
distinction of two opposite ends of a relationship and the only possible
basis for relationship in the Godhead is the relation of origin to what
is originated, a relation set up by some *procession* such as the conception
of the Word, the generation of the Son. So the Holy Spirit too must be
distinct in its relation to its origin and its origin, says St Thomas, lies in
that other immanent operation of the intellectual being, the operation
of the will, the operation of love.

This, however, is where the difficulties begin. It is not too difficult to
see how in understanding himself the Father forms a concept of himself
which being real in God is itself God; it is much less easy to see how
anything is formed in the operation of the will. This is especially so if
we remember Aquinas' own often repeated doctrine that while truth is
in the mind, goodness is in things. The act of understanding is a taking
into the mind of the form or nature of things and this is the formation
of a concept; but the act of loving is a going out towards the thing, a
being attracted to it or an enjoyment of it. It is not at all clear what
it is that is originated in this act of the will. Remember that the Holy
Spirit is not *what* is loved, any more than the concept or word or Son is
what is known; what is known and loved is the divine nature itself, it is
a question of *self*-knowledge and *self*-love; the Word is what is formed in
this self-knowledge and the Holy Spirit is what is formed in this self-love.

Well, says Aquinas, we ought not to think of the Holy Spirit as a
likeness of what is loved in the way that the concept is a likeness (in this
case a perfect likeness) of what is known; rather it is tendency towards,
a *nisus* or impulsion towards, even a kind of excitement – an enjoyment.
This, Aquinas thinks, is formed in the act of loving. This is the term of
the act of what he calls *spiratio*, breathing forth. It becomes, then, difficult
to speak of the Holy Spirit as a 'thing' that is formed, and I remember
Victor White always used to regard this as one of the great strengths
and glories of Aquinas' teaching on the Trinity. With the Holy Spirit, as
least, we are in no danger of seeing God as a 'person' in the modern
sense. Here God is a movement, an impulse, a love, a delight. 'This is
my beloved Son in whom I am well pleased' (Luke 3: 22).

It is essential to Aquinas' doctrine that the Holy Spirit proceeds from
both the Father and the Son, and not merely from the Father. The reason
for this is that the only distinction admissible in the Trinity is that of
being at opposite ends of a relation based on a procession of origination.

If the Holy Spirit does not proceed from the Son there is no such relation between them and therefore no distinction between Son and Holy Spirit.

Thus in Aquinas' account there are two *processions* in God, one of the intellect, God's knowing himself, which is generation, and one of the will, God's enjoying himself, which is spiration. Each of these gives rise to a relationship with two (opposite) ends, the origin and the originated. There are thus four of these *relations*. This does not, however, result in four distinct persons, for in order to be distinct a person must be at the opposite ends of a relation from *both* other persons. The Father is opposed to the Son by generating and to the Spirit by spiration. The Son is opposed to the Father by being generated and to the Spirit by spiration. The Spirit is opposed to both the Father and the Son by being spirited, or *processio* (in a new sense).

This does not commit Aquinas to the *filioque* in the sense in which it is found objectionable by the Eastern churches. The root of their complaint, as I understand it, is that the *filioque* seems to take away from the Father as unique source or principle of the Godhead. However, the Greek Orthodox theologians who in 1875 came to an agreement with the Old Catholics[4] expressed their faith by saying, 'We do call the Holy Spirit of the Son and so it is proper to say that the Holy Spirit proceeds from the Father through the Son.' But that last clause is an exact quotation from Aquinas:

Quia igitur Filius habet a Patre quod ab eo procedat Spiritus Sanctus, potest dici quod Pater *per* Filium spirat Spiritum Sanctum; vel quod Spiritus Sanctus procedat a Patre *per* Filium, quod idem est.[5]

Because the Son owes it to the Father that the Holy Spirit should proceed from him, it can be said that the Father through the Son breathes forth the Holy Spirit, or that the Holy Spirit proceeds from the Father through the Son, which is to say the same thing.

I think it will be clear that Aquinas' doctrine gives us no warrant for saying that there are three persons in God; for 'person' in English undoubtedly means an individual subject, a distinct centre of consciousness. Now the consciousness of the Son is the consciousness of the Father and of the Holy Spirit, it is simply God's consciousness. There are not three knowledges or three lovings in God. The Word simply is the way in which God is self-conscious, knows what he is, as the Spirit simply

---

[4] Ibid., p. 186.   [5] *Summa Theologiae* 1a q36 a3 *corp.*

is the delight God takes in what he is when he is knowing it. If we say there are three persons in God, in the ordinary sense of person, we are tritheists.

For Aquinas the key to the Trinity is not the notion of person but of relation, and in fact in my account of his teaching I have not found it necessary to use the word 'person' at all. Aquinas quotes with ostensible approval Boethius' definition of a person as 'an individual substance of rational nature'. But, as speedily emerges, the 'persons' of the Trinity are not individuals, not substances, not rational and do not *have* natures. What Aquinas labours to show is that in this unique case 'person' can mean relation. This he does out of characteristic *pietas* towards the traditional language of the church. But of course even in Aquinas' time *persona* did *not* mean relation and most emphatically in our time 'person' does not. For our culture the 'person' is almost the opposite of the relational; it is isolated bastion of individuality set over against the collective. Even if we criticise the individualism, even if we try to put the human being back into a social context as part of various communities, the notion of person does not become relational enough to use in an account of the Trinity. Aquinas could have made better use of the original sense of *prosopon* of *persona* as the player's mask, and his doctrine of the Trinity might be more easily grasped if we spoke of three *roles* in the strict sense of three roles in a theatrical cast – though we have to forget that in the theatre there are people *with* the roles. We should have to think just of the roles as such and notice how they each have meaning only in relation to and distinction from each other. We could speak of the role of parenthood, the role of childhood and the role of love or delight. This is not to speak of the Trinity as a matter simply of three aspects of God, three ways in which God appears to *us*, as Sabellius is alleged to have taught, for essential to this whole teaching is that God turns only one aspect to us, *opera ad extra sunt indivisa*; it is in his immanent activity of self-understanding and self-love, delight, that the roles are generated.

These roles, firmly established in the life of the Godhead, are then reflected (I prefer the word 'projected' – as on a cinema screen) in our history in the external missions of the Son and the Spirit by which we are taken up into that life of the Godhead. In this way the obedience of Jesus is the projection of his eternal Sonship and the outpouring of the Spirit is the projection of his eternal procession from the Father through the Son. It is because of these missions in time that the life of the Trinity becomes available to us: I mean both in the sense that we know of it, believe in it, and in the sense that we belong to it. These are of course the same thing. It is because we share in the Holy Spirit through faith and charity and the other infused virtues that we are able to speak of the Trinity at all. It is not therefore adequate to speak of God's redemptive act as an *opus ad extra*. It is precisely the act by which we cease to be *extra* to God and come within his own life.

5

Vere tu es Deus absconditus: *the hidden God in Luther and some mystics*

Bernard McGinn

Vere tu es Deus absconditus – 'Truly, you are a God who hidest thyself.'[1] In commenting on this verse from Isaiah 45:15 in his exegesis of the book, Martin Luther drew a parallel between the prophet's time and his own. The divine promise of restoration to Jerusalem, despite the trials of Isaiah's era, led the seer to exclaim that God's ways were beyond the power of reason, 'The flesh sees nothing and concludes: Nothing produces nothing.' But the eyes of faith see differently. 'So today', Luther continues, 'we see in the Word the progress of the Church of God against the force and schemes of all tyrants. Since faith is the conviction of things not seen, the opposite must appear to be the case.'[2]

Throughout his later *Lectures on Genesis* (1535–45) the reformer often employs the theme of divine hiddenness, citing the Isaian text in four of these discussions.[3] In order to grasp the meaning of these and other passages, it is useful to note that Luther seems to have distinguished between two forms of God's hiddenness: God's hiding of himself *sub contrariis*, that is, under contrary signs; and God's hiding of himself in the dark mystery of predestination.[4]

The first hiddenness, cloaking *sub contrariis*, shows how the tribulations endured by the patriarchs, so often in conflict with the promises God had made to them, provide the model for us, their heirs in belief. Thus, in his long exegesis of the Joseph story, Luther summarises: 'Therefore,

---

[1] I wish to thank my colleague Susan E. Schreiner for her help and suggestions in developing this paper, especially the section devoted to Luther.

[2] I will cite from *Luther's Works*, edited by Jaroslav Pelikan et al. (Saint Louis: Concordia, 1959–). The comment on Isa. 45:15 is found in the *Lectures on Isaiah* (1527–30) in *Works* 17:131–2. Where necessary, I will also note the original Luther texts as edited in *D. Martin Luthers Werke: Kritische Gesamtausgabe* (Weimar: Böhlau, 1883–), cited as WA followed by volume and page.

[3] Luther uses Isa. 45:15 in *Works* 3.121 (on Gen. 17:8), *Works* 4.7 and 356 (Gen. 21:1–3 and 25:22), and *Works* 6.356 (Gen. 25:22).

[4] Much has been written about Luther's theology of God's hiddenness. For an insightful survey of the two forms, see B. A. Gerrish, ' "To the Unknown God": Luther and Calvin on the Hiddenness of God', *Journal of Religion*, 53 (1973), pp. 263–92.

we should know that God hides himself under the form of the worst devil. This teaches us that the goodness, mercy, and power of God cannot be grasped by speculation but must be understood on the basis of experience.'[5] The appeal to the experience of the person of faith was crucial for Luther, who always contrasted such experience with the 'original sin' of proud speculation. If the patriarchs were models for the former, Adam and Eve, who sought to know the *reason* why God had forbidden them to eat the Tree of Knowledge, were the ancestors of all those who sought to penetrate the mystery of the divine nature through their own efforts and who refused to be instructed by experiencing the God who reveals himself so paradoxically *sub contrariis*.[6]

Discussing the *crux interpretationis* of Genesis 6:5–6 (God's repentance at having created humanity), Luther employed the scholastic distinction between the 'will of good pleasure' (*voluntas beneplaciti*), that is, 'the essential will of God or his unveiled majesty', and the 'will of the sign' (*voluntas signi*), quoting Exodus 33:20, another favourite proof-text on God's hiddenness: 'Man shall not see me and live.' Any investigation of the will of good pleasure must be avoided, 'unless you are a Moses, or a David, or some similar perfect man'. Even these privileged ones never looked at the will of good pleasure without *also* beholding what is necessary for all in order to be saved, the will of the sign, that is, the coverings, masks, or signs under which God gives himself to us. These signs, however, often induce terror in us. It is only in the *true* will of good pleasure, namely the incarnate Christ who portrays the mercy that God wishes to show us, that we can have hope in the midst of the darkness of life. Luther concludes:

> The incarnate Son of God is, therefore, the covering in which the Divine Majesty presents himself to us with all his gifts, and does so in such a manner that there is no sinner too wretched to be able to approach him with the firm assurance of obtaining pardon. This is the one and only view of the divinity that is available and possible in this life.[7]

Christ, the unveiling of the veiled divinity, is what Luther called the 'emptied form of God'.[8] In divesting himself of his divine majesty and taking on a human form, he encourages our approach to him. The full humanity of the Saviour realised in his suffering and death on the cross

5 *Works* 7:175, commenting on Gen. 41:40.
6 On Adam and Eve, see, e.g., the comments on Gen. 26:9 (*Works* 5:42–3).
7 *Works* 2:46–9.
8 See the comment on Gen. 21:18 in *Works* 4:61–6.

illustrates another aspect of God's hiddenness *sub contrario*. The cross is the greatest sign of how God works through contraries. The irony and paradox of this aspect is underlined in the *Lectures on Genesis* where Luther says: 'Thus, when Christ himself is about to enter into glory, he dies and descends into hell. There all glory disappears. He says to his disciples (John 14:12): "I go to the Father," and he goes to the grave. Let us constantly meditate on such examples and place them before our eyes.'[9]

This message was scarcely new for Luther. In the *Heidelberg Disputation* of 1518, citing Isaiah 45:15 again, he had insisted that, 'Because men misused knowledge of God through works, God wished again to be recognized in suffering and to condemn wisdom concerning invisible things by means of wisdom concerning visible things, so that those who did not honour God as manifested in his works should honour him as he is hidden in his sufferings.'[10] '*CRUX sola est nostra theologia*', as Luther once exclaimed.[11] The reformer's theology of the cross provides the necessary context for this aspect of his appeal to the *Deus absconditus*.

In some places in the Genesis lectures and elsewhere, however, Luther speaks of another form of divine hiddenness, the God hidden *behind* his revelation in his predestinating will. Genesis 26:9 provides an unexpected place to launch into a discussion of 'doubt, God, and the will of God'. Against those who had revived the old complaint that if God predestines everything, nothing we do, either of good or ill, really counts, Luther responded with force, citing the distinction he made in *On the Bondage of the Will* between the hidden and revealed God. 'With regard to God', he says, 'insofar as he has not been revealed, there is no faith, no knowledge, and no understanding. Here one must hold to the statement that what is above us is none of our business.'[12] What is important, says Luther, is to believe that God does disclose himself, while still remaining the same God. 'I will be made flesh, or send my Son. He shall die for your sins and rise from the dead. And in this way I will fulfill your desire, in order that you may be able to know whether you are predestined or not.'[13]

---

[9] *Works* 4:357. There is a similar passage in the section on Gen. 45:5: 'Before the world Christ is killed, condemned, and descends into hell. But before God this is the salvation of the whole world from the beginning all the way to the end' (*Works* 8:29).

[10] *Heidelberg Disputation* 20 (*Works* 31:52).

[11] See WA 5:176.2–3. For a study, Alister E. McGrath, *Luther's Theology of the Cross. Martin Luther's Theological Breakthrough* (Oxford: Blackwell, 1985).

[12] Luther is probably referring to the section in *The Bondage of the Will* commenting on Ezek. 18:23 (*Works* 33:138–40).

[13] Commentary on Gen. 26:9 (*Works* 5:42–7). The passages cited are from 44–5.

In stressing this possibility of some knowledge that we are predestined, the Luther of the *Lectures on Genesis* appears to be in a more optimistic mood than in *On the Bondage of the Will*. In the *Lectures* any consideration of the hidden God of predestination is quickly passed over so that the believer can be invited to place all his trust in the love revealed in Christ. Luther puts it this way, 'If you cling to the revealed God with a firm faith, so that your heart is so minded that you will not lose Christ even if you are deprived of everything, then you are most assuredly predestined and you will understand the hidden God.'[14] But Luther was not always so ready to pass over the terror induced by the thought of the hiddenness of predestination. When we look back to *On the Bondage of the Will* of 1525 we see that while Luther here too insists that 'the secret will of the Divine Majesty is not a matter for debate',[15] he was more willing to emphasise the contrast between the dread image of the God of predestination and the God revealed in Jesus. 'God does many things that he does not disclose to us in his word', Luther says. 'He also wills many things which he does not disclose himself as willing in his word. Thus he does not will the death of the sinner according to his word, but he wills it according to that inscrutable will of his.'[16] Our role is not to enquire, but to 'fear and adore'. More powerfully, Luther also allows for a conflict between the incarnate revealing God and the hidden predestinating God. Jesus' tears over Jerusalem (Matt. 23:37) provide the exegetical focus for this contrast: 'It is likewise the part of this incarnate God to weep, wail, and groan over the perdition of the ungodly, when the will of the Divine Majesty purposely abandons and reprobates some to perish.'[17]

There are also places in his biblical commentaries where Luther paid witness to the existential dread that the enigma of the hidden God's abandonment of sinners induces in believers. For example, Psalm 6:4 ('Turn, O Lord, save my life') for Luther implies that God can indeed turn *away* from us. 'A turning away on the part of God implies an inner rejecting and forsaking. Then a horrible terror and, as it were, the beginning of damnation, is felt.' In this situation, as Luther went on to say, explaining verse 5 ('In hell who will give you thanks?'), the saints have to continue to praise and to have a good will toward God, knowing that that alone separates them from the damned. Here the reformer taps into the theme of the *resignatio ad infernum* theme based on Romans 9:1–3,

---

[14] Ibid., 46.
[15] See WA 33:139–47, where this quotation is on p. 145. On p. 147 Luther uses the familiar texts about not prying into God's will found in Rom. 9:19–21 and Isa. 58:2.
[16] WA 33:140.　　[17] WA 33:146.

claiming that the saints 'are more concerned about losing God's gracious will, praise, and honour than about being damned'.[18]

While it is possible to distinguish two forms of God's hiddenness in Luther, their existential character can often be hard to separate. The saints who suffer 'the beginning of damnation' may wonder if they will also endure its conclusion. God's action toward us may be so *sub contrario* that it is hard to discern any salvific purpose. In the *Lectures on Genesis* Luther admitted that God 'conducts himself . . . toward the godly so that it seems that he does not know us at all'. The faithful who hear the text (Ps. 120:4), 'He who keeps Israel will neither slumber nor sleep', may justly wail, 'He is not only sleeping, but even snoring.'[19]

A good illustration of the affliction involved in every form of divine hiddenness can be found in a passage from near the end of the *Lectures on Genesis* where Luther exegetes Genesis 45:5, Joseph's speech to his brothers about how their intent to kill him actually led in God's providence to his ability to preserve their lives. The reformer says that Joseph, Jacob, and his sons, like Moses in Exodus 33:23 (another favourite hiddenness text), did not see God's face, but only his back – 'When Joseph was sold and his father was grieving, God's face was hidden. Nor did any god appear, but the whole world seemed to be full of devils.' The saints, however, are not scandalised by the face with which God meets them: 'He is, indeed, the God of life, glory, salvation, joy, and peace; and this is the true face of God. But sometimes he covers it and puts on another mask by which he offers himself to us as the God of wrath, death, and hell.'[20]

The saints can endure this experience of terror because their lives are founded upon faith, and faith, as Brian Gerrish suggests, is not a resolution of the contrast between the two masks of God, but a flight *away* from the hidden God of predestination *toward* the God 'hiddenly' revealed in Jesus.[21] Such a flight was a fact of experience for Luther. In a passage from his early *Offerings on the Psalms* (1519–21) he spoke of 'the dread and horror of conscience before the face of God's judgment' that Christ underwent in the garden, and that Job, David, King Ezechias, and others had spoken of. 'All other temptations', he said (one thinks from personal experience), 'are little exercises and preludes of this consummate one. In them we get used to fleeing to God against God.'[22]

[18] *Works* 14:142–3.
[19] Commentary on Gen. 37:18–20 (*Works* 6:359–60).
[20] *Works* 8:30–1.   [21] Gerrish, '"To the Unknown God"', 290–1.
[22] *Operationes in Psalmos* on Ps. 6:2 (WA 3:204.25–7). McGrath (*Luther's Theology of the Cross*, p. 173, n. 75), who argues that the hiddenness of predestination does not appear in Luther's thought until

Luther's views on the hiddenness of God are well known. The many treatments of this theme have laid out the issues and explored the tensions in this important part of the reformer's thought. It is not my intention to try to unveil more about Luther's view of God's veilings. Rather, I would like to put the reformer's treatment of the theme into a context, specifically the context of the development of the hidden God in the Christian mystical tradition. This is not to claim that Luther was a mystic. Rather, a survey of some examples of mystical hiddenness will underline Luther's difference from the mystics, though it will also, I hope, raise some questions worth pondering about the different ways in which the God who hides himself has affected those who have tried to reach out to him in faith.

Luther's relationship to mysticism remains an issue subject to much discussion and disagreement. While it is clear that Luther adapted a number of important mystical themes into his theology, he did so in such a manner that he usually transformed them into something new.[23] Luther's distance from the primary negative, or apophatic, mystical tradition in the West, that of Dionysius the Areopagite, is already evident in his terminology for God. The reformer prefers the term *Deus absconditus* suggested by Isaiah 45:15, or sometimes *Deus nudus*, over the *Deus ignotus* found in Acts 17:23 and *Deus incognoscibilis/incognitus* of Dionysius' *Mystical Theology* (Dionysius never cites Isa. 45:15). The goal of Dionysian anagogy, as the end of the first chapter of that work puts it, is to reach a state where 'being neither oneself nor anyone else, a person is united according to his better part to the Wholly Unknown (*tô pantelôs de agnôstô*) by a cessation of all knowing, and knows beyond the mind by knowing nothing'.[24] Luther, moreover, was explicit about his dislike of Dionysius.[25] In his early *Lectures on the Psalms* (1513–16) Luther had, indeed, praised Dionysius' view of negative theology, identifying 'the anagogic darkness'

1525 and the dispute with Erasmus, interprets this early text differently from Gerrish – 'Man thus flees *ad deum* (the reality) *contra deum* (the appearance).'

23 In this connection, see especially Heiko A. Oberman, '*Simul Gemitus et Raptus*: Luther and Mysticism', *The Reformation in Medieval Perspective*, edited by Steven E. Ozment (Chicago: Quadrangle Books, 1971), pp. 219–51. Gerrish, ' "To the Unknown God" ', 265, says that 'the language of the mystical tradition remained always congenial to him [Luther] in some respects'.

24 *De mystica theologia* 1 (J.-P. Migne, *Patrologia Graeca* [Paris, 1857–66], 3:1001A; hereafter cited as PG).

25 On Luther's attitude toward Dionysius, see Paul Rorem, 'Martin Luther's Christocentric Critique of Pseudo-Dionysian Spirituality,' *Lutheran Quarterly* 11 (1997), pp. 291–307. For a survey of Reformation attitudes towards the Dionysian corpus, including Luther, see Karlfried Froehlich, 'Pseudo-Dionysius and the Reformation of the Sixteenth Century,' *Pseudo-Dionysius. The Complete Works*, translated by Colm Luibheid (New York: Paulist Press, 1987), pp. 33–46.

as one of five possible meanings of 'the darkness of God's hiding place' mentioned in Psalm 18:11.[26] He also saluted Dionysius' negative theology as a *vera cabala* superior to scholastic affirmative babblings.[27] But it is unlikely that even at this early stage Luther's *Deus absconditus* was much like the Dionysian *Deus incognitus*. The religious world that undergirds the Dionysian project was far from the anxieties of *Anfechtung* that marked the emerging reformer's view of the meaning of God's hiddenness.[28] Dionysius' 'Wholly Unknown' God is not the fear-inducing hidden God of Luther's experience. The reformer makes this clear in the sharp attack he issued against the *Mystical Theology* and the commentaries on it found in his next interpretation of the Psalms, written between 1519 and 1521. Here speaks the Luther we all know: 'This is a mere provocation of a self-inflating and show-off knowledge, that someone could believe himself a "mystical theologian" if he were to read, understand, and teach this stuff, or rather seem to himself to understand and teach it. By living, yet more, by dying and being damned, you become a theologian, not by understanding, reading, and speculating.'[29] After this Luther never wavered in his opposition to Dionysian theology. He continued to see the *theologia crucis* as diametrically opposed to the Dionysian ascent into the divine darkness.

If the history of negative forms of mysticism were restricted to the Dionysian corpus and its influence, a comparison with Luther would be little more than an exercise in contrasts. There are, however, other aspects of negation in the annals of Christian mysticism that offer intriguing analogues to aspects of Luther's theology of the *Deus absconditus*.[30] Some of these mystical writings would have been familiar to Luther; others not. While none of them should be looked upon as a direct source for Luther's teaching, in several cases they offer fruitful comparisons both

[26] *Dictata super Psalmos* (WA 3:124). On the role of the *Dictata* in the evolution of Luther's exegesis, see James Samuel Preus, *From Shadow to Promise. Old Testament Interpretation from Augustine to the Young Luther* (Cambridge, MA: Belknap Press, 1969).

[27] *Dictata super Psalmos* (WA 3:372), a scholion on Ps. 64:2. Here he even says that *theologia extatica et negativa* 'makes the true theologian'.

[28] For a brief introduction to the meaning of *Anfechtung* ('temptation-assault-testing'), see McGrath, *Luther's Theology of the Cross*, pp. 170–4.

[29] *Operationes in Psalmos* (WA 5:163.26–9).

[30] It may be helpful in this connection to distinguish three forms of negation in Christian mysticism: (1) the negativity of apophasis, that is, the 'unsaying' of all forms of human speech in relation to God; (2) the negativity of detachment, i.e., the cutting away of attachments to self and world in order to be open to God; and (3) the negativity of dereliction and suffering in which anguish and even damnation become the way to God. Dionysius is a classic representative of the first form of negativity. The mystics to be considered in what follows exemplify the third form.

to the existential attitude Luther displayed toward the God who hides himself, as well as to the theological message he drew from it.

In the same *Offerings on the Psalms* in which he attacked Dionysius, Luther speaks of the experience 'of fear and horror of conscience before the face of God's judgment'. He says, 'The conscience that has been rebuked and convicted soon feels that it has been threatened with its eternal damnation. Only one who has tasted it understands this supreme feeling, and therefore we are not worthy to treat it. Job suffered it more than others, and suffered it often.'[31] It is surprising that Luther never wrote a commentary on Job – perhaps this most tortured book of the Bible was too close to his own experience. But the reformer must have been familiar with the most famous commentary on the book, Gregory the Great's *Moralia in Iob*.

Gregory has sometimes been spoken of as a 'mystic of light', and his frequent reference to God as 'uncircumscribed Light' (*lumen incircumscriptum*) lends weight to this.[32] But this monk turned pontiff delighted in the interplay of polarities – light/darkness, inner/outer, silence/sound, presence/absence, joy/fear, and elevation/temptation. While Gregory is not an apophatic theologian in the tradition of Dionysius, his sense of the overwhelming majesty of God, especially as revealed to Job, led him to the conviction that contemplative experience of God was often a dark and terrible thing. Many aspects of the Pope's understanding of the redemptive nature of suffering found in Job would have appealed to Luther, though as far as I know, the reformer does not cite the Pope in this connection.[33]

According to Gregory, the path to contemplation of God begins and ends in fear, at least as long as we are still in this life. In his *Commentary on First Kings* he says, 'The ascent to contemplation is ordered if it begins in fear',[34] that is, in the compunction of tears by which we express sorrow for sin. But Gregory's own experience, as well as his reading of Job, convinced him that fear was present at the end, as well as at the beginning of the itinerary of contemplation. Like Augustine, Gregory often

[31] *Operationes in Psalmos* on Ps. 6:2 (WA 5:203.1, 11–14).

[32] On Gregory the Great's mysticism, see Bernard McGinn, *The Growth of Mysticism. Gregory the Great through the Twelfth Century* (New York: Crossroad, 1994), Chap. 2. On 'incircumscription', see Friedrich Ohly, '*Deus incircumscriptus*', *Mittellateinisches Jahrbuch* 27 (1992), 7–16.

[33] For an account of the *Moralia in Iob*, see Susan E. Schreiner, *Where Shall Wisdom Be Found? Calvin's Exegesis of Job from Medieval and Modern Perspectives* (Chicago: University of Chicago Press, 1994), chap. I.

[34] *In I Reg.* 1.68 (*Corpus Christianorum* 144:93).

spoke of the brevity of any experience of heightened contact with God,
because the human gaze will always be 'beaten back' in its attempts to
comprehend the divine mystery. As a passage in Book 24 of the *Moralia*
puts it:

> In the very act of directing its attention [to the Truth], the intellectual soul's
> effort is beaten back (*reverberatur*) by the encircling gleam of its immensity. The
> truth fills all things; it encircles all things. Therefore, our minds can never be
> expanded to comprehend the unbounded bounding [of God], because it is
> hemmed in by the imperfection of its own bounded existence.[35]

Gregory, however, went further by bringing a form of divine hiddenness into the experience of the height of contemplation itself. Exegeting
Job 4:13, Eliphaz's account of his seeing God 'In the horror of a vision
by night' (*in horrore visionis nocturnae*), the Pope described the 'shuddering
of secret contemplation' (*pavor occultae contemplationis*) in some detail. The
higher the contemplation of eternal things, the more the human mind
is struck with dread over its own guilt and imperfection before God. In
this life we cannot behold the brightness of the divine daylight; hence
God remains in a *visio nocturna* in which 'we go darkling under a doubtful
seeing' (*sub incerta contemplationis caligamus*). In this darkness we are 'ter-
rified and filled with greater fear' than we were before we had contact
with God.[36] Gregory insists on the strict correlation between height and
fear – a kind of contemplative acrophobia: 'The human soul is lifted high
by the engine of its contemplation so that the more it gazes on things
higher than itself the more it is filled with terror.'[37] Gregory, of course,
also spoke of the joy and delight found in contemplation, but the figure of
Job and his dark experience of God showed him that *contemplatio* involved
a paradoxical coincidence of opposites in which fear was as great – and
perhaps even more useful – for fallen humanity as any delight in God's
presence. Precisely for that reason he also insisted that contemplatives
were subject to greater temptations than non-contemplatives. The very
elevation of their attentive gaze at God makes temptation a necessary
form of humility to curb any pride they might take in such experiences.[38]

---

[35] *Moralia in Iob* 24.6.12 (*Corpus Christianorum* 143B:1196.41–6). The theme of the *reverberatio* appears
often in the *Moralia* and in Gregory's other writings discussing contemplation; cf. e.g., *Moralia*
23.21.41, and *Homiliae in Ezekielem* 2.1.17–18.

[36] These passages are from *Moralia* 5.30.53 (*Corpus Christianorum* 143:254–5).

[37] *Moralia* 5.31.55 (*Corpus Christianorum* 143:258.80–2). For other texts on divine incomprehensibility
and its effect on the contemplative, see, e.g., *Moralia* 10.8.13–9.15, and especially the exegesis of
Job 33:15 in *Moralia* 23.20.37–21.43.

[38] On the temptations that come to contemplatives, see especially *Moralia* 10.10.17, and *Homiliae in
Ezekielem* 2.2.3.

The thirteenth century witnessed an important revival and development of apophatic mysticism. This renewal was mostly tied to the Dionysian corpus, as new translations were made, commentaries produced, and Dionysius' writings and their attendent scholia became a textbook at the University of Paris.[39] These new forms of apophatic negativity have been much studied, but we must remember that not all ways of presenting the unknown and hidden God found in the mystical texts of the later middle ages are Dionysian in nature. This is especially true of the writings of the women mystics who proliferated after 1200.[40] Some of these mystics provide intriguing analogies with Luther's emphasis on the terror that faithful and ardent lovers of God find in their experience of his absence.

It is important in this connection to emphasise the difference between the negativity of apophasis and the negativity of dereliction, though, to be sure, individual mystics could make use of both these traditions. The usefulness of the distinction, however, is evident by looking at the mysticism of Meister Eckhart. The German Dominican is the premier exponent of divine nothingness; his entire mysticism is founded on the teaching that there is no 'God', at least as humans could ever conceive him. Eckhart is one of the few mystics who cites Isaiah 45:15 fairly frequently (eight times) as a scriptural source for divine unknowability.[41] Nevertheless, Eckhart's view of God's hiddenness has nothing of the tortuous character of Luther's *Deus absconditus*, or of what we find in some of Eckhart's mystical contemporaries. The divine nothing (*niht*) that Eckhart preaches, unlike the God attained in Gregory's contemplative ascent, or the predestinating God of Luther, does not induce fear and anxiety in the mystic. For the Dominican, sinking into the indistinct nothingness of God (*sink all mîn iht in gotes nît*, as the *Granum sinapis* poem puts it) does not result in anything like Luther's *Anfechtung*, or mystical dereliction.

---

[39] For a brief sketch of the history of Dionysianism, see Paul Rorem, *Pseudo-Dionysius. A Commentary on the Texts and an Introduction to Their Influence* (Oxford: Oxford University Press, 1993), Afterword. The classic study of the formation of the university text of Dionysius is H. F. Dondaine, *Le corpus dionysien de l'Université de Paris au XIIIe siècle* (Rome: Edizioni di storia e letteratura, 1953).

[40] For an introduction to these figures, see Bernard McGinn, *The Flowering of Mysticism. Men and Women in the New Mysticism – 1200–1350* (New York: Crossroad, 1998).

[41] Eckhart's writings have been edited in *Meister Eckhart. Die deutschen und lateinischen Werke* (Stuttgart: Kohlhammer, 1936–), using the abbreviations DW for the German works and LW for the Latin. Eckhart cites Isa. 45:15 three times in his sermons: Pr. 15 (DW 1:253.4–6), Pr. 79 (DW 3:369.6–7), and Sermo IV n. 89 (LW 4:86.2–6). The text also appears in the Latin commentaries five times: *Expositio libri Genesis* n. 300 (LW 1:435.12–13); *Liber Parabolorum Genesis* n. 47 (LW 1:516.2–3); and *Expositio Evangelii secundum Ioannem* nn. 75, 195, and 304 (LW 3:63.1–5, 163.9–12, 253.10–12). Eckhart also uses the term *Deus absconditus*, taken from Maimonides's *Dux neutrorum* in *Expositio Libri Exodi* n. 237 (LW 2:195.11).

It is rather the cessation of all experience, i.e., the forms of particularised consciousness that are the hallmarks of created being. For example, in his vernacular Sermon 15, Eckhart concludes a wide-ranging treatment of the divine nature and its relation with the humble/detached person with a characteristic flight of apophatic rhetoric about God. Eckhart says:

The last end of created being is the darkness and unknowing of the hidden divinity, in which the light that the darkness does not comprehend shines forth (cf. John 1:5). Therefore, Moses said, 'He who is sent me' (Exod. 3:14) – he who is without name, who is a denial of all names, and who never acquired a name. And therefore the prophet said: 'Truly you are the hidden God' (Isa. 45:15), in the ground of the soul, where God's ground and the soul's ground are one ground. The more one seeks you, the less one finds you.[42]

This is a powerful statement of the darkness of God, but not of the torture of the believer in the face of the divine mystery.

Though many of the thirteenth-century women mystics, like Eckhart, aspired to a unitive goal beyond distinction and all human modes of knowing and willing, their accounts of how the unknown God is encountered often contain strong doses of a mystical dereliction not found in Eckhart. For many of these women the experience of estrangement from God was central to their teaching. As they describe it, in this torture God not only vanishes, but also at times appears not as the God of love but the God of vengeance and damnation. The mystic experiences herself as not just sinful, and therefore distant from God, but as sin itself, the direct object of divine wrath. Such modes of mystical consciousness are found in many thirteen and fourteenth-century women.

An example can be found in the Italian Franciscan tertiary, Angela of Foligno, whose complex mystical itinerary of thirty stages (*passus*) was completed between the years 1285 and 1296 and recorded by an Italian friar in the book known as the *Memoriale*.[43] Having attained the status of 'mother and teacher', Angela functioned as the leader of a circle of clerical and lay devouts until her death in January, 1309. The *Instructions*, which record her late teachings, pay witness to the role of the unknown God in her life. On her deathbed she cried out: 'O unknown Nothing! O unknown Nothing! In truth the soul can have no better vision in this life than to see its own nothing and to stay in its prison.'[44] Though this

---

[42] Pr. 15 (DW 1:252.1–253.6).

[43] For an account of Angela, see McGinn, *The Flowering of Mysticism*, pp. 141–51.

[44] *Instructio* XXXVI in *Il Libro della Beata Angela da Foligno*, eds. Ludger Thier and Abele Calufetti (Grottaferrata: Collegii S. Bonaventurae, 1985), p. 734. For more on the *Deus incognoscibilis*, see

text lacks direct appeal to Christ crucified, the role of *imitatio passionis* in Angela's mystical itinerary has much to do with how she understands the role of negation. In comparison with Luther, it would not be too much to speak of Angela as presenting a mysticism *sub contrario*. Like the reformer, the Italian tertiary insisted that it was only by meeting Christ under the contrary sign of the cross that one could begin to discern God's loving purpose. Of course, passion-centred mysticism was widespread in the late middle ages. What makes Angela an interesting case is her description of states that go beyond sharing Christ's physical sufferings to penetrate into the realm of dereliction and despair in the face of the God who hides himself.

The two highest stages of the mystical itinerary recounted in the *Memoriale*, the sixth and seventh 'supplementary stages', are quite complex, but a brief account will suggest how Angela unites apophatic theory with abandonment by God. The sixth step describes Angela's experience of living damnation – a terror similar to what Luther found in Job.[45] After having enjoyed traditional forms of erotic union and ecstasy with Christ in the previous stages, in stage six Angela is afflicted by tortures and demonic assaults both in body and in soul. 'Concerning the torments of the soul which demons inflicted on her', we are told, 'she found herself incapable of finding any other comparison than that of a man hanged by the neck who, with his hands tied behind him and his eyes blindfolded, remains dangling on the gallows and yet lives, with no help, no support, no remedy, swinging in the empty air.'[46] Though it is the demons who torture Angela to the point of madness and despair, so that she rages against herself, physically beating and burning her sinful body, it is God she blames for having abandoned her. She turns the tables on Christ, imitating his cry of dereliction on the cross, repeatedly wailing, 'My son, my son, do not abandon me, my son!' (see Matt. 27:46). Angela cries out for death, beseeching God to send her to hell – 'Since you have abandoned me, make an end to it now and completely submerge me.' Echoing what Luther was later to say about the saints' experience of damnation, Angela claims: 'I see myself as damned, but I am in no way preoccupied with this damnation; rather, what concerns me and grieves me most is having offended my Creator.'[47]

Instructio XXXII (ed., pp. 664–6). For a translation of Angela's book, see Paul Lachance, *Angela of Foligno. Complete Works* (New York: Paulist Press, 1993).

[45] See *Memoriale* chap. VIII (ed., pp. 336–52).

[46] Ibid. (ed., p. 338). Luther has an early sermon in which he speaks of the experience of faith as similar to that of Christ hanging from the cross with no support for his feet (WA 1:102.39–41).

[47] Ibid. (ed., pp. 340–4).

Angela remained in this stage for about two years (*c.* 1294–6). Paradoxically, the mystical dereliction of the sixth step overlapped with the
seventh and final mystical *passus*, an indescribable encounter with God,
the All-Good, 'in and with darkness' (*in et cum tenebra*), her own characterisation of God's total unknowability.[48] In the highest form of this state,
which Angela attained only three times, she says that she went beyond
love to a condition in which 'the soul sees nothing and sees everything;
the body sleeps and speech is cut off'. All the previous favours she received from God become unimportant here. In the darkness she stands
in the midst of the Trinity and remembers no form, not even that of the
God–man. She hears the words, 'You are I and I am you' (*Tu es ego et ego
sum tu*).

Mystical dereliction and *resignatio ad infernum* played an important
role among thirteenth-century women mystics in northern Europe too.
Examples exist in many hagiographical accounts. An interesting case can
be found in the *Life of Margaret the Cripple*, an anchoress of Magdeburg
active about 1260.[49] Margaret is portrayed as making her daily experiences of 'pain, abjection, and poverty' the centre of her mystical contact
with Jesus – a mysticism of suffering rooted in the paradox of the cross. –
Margaret's message is that it is suffering not sweetness, desolation not
consolation, that bring us to God. At one place in the *Life* God tells her:
'If solace were solace to you, then I would not have given you that kind
of solace; but because your solace is desolation, I have consoled you in
this fashion.'[50] We noted before that Luther adopted the Pauline notion
of *resignatio ad infernum* (Rom. 9:1–3) to understand how the saints act in
the midst of the despair brought on by God's hidden predestinating will.
Many thirteenth-century women mystics also spoke of their willingness
to accept damnation if such were God's will. This theme appears more
often in the *Life of Margaret* than in any other text.

Some decades before Angela of Foligno, the German beguine
Mechthild of Magdeburg wrote her *Flowing Light of the Godhead* with the
assistance of her Dominican confessor. The *Flowing Light* does not present
a developed apophatic theory, but it does contain some remarkable chapters devoted to mystical dereliction, what Mechthild called *gotesvremedunge*

---

[48] *Memoriale* chap. 9 (ed., pp. 354–64). Angela's account of this experience of the divine darkness
does not use traditional Dionysian vocabulary, but is an original form of apophasis.

[49] See *Johannes von Magdeburg, O.P.: Die Vita der Margareta contracta, einer Magdeburger Rekluse des 13.
Jahrhunderts*, ed. Paul Gerhard Schmidt (Leipzig: Benno, 1992). For a more detailed account, see
McGinn, *The Flowering of Mysticism*, pp. 194–8.

[50] *Vita* chap. 56 (ed., p. 64).

(estrangement from God), or *verworfenheit* (rejection). Mechthild is justly regarded as one of the most daring exponents of bridal language in medieval mysticism. The frequent erotic raptures in which she 'soars into God', however, need to be balanced with the role that suffering, rejection, and estrangement play as the more decisive identification with Christ. As she puts it in *Flowing Light* 6.20:

God bestowed upon me the favor that is written down in this book in a three-fold manner. First of all with great tenderness; then, with high intimacy; now with intense suffering. I much prefer to remain in this state than in the other two . . . But the nature of love is such that it first of all flows in sweetness; then it becomes rich in knowledge; in the third place it becomes avid in rejection.[51]

Here I will analyse only one of the chapters which witness to the role of estrangement from God in Mechthild. In *Flowing Light* 4.12 Mechthild begins with a dialogue in which the soul as bride of God, disturbed from her sleep in the Trinity by the departure of her Beloved, refuses to take consolation from any creature. The soul declares that her 'nobility' (*edelkeit*), that is, the status she enjoyed in God before creation, can only reach satisfaction by once again being drawn into the Trinity to die a 'mystical death'. But the beguine also says that she is willing to give up even the taste of God as long as *he* will continue to be praised in all his creatures. This admission sets the stage for a second dialogue, in which, after eight years of divine consolation, Mechthild learns the deeper consolation of giving up all consolation in the experience of estrangement from God.

Here God consoles her 'beyond her soul's nobility', that is, to a deeper level than consolation in one's pre-created state, by allowing her to fall down to the level of the souls suspended in purgatory and even those rejected in hell.[52] Mechthild's desire now is not for consolation. She says: 'Oh, leave me, dear Lord, and let me sink further for your honour.'[53] Now soul and body enter into a great darkness without light or any kind of knowledge in which the beguine loses all intimacy

---

[51] *Mechthild von Magdeburg. 'Das fliessende Licht der Gottheit'*, ed. Hans Neumann, 2 vols. (Munich: Artemis, 1990–93). FL 6.20 (1:229–230). See the translation by Frank Tobin, *Mechthild of Magdeburg. The Flowing Light of the Godhead* (New York: Paulist Press, 1998). What follows is based on my treatment of Mechthild in *The Flowering of Mysticism*, especially pp. 239–43.

[52] In FL 4.5 (ed., pp. 156–9) Mechtild has another account of how 'sinking Humility' brings both body and soul down to the place called *unter Lucifers zagel*, namely, hell.

[53] Ed., p. 124.45–7.

with God. She converses with a series of personifications, including Estrangement herself:

After this came Constant Estrangement from God and enveloped the soul so completely that the blessed soul said: 'Welcome, very Blessed Estrangement. Fortunate am I that I was born – that you, Lady, shall now be my chambermaid, for you bring me unusual joy and incomprehensible marvels and unbearable delight as well. But, Lord, you should take delight from me and let me have Estrangement from you.'[54]

God's honour is now fulfilled in her, she says, and although she is estranged from him, 'now God is with me in a marvellous way'. The beguine ends her account with a description of how she entered into a great darkness in which 'her body sweated and writhed in painful cramping'. Here she overhears a conversation between Christ and Lady Pain in which the Lord reminds Pain that although she is the devil's servant, she was his 'closest garment' when he was on earth. Pain serves as Mechthild's messenger to remind her audience that humility, pain, and estrangement from God are actually the best way to God.[55] As often in her book, Mechthild concludes the chapter with a summarising couplet:

> Mere ie ich tieffer sinke
> Ie ich suesser trinke.
> [The deeper I sink
> The sweeter my drink.]

Another example of a northern European female mystic who emphasised the role of estrangement from God is the French beguine Marguerite Porete, who was executed for heresy in 1310 for continuing to disseminate her book, *The Mirror of Simple Annihilated Souls*, after it had been judged to contain serious errors.[56] Marguerite differs from most other late medieval women mystics, both in her boldness and in her

---

[54] Ed., p. 125.65–9.

[55] On the role of suffering in Mechthild, see Margot Schmidt, ' "Frau Pein, Ihr Seid mein nächstes Kleid." Zur Leidenmystik im "Fliessenden Licht der Gottheit" der Mechthild von Magdeburg', *Die Dunkle Nacht der Sinne. Leiderfahrung und christlicher Mystik*, ed. Gotthard Fuchs (Düsseldorf: Patmos, 1989), pp. 63–107.

[56] Marguerite's text has been edited by Romana Guarnieri and Paul Verdeyen, *Marguerite Porete. Le Mirouer des simples ames* (Turnholt: Brepols, 1986. *Corpus Christianorum. Continuatio Mediaevalis* LXIX). There is an English translation by Ellen Babinsky, *Marguerite Porete. The Mirror of Simple Souls* (New York: Paulist Press, 1993). For what follows, I have used aspects of the treatment of Marguerite developed more fully in *The Flowering of Mysticism*, pp. 244–65.

opposition to some of the themes common to women, such as emphasis on visionary experience. Marguerite can also be said to possess the most profound apophatic theology of any of the medieval women mystics. Her God of absolute annihilation exceeds, even deconstructs, every effort to express him.[57] For the French beguine, personal annihilation is the goal of the mystical quest. Her descriptions generally avoid the language of tortured dereliction that we find in Angela and Mechthild,[58] but there is an interesting analogy to the other women, as well as to Luther, in the stress she gives to the necessity for a mystical descent into sinfulness in order to attain annihilating union with God.

Marguerite inverts the standard language about the fall of humanity to claim that the soul, like the Divine Word who emptied himself in taking on humanity, must empty itself *into sin* in order to be united with God. In chapter 40 Love describes a person 'abyssed in humility', who 'has injustice in nothing and nevertheless knows that he has justice in nothing. He who exists in this knowledge of his injustice, sees so clearly that he sees himself beneath every creature in the mire of sin'. As a slave to sin, such a soul is beneath even the demons. And yet, by recognising her complete sinfulness, 'this soul has become nothing and less than nothing in all respects', and has therefore reached its goal.[59] A more lengthy discussion of the same descent that is really ascent to union occurs in chapters 102–9. Here, especially in chapters 107–8, Marguerite boldly redefines sin as any and all removal of the will from God. If sin is every act in which the soul does not strive to do the absolute best, it must be a constant condition until such time as the will is totally annihilated. Soul says, 'As long as I have had a will, I have not stopped [removing it from God], until I totally lost the will and nakedly restored it to him who gave it to me freely of his goodness.'[60] Finally, in chapter 117, the beguine praises the 'Superexalted Spirit', who has so completely emptied herself into the pit of sin and wretchedness that God must come to dwell in her

---

[57] Two helpful accounts of Marguerite's apophaticism and its relation to Meister Eckhart are Michael A. Sells, *Mystical Languages of Unsaying* (Chicago: University of Chicago Press, 1994), chaps. 5–7; and Amy Hollywood, *The Soul as Virgin Wife: Mechthild of Magdeburg, Marguerite Porete, and Meister Eckhart* (Notre Dame: University of Notre Dame, 1995).

[58] The closest she comes to this is in her description of the pain the Soul suffers in being unable to answer the testing questions of Love in chap. 131 (ed., pp. 384–8).

[59] *Mirouer*, chap. 40 (ed., p. 127). My translation here is based on the Latin rather than the French text. Although most students of Marguerite prefer to use the French version, it is important to remember that all the surviving versions are translations from the lost Old French original.

[60] *Mirouer*, chap. 108 (ed., p. 293).

and thus make her 'an exemplar of salvation' and more. With typical daring she puts it this way:

> And through this I am an exemplar of salvation, and even more [I am] the salvation itself of every creature and the glory of God. And I will tell you how, why, and in what. First, because I am the height of all evil, for I contain of my own nature what is wretched, and therefore I am total wretchedness. And he ... is the height of all goodness ... Since I am total wretchedness and he is total goodness, it is necessary for me to have the totality of his goodness before my wretchedness can be terminated.[61]

Though Luther, like Marguerite's inquisitors, would scarcely have been happy with her claims to be the cause of salvation for others, the beguine's acceptance of her total sinfulness and distance from God has a surprising similarity to his famous expression, *Pecca fortiter*.

   This brief look at four thirteenth-century women mystics on the experience of desolation and abandonment by God scarcely exhausts the role of this theme in late medieval mysticism. Many other examples could be cited, such the Franciscan nun, Catherine of Bologna, who, a century before Luther, stressed God's hiddenness under the contrary sign of temptation to despair in her book, *The Seven Spiritual Arms*.[62] Nor is it only among women that we find this form of mystical consciousness. Angela of Foligno's contemporary, the lay Franciscan Jacopone da Todi, speaks of his abandonment by God in ways that parallel what we have seen in the women.[63] There is even a male mystic whose account of the suffering that strikes the saints in the face of the God who withdraws and hides himself was well known to Luther. This is the student of Eckhart, John Tauler.

   In listing examples of those who provide models of the suffering induced by God's absence in his comment on Psalm 6:2 in the *Offerings on the Psalms*, Luther says, 'Finally, the German theologian, John Tauler, speaks of it often in his sermons.'[64] Tauler, who combined Eckhart's language of the divine nothingness with the more experiential accents

---

[61] *Mirouer*, chap. 117 (ed., pp. 310–12).

[62] *Caterina da Bologna. Le Sette Armi Spirituali*, ed. Cecilia Foletti (Padua: Antenore, 1985), pp. 118–19, 154–55.

[63] On Jacopone, see *The Flowering of Mysticism*, pp. 125–32. Another male mystic of the fourteenth century who has a sense of the terror that accompanies the highest forms of contemplation is the anonymous author of *The Cloud of Unknowing*. In chap. 69, speaking of the 'spiritual experience' (*goostly felyng*) of the nothing that is achieved nowhere, he says that this is accompanied by an intense consciousness of all the sins that the mystic has ever committed. 'It seems to him', the text continues, 'sometimes, in this labor, that to look upon it is like looking upon hell' (*The Cloud of Unknowing and Related Treatises*, ed. Phyllis Hodgson (Exeter: Catholic Records Press, 1982), p. 68).

[64] WA 5:203.16–17. On Luther's praise for Tauler, see also the letter to Spalatin of 14.12.1516 in WA Br.1, Nr. 30.58.

of the women mystics, has long been recognised as one of the major
points of contact between Luther and the medieval mystical tradition.
But Tauler also illustrates the limits of Luther's connection to mysticism
and to mystical hiddenness and dereliction.

The annotations that Luther made in his copy of the 1508 edition
of Tauler's sermons during 1515 and 1516 provide evidence both of his
interest in this 'German theologian', as well as his break with central
themes of Tauler's Eckhartian anthropology of the divine ground of
the soul.[65] Luther appreciated Tauler's devotion to the crucified Christ
and the practicality of his vernacular preaching; but he read Tauler in
his own way, as can be seen in his lengthy comments on Sermon 45
(Predigt 41 in the modern Tauler edition of Ferdinand Vetter).[66] Here,
he praised the Dominican's teaching that the birth of God in the soul
can only take place if one gives up all one's own plans for achieving
goodness and 'bear your suffering to the end . . .', ' . . . because standing
by this storm, the birth [of God] is close and God will be born in you'.[67]
Luther summarises Tauler's message thus: 'Therefore, all salvation is in
resignation of the will in all things, as he teaches here, both in things
spiritual and in things temporal – and in naked faith in God.'[68] Tauler's
notion of resignation of the will, however, leads back into the *Seelengrund*,
an ontological conception foreign to Luther's anthropology.[69]

When it came to the suffering and terror induced in even faithful
Christians by the God who hides himself, the reformer found an ally in
the Dominican preacher, though, of course, Luther did not need Tauler
to discover the importance of this form of trial. Two of the sermons found
in the 1508 edition that Luther commented on demonstrate the basis for
the reformer's remark, quoted above, that Tauler 'often spoke of it',

[65] These annotations, 'Luthers Randbemerkungen zu Taulers Predigten', can be found in WA
9:95–104. For a study of their relation to modern texts of Tauler, see Steven Ozment, 'An Aid
to Luther's Marginal Comments on Johannes Tauler's Sermons', *Harvard Theological Review*, 63
(1970), 305–11. Ozment's book, *Homo Spiritualis. A Comparative Study of the Anthropology of Johannes
Tauler, Jean Gerson and Martin Luther (1509–16) in the Context of Their Theological Thought* (Leiden: Brill,
1969), shows how Luther broke with Tauler's Eckhartian anthropology. For more on the relation
of the two theologians, see Bernd Möller, 'Tauler und Luther', *La mystique rhénane* (Paris: PUF,
1963), pp. 157–68.
[66] Ferdinand Vetter, *Die Predigten Taulers* (Zürich: Weidmann, 1910; reprint 1968), pp. 170–6.
[67] These two phrases are from Tauler's Sermon 41 (ed. p. 172.8–14). Luther's comments on this
sermon in the 'Randbemerkungen' (pp. 101.14–103.19) are the longest he devotes to any of the
Dominican's homilies. The reformer uses the sermon as a basis for a discussion of God's action
toward us *sub contrario*.
[68] 'Randbemerkungen' (p. 102.34–6).
[69] See the discussion in Ozment, *Homo Spiritualis*, pp. 199–203, showing how the reformer glides
over the anthropological differences between himself and the Dominican.

that is, the suffering of those believers who experience the hiddenness of torturing God.[70]

One of the sermons that Luther deemed worthy of notation was the fourth in the 1508 edition (Predigt 3 in Vetter).[71] This homily for Epiphany discusses the various types of myrrh, one of the gifts offered to Christ by the Magi. According to Tauler, there are three kinds of myrrh: first, recognition of the fleetingness of the world's pleasures; second, all the general sufferings sent by God; and third, 'a totally bitter myrrh God gives, inward anguish and inward darkness'. Tauler says, 'The person who wills to accept this and to suffer it, will have flesh and blood and nature destroyed . . . God comes to him with terrible temptations and in wonderful and unusual ways that no one knows who has not experienced them.'[72] In his glosses Luther interpreted this third myrrh as 'the suspension of grace and the Spirit', and said that the 'terrible suffering' it entailed was because those who experience it 'do not ascend into God; as Job says, "The Lord gives, and the Lord takes away"' (Job 1:21).[73]

Another sermon that shows Luther's interest in Tauler's view of estrangement from God is Sermon 41 (Vetter, Predigt 37) for the Third Sunday after Trinity. This contains one of Tauler's most powerful passages about the tortured love of those whom God abandons, a text Luther so admired that he made no less than eleven notations on a brief passage that takes up only fifteen lines in the modern edition. In this piece Tauler identifies the lost drachma of Luke 15:8 with the human soul, imprinted with God's image. When it is lost, the woman, that is, Divine Wisdom, lights the lantern of love and turns the whole house upside down to retrieve it. The lantern of love lit in the heart is not powerful emotions of joy, as many think; it is an experience of tortured love not unlike what we have seen in Angela and Mechthild. Tauler describes it thus:

This is love, that a person is burning in seeking and in lacking, and in a feeling of being abandoned; one remains in constant torment, but content to be tormented. In this torment a person is melted and consumed by the fire of desire for God, and yet is in equal contentment [*gelossenheit*]. This is love; it is not what you imagine it to be. It is the lighting of the lantern.[74]

---

[70] These texts by no means exhaust Tauler's rich treatment of the role of suffering in the path to God, especially his teaching on *gotliden/deipassio*. For some useful studies, see Christine Pleuser, *Die Benennungen und der Begriff des Leides bei Johannes Tauler* (Berlin, 1967); Alois M. Haas, '"Trage Leiden geduldiglich". Die Einstellung der deutschen Mystik zum Leiden', *Gottleiden – Gottlieben. Zur volkssprachlichen Mystik im Mittelalter* (Frankfort: Insel, 1989), pp. 127–52, and '"Die Arbeit der Nacht". Mystische Leiderfahrung nach Johannes Tauler', *Die Dunkle Nacht der Sinne*, pp. 9–40; and Louise Gnädinger, *Johannes Tauler. Lebenswelt und mystische Lehre* (Munich: Beck, 1993), pp. 251–86.
[71] *Die Predigten Taulers*, pp. 16–20.   [72] Pr. 3 (ed. p. 19.4–9).
[73] 'Randbemerkungen' (p. 99.29–34).   [74] Pr. 37 (p. 143.18–23).

In commenting on this passage, Luther has a long note illustrating Tauler's point through a comparison with carnal love, which proves itself more when it 'suffers hard and difficult things for the beloved's sake' than when it 'enjoys the beloved in sweetness and benefits'. The abandonment he glosses as 'dereliction from God through suspension of grace' (*derelictione a deo per suspensionem gratiae*).[75] In another strong passage not commented on by Luther, Tauler, like the reformer, uses the figure of Job as an example of the just man who, because of his sin, 'wanted to go wandering in the deepest ground of the abyss, in what was most painful and in the darkest place of hell . . . And he wanted to suffer this in the greatest and sharpest suffering, and never to leave it.'[76]

My purpose in looking at Luther's comments on Tauler in the light of what I have called mystical dereliction is not to re-open the question of Luther's relationship to mysticism. It does seem, however, that the reformer's appeal to the *Deus absconditus* is different from that of the mystics, though Luther could cite texts about mystical estrangement from God, such as those he found in Tauler, for his own purposes. After an initial hesitation in his earliest writings, the reformer quickly adopted an attitude of opposition to traditional Dionysianism and its apophatic teaching. Nevertheless, Luther had his own form of experiential negative theology of the *Deus absconditus*. What attracted him to certain mystical texts, such as Tauler and the *Theologia deutsch*,[77] was not their Eckhartian apophaticism of divine nothingness and union without distinction, but the way in which these German theologians stressed how God works *sub contrariis* as the hidden God who demands that believers must surrender all self-will, imitating Christ's suffering on the cross, in order to be justified.

Luther, however, had a second form of the *Deus absconditus*, the dreadful hidden God of predestination. Existentially, Luther's language about the terror induced even in the saints by this *Deus absconditus* finds parallels in mystical literature, but Luther clearly did not depend on the mystics for this aspect of his thought. Indeed, the reformer related to this hidden God in a way different from how the mystics did. Luther seems to have reversed the polarities of the mystical relationship between the believer and the *Deus absconditus* experienced as the God who consigns to suffering and even to hell. The mystics embraced the God who absents himself and condemns to hell, seeking ever-deeper contact with

---

[75] 'Randbemerkungen' (pp. 100.34–101.4).
[76] Pr. 46 (ed. p. 205.21–5). Tauler is commenting on Job 17:16.
[77] On the relation between the *Theologia deutsch* and Luther, see Alois M. Haas, '"Theologia deutsch", Meister Eckhart und Martin Luther', *Gottleiden – Gottlieben*, pp. 286–94.

his absent presence. Luther fled *from* the God who hides himself in the mystery of predestination in order to take refuge in the God hidden *sub contrario* on the cross.

This difference between Luther's view of the *Deus absconditus* and what we have found in some mystics has ramifications for our understanding of mysticism. For those who then and now have dedicated their lives to seeking the unknown and hidden God, no trial may seem worse than the loss of God, save possibly the conviction that the hidden God has from all eternity decided to forbid his presence to those who most love him. Many students of mysticism have been acquainted with this aspect of mystical consciousness through John of the Cross's powerful descriptions of the 'Dark Night of the Spirit'. However, even this brief look at the theme of mystical dereliction in the late middle ages shows what a long pedigree such forms of divine hiddenness have had in western mysticism.

Luther felt as if he were damned – an experience that drove him almost to despair. Many of the mystics we have looked at speak in similar ways about God's absence, about estrangement from God, and about a damnation so painful that we do not do it justice by speaking of it as a '*resignatio*' *ad infernum*. Nevertheless, the mystics did something rather different with this despair than Luther did. They do not flee from the God whose hiddenness so tortured them; they seek it out in confidence that it is only through the full embrace of God's absence, even in hell itself, that God can be attained.[78] True consolation is in desolation – 'Welcome, very blessed Estrangement', as Mechthild of Magdeburg put it.

---

[78] Obviously, a further issue, one too large to be examined here, is the exploration of the reasons for this difference between Luther and the mystics. Part of this gap rests in the diverse anthropologies; equally significant, of course, are changes in the doctrine of predestination.

6

The deflections of desire: negative theology in trinitarian disclosure

Rowan Williams

I

The spirituality of the first Christian centuries was shaped by two convictions – that Christian identity was a matter of coming to share by
God's gift the relation that eternally subsists between the Logos and the
divine Source; and that what we encounter in prayer is never capable of
being reduced to a finished conceptual scheme, however much we may
labour to remove obvious inadequacies and misunderstandings in our
speech about God. Both convictions have roots in pre-Christian concerns about the relation between God and 'being' in general or between
God and mind; but these themes are given new and pretty specific content in relation to the figure of Jesus of Nazareth: the language of divine
relatedness gradually supersedes that of a descending scale of participation in divinity, and the personal quality of relation between Logos and
Source becomes determinative for trinitarian language.[1] As the scheme
was slowly matured in the fourth and fifth centuries, however, emphasis
was laid upon the idea that the divine *essence* constituted the mysterious heartland of Godhead.[2] No one could ever produce or dream of
producing a definition of what is involved in being God; occasionally
Isaiah 53:8 ('Who shall declare his generation?') was used to reinforce
the mysterious character of the bringing into being of the Logos;[3] but

---

[1] For a more detailed discussion, see R. Williams, *Arius, Heresy and Tradition* (London: 1987), especially
the conclusions to Parts II and III (pp. 175–8 and 230–2).
[2] This is characteristic of the Cappadocian Fathers; see, for example, Basil of Caesarea, *De spiritu
sancto* 9 (PG 32, 108D), Gregory Nazianzen, Or.38.7 (PG 36, 317B), Gregory of Nyssa, *De vita Moysis*
2 (PG 44, 404B), among many other examples. There is much helpful orientation on the historical
and polemical background of all this in T. A. Kopecek, *A History of Neo-Arianism* (Cambridge,
Mass.: 1979), especially chs. 5 and 6.
[3] For example, it is used by Alexander of Alexandria in his first letter about the teaching of Arius,
preserved in a number of sources, including Theodoret's *Historia ecclesiastica* 1.4 and published by
H. G. Opitz in *Athanasius Werke* III.1: *Urkunden zur Geschichte des Arianischen Streites* (Berlin/Leipzig:
1935), text no. 14; ET in Williams, pp. 249–51.

on the whole, despite assertions of the incomprehensibility of the divine relations in various respects, the weight of the negative moment in theological speech was laid on the side of divine *ousia*, that inaccessible core of life in virtue of which God is God.

But as soon as you have put it like that, the problems are evident. Does this mean that there is a 'something' that makes God what God is, over and above the relations of Father, Son and Spirit? Or that the level of divine essence is in some sense higher or deeper than that of the divine persons? Both ideas found their defenders in theological history; both come awkwardly near to suggesting that there is something secondary about trinitarian language. The reaction to Arius ruled out the idea that God was really and essentially a single divine agent beyond relation in his own being; but some features of the language that subsequently developed, Eastern as much as Western, could well have led back to an uncomfortably similar picture, in which the unutterable and unrelated comes first. A recent French writer speaks of the 'prechristian or pretrinitarian' character of some such negative theologies, associating then with the neoplatonic heritage (and treating Eckhart as typical of this trend, a judgement open to challenge).[4] This is not wholly fair, to the extent at least that the simply *grammatical* observation that what makes God to be God cannot be the subject of a human conceptual definition is not the exclusive property of Neoplatonists but is the common sense of all reflective religion. But we cannot deny a certain risk of polarising hidden essence and revealed persons. It should be clear that any division of God's life into the bit you can see and the bit you can't see is unsustainable. And the revealing mistake in such a rendition of trinitarian faith is perhaps in this: that we acknowledge the inseparability of revelation and hiddenness in our encounter with God, yet feel that its character *as* encounter can only properly be salvaged by holding to a model of God as three more or less perceptible objects, united by a life whose nature evades all description. The impulses to safeguard the personal and the apophatic are proper instincts; the difficulty lies in not allowing the negative moment to reach into our discourse about the persons and reconstruct this. In other words, how are we to understand negative theology as it applies to the *relations* of divine life? This demands more than affirmations that the *mode* of divine relating is incomprehensible, and it equally demands something quite different from saying that divine relatedness is what

---

[4] Y. Labbé, 'La théologie négative dans la théologie trinitaire', *Revue des sciences religieuses*, 1993, 4, pp. 69–86 ('préchretien ou prétrinitaire' and reference to Eckhart, p. 70).

must be denied in order to get at the inmost truth of divine life. But to tease this out requires attention to the ways in which, in the literature of Christian contemplation, such pervasive negativity is indeed allowed to transform the whole discourse. If it is true that the structures of Christian prayer prompt and shape and confirm Christian speech about God as trinity, then the enormously important dimension of 'negative' rhetoric in writing about prayer and growth in the spirit must play its part.

This discussion concentrates on St John of the Cross, for two reasons. Most discussions of John overlook or marginalise what he has to say, explicitly and not so explicitly, about the life of the Trinity, and it is at least worth reading with care what he does say. But it is specially important to do this because he is by common consent among those who have most systematically pressed the priority of negation, in word and life, within Christian practice. What he sees as significant in trinitarian theology is therefore of particular interest; and I shall suggest that in fact he offers a trinitarian theology of negation that avoids precisely those traps which beset a scheme in which the divine essence is the real locus of the negative moment.

II

The *Romanzas* of St John are among the less well known of his works.[5] A sequence of nine fairly brief and strictly versified meditations, culminating in a poem on the nativity, they can at first sight appear just a little mechanical in form, while their content is a closely reasoned scholastic theology expressed in the lyrically intense terms familiar from John's other poems. However, the more closely you examine them, the more remarkable they appear. They move rapidly from contemplation of the mutuality of the persons of the Trinity to an evocation of the purpose of creation as the provision of a bride for the Son; by this provision, the Father is enabled to extend his own love 'beyond' the life of the Son, to create for the Son a 'lover' for his joy, and to bring this lover/beloved within the life of the Godhead. This act does not augment the joy of the trinity but represents its inner character of rhythm, remaking it at another level. The imagery boldly assimilates the relation of Father and

---

[5] See E. Allison Peers, *The Complete Works of St John of the Cross* (London: 1943), vol. 2, pp. 455–65. They are given their proper weight as guides to this thought in what is one of the best general guides in English to St John, *The Impact of God. Soundings from St John of the Cross*, London 1995, by Iain Matthew, especially ch.17. I must gratefully acknowledge an enormous debt to Fr Matthew in my understanding of these texts.

Son to more than the conventional pattern – though it builds, of course, on earlier hints in the Augustinian tradition. Father and Son indwell one another 'like the beloved in the lover'; later on, the word used is *quería*, which carries unmistakable associations of 'desiring'. And the theologically eccentric language of a 'growth' of love eternally between the three persons suggests again the idea of desire, 'erotic' movement towards a goal, despite the orthodox terminology alongside this of a perfect and immutable love. The extreme compression demanded by the simple metrical structure makes interpretation difficult at several points; but the argument appears to be something like this.

Father and Son are 'in' each other, as lover and beloved, and the love uniting them is equal to them. Yet in the trinity there is *one* lover and *one* beloved: all three are one lover, all three are one object of love, since the being or essence (*ser*) of the three is identical with each one. It is as if the *ser* of the Godhead is being identified with the formal pattern of indwelling itself – not with a 'nature' beyond or behind the three, but with the movement of one into another in desire. In one sense therefore, love itself is the *esencia* of God (*un sol amor tres tienen, Que su esencia se decía*: 'a single love unites the three, a love which we may recognise as the divine essence'). The love specifically uniting Father and Son is, as we shall shortly see, the love that is the 'excess' of what each desires in the other; it is thus constituted as an equal presence or agent within the pattern of divine agency. But at the same time – and potentially confusingly – the love of the Father, the love of the Son and the excess of their mutual love which is the Spirit also constitute the divine life or essence, three agents of one love, one recipient of love in three modes. The ambiguity of the Spirit's role and designation is notable; but there is an important point behind what seems a confusion. The single life of the Godhead is the going-out from self-identity into the other; that cannot be a closed mutuality (for then the other would be only the mirror of the same); the love of one for other must itself open on to a further otherness if it is not to return to the same; and only so is the divine life 'as a whole' constituted as love (rather than mutual reinforcement of identity). If so, the designation of both Spirit and divine essence as love makes sense: it is the Spirit as excess of divine love that secures the character of God-as-such.[6]

---

[6] See particularly John Milbank, 'The Second Difference' in his collection, *The Word Made Strange: Theology, Language, Culture* (Oxford: 1997), pp. 171–3. Milbank argues that the recognition of the Spirit in the Trinity is the ground of a recognition relative to the whole business of understanding thought itself and relation itself, in that 'Judgement concerning significant form, and the guidance of formal structuration, can never be exhaustively specified by analysis of the

The second of the poems imagines the Father's address to the Son in eternity, beginning to sketch the notion of 'excess'. The Son is not only the cause of the Father's joy in himself; he is the potential cause of joy in other beings. The Father, rejoicing in the Son, envisages beings who can participate in the Son's life and status, can receive the same gift that the Father gives the Son eternally. Again, the Father desires that the Son be loved by others than himself, others who will learn to rejoice in the miracle of the Father's self-bestowal to the Son. This is the main burden of the third *Romanza*, at the end of which the Son looks forward to holding the partner thus proposed for him by the Father in his arms, so that she may be 'burned' by the Father's love. The fourth poem begins very strikingly by affirming simply that the Father's consent to all this is, instantaneously, the creation of the world; and the rest of the sequence details the narrative of creation up to the point where it reaches its destiny, where the Son completes creation by his taking flesh, satisfying the yearning of creation and bringing about the miraculous exchange of divine joy and human pain that is the essential gift of the incarnation.

It is a complex pattern, constantly weaving back upon itself; but it is also a coherent framework within which to understand the whole of John of the Cross's theology. Briefly put: the human relation with God lives in a tension between the nuptial and the filial. The eros of the created self for God, understood as the longing for communion with the Word, is a desire not for the Word or Son as terminus of prayer and love, but *a desire for the desire of the Word* – i.e. for the Word's own desire for the Father and the relation in which that desire exists, the relation we call 'filial'. Union with the divine partner is union with that partner already and eternally in relation to the Source from which the partner originates. But the love of the Son for the Father is itself a desire for the desire of the Father, and so for the Father's excess of love 'beyond' what is directed to the Son. Thus we, incorporated into this relation to the Father, share the 'deflection' of the Son's desire towards the Father's excess of love: we are taken into the movement of the Spirit.

Contemplative living in the trinitarian life is therefore a transcription into the circumstances of the world of the divine excess and displacements

structures themselves. There is a dynamic surplus that surpasses the formal object and constitutes "subjectivity"' (p. 188). In other terms, structures 'give' themselves to be repeated or participated; above all, one might say, the 'structure' of mutual love is intelligible only by being the bestowal of love. That which is to be understood is understandable only if it is more than a structure of closed reciprocity. This needs fuller discussion than can be given here, and Aquinas' account of trinitarian relation in ST I. xxvii and xxxvii–xxxviii is more suggestive than has sometimes been recognised.

of love. The relation of Father, Son and Spirit is never reducible to the indwelling of two loving subjects; the movement that is divine life or essence is not only a self-bestowal in or into the being of an other, but the overflow beyond that immediate other. Just as – to put it in anthropomorphic terms – what the Son loves in the Father is *more* than the Father's love for the Son, so our love for God is more than the search for a divine other whose love for us satisfies and completes what we are – more than the search for a fantasised partner in whom our eros will decisively find its goal and end. Our love is deflected into the same excess as God's love shows. The tension between nuptial and filial in our contemplative stretching-out Godwards itself becomes a clue to how we might speak of God's own self-relatedness as trinity (and, incidentally, it puts certain questions against too wooden a reading of the scholastic language of subsistent and opposing relations in the Godhead).[7] To move into the divine life is to find desire reconstituted; as that happens, the vision of the divine life is also reconstituted into this pattern of a ceaseless or circling deflection, an emptying of 'desire' that seeks *closure* with a determinate other, and an opening therefore on to the dimension or a love that is always directed to but never determined by a specific other – the dimensions of a love that can properly be called endless.

Turn from the *Romanzas* to the more 'mainstream' works of John of the Cross, and it becomes possible to read them with rather different eyes. The negativity of John appears rather as what I have been calling the deflection of love towards the desire of the other (towards the other *of* the other). The *Ascent of Mount Carmel/Dark Night of the Soul* is dominated by the idea that the way in which my self-identity is constituted (by memory, intelligence and will in the Augustinian and scholastic anthropology) must be radically restructured by encounter with grace (so that memory, intelligence and will become hope, faith and love). To start with, my self is determined by what I want, and that wanting determines and limits who I am. The self I am aware of is a self bound to gratification by means of eros terminating in this or that object. When I am transformed into the subject of hope, faith and love, no determinate object is presented to my eros, because God is that in which these virtues terminate, and God is no determinate object. But this in turn means – painfully – that the way in which I can be a coherent object to myself begins to be very confused: the privation of specific, determinate goods for my subjectivity produces the sense of a dissolution of selfhood

---

[7] As found in Aquinas; see especially ST I xxix and xxxvi.

itself – the appalling darkness, suffering and disorientation evoked in the treatise on the night of the spirit.

The model for this is the dereliction of Jesus on the cross: if Jesus is the way to the Father, our way involves the same death he endured. On the cross, Jesus is left without any perceptible consolation or sense of support from the Father; the Father, we might say, has ceased to be in any way a graspable *other* for the subjectivity of Jesus. And in this emptying out of the sense of the Father as the term of any kind of gratification, what is achieved is the total reconciliation of humanity with God. When the negation of all determinate consolation is arrived at, what is 'left' is the purpose and act of God.[8] The experience under examination (though 'experience' is not exactly the right word here) is that reconstruction of what the otherness of God might mean that occurs in contemplative practice. John of the Cross treats this as a centrally Christological and trinitarian matter: this is how the *non aliud* of God's difference is concretely encountered *because* this is the *non aliud* of the presence of the trinitarian persons to each other. In the life of God, love is always deflected from the 'object' that would close or satisfy, that would simply be the absent other imagined as the goal of desire; the other is always engaged beyond, engaged with another otherness. So to be included in the love of the Son for the Father is to participate in a love without satisfaction or closure – an endless love; and for us as creatures, that *can only* be felt as pain and privation before it is recognised as freedom (and continues as pain even within the recognition). Even for the human subjectivity of Jesus, the *non aliud* of the Father's reality, the excess and elusiveness of the Father's love, appears concretely as the black void of Gethsemane and Calvary, the 'annihilation' of the dereliction on the cross. Divine love is most free in Jesus at the moment when the Father is no longer a determinate other over against him but an absent love that will not stand still to be consolingly viewed. It is a love now wholly active *in* the otherness of Jesus (as in the otherness of the eternal Word), identified with *his* outpouring of his being in love. The Son loves what the Father loves, and so loves the Father's complete bestowal of love upon and in his own substantive being; ultimately then, he must love the absence of a love that is given to him as if from a consoling or satisfying other, because he must love the excess of the Father's love, that which

[8] See in particular, *The Ascent of Mount Carmel* II.vii.11: 'Thus [Christ] wrought herein [in the dereliction of the cross] the greatest work that He had ever wrought . . . either upon earth or in Heaven . . . And when [the believer] comes to be reduced to nothing . . . spiritual union will be wrought between the soul and God' (p. 92 in vol. 1 of the Allison Peers translation).

escapes simply being a mirror of his own identity. The Son's love must enact the Father's, not simply reflect it back to him; so on Calvary it acts in an experienced darkness with respect to the knowledge or feeling of a divine other.

These apparently convoluted explorations are an attempt to draw out an exceptionally deep and resourceful understanding of the relation between contemplative language and discipline and the conceiving of plurality in the divine life. It should be clear that the negative moment in John's teaching is fundamentally bound to the nature of trinitarian relationship, in which the divine subsistents are in no way 'objects' to each other as in an interpersonal relation within the world. Their life is a pattern of gift and reception so radical that we have no finally suitable analogies; their love is a giving 'into' the otherness of a love that does not simply return upon itself. We are faced not so much with logical paradox as with a plain lack of adequate categories for speaking about something *like* subjectivity that cannot be accounted for in the terms of our standard discourse of sameness and otherness, subject and object. The 'language' available for this can only be, for John, the practice of contemplative and practical dispossession. What escapes conceptual description is not the interiority of the divine essence but the movement of 'love beyond desire', which we can only make sense of (insofar as we can make sense of it at all) in the context of the unconsoled commitment and objectless longing of contemplation.

John's *Ascent/Night* is generally none too specific on the matter of trinitarian theology; we have to reconstruct the outlines from terse and involved passages like the discussion of Christ's dereliction. But the *Living Flame of Love* makes the connections more overtly. Here we find the same model of the self rebuilt in hope, faith and love as is found in the *Ascent/Night*: III.18ff (references in the text are to the first redaction) describes how the 'caverns' of memory, intelligence and will are opened up to God in an infinite thirst or yearning, whose object is the infinity of God's wisdom and love. Yet (says John) the soul that truly desires God already possesses God; whence then the pain of our yearning? John distinguishes the possession given simply by grace – the unity of will that results from creation's surrender to God – and the possession in which created *nature* itself is transformed into the life of God. In the former (the state of 'betrothal' in John's scheme), my created desire is more and more decisively aligned with God's will; but is still in process of change, being assimilated to the divine life. Pain and frustration are unavoidable, since desire is still being felt as real lack or absence, even in the soul well advanced on the road.⁹ In the state of 'communication', in which the divine life is being concretely made over to the creature (spiritual 'marriage'), there is no gap between desire and possession: as with the angels, desire itself becomes 'satisfying', an occasion of joy in which we consent to our own endless progression into God's depths.[10]

In both stages, however, the same reality underlies what is going on. The eternal Word is coming fully to life in the created self, under the agency of the Spirit, who works to wean us away from particular gratification, to prepare us for the fullness-in-absence of the love of the Word to the Father. Later on in the commentary on the same stanza (66), John begins to discuss this in terms of the implanting in us of divine desire. The transfigured faculties of the soul 'turn to God in God' (67); because of what the soul is receiving from the divine Bridegroom, and because of the resultant unity of will between soul and Word, 'the soul . . . is giving God in God to God Himself' and is able 'through the grace that God gave to it of Himself' to 'give and communicate Him to whomsoever it desires; and thus it gives Him to its Beloved, Who is the very God that gave himself to it'. In other words, the presence of God in the soul is the freedom to give what has been given; and in giving what has been given, God gives God to God. What is given is what has been received; the terminus of the gift is the giver himself, *through* the act of giving to another. In this absorption into the divine action of bestowal on a bestowing other, loving a loving other, what comes to life in the soul is not the reality of the Word in some kind of abstraction, but the integral life of the Godhead – the Word directed in love to the Father's love which loves the Word's love, issuing in the Spirit's love which turns to the Father's love; and so on. The soul's relation to the Father is thus inseparable from the other-directed love that communicates divine life to the world. And the coming-to-be of the Word in the created self is identical with the 'communication' of Father, Son and Spirit together (70).

The analogy between the relation of Father and Word and Word and soul is touched upon more than once in these passages; Jn 17.10 and 26 are the texts quoted here ('All my things are Thine and Thine are Mine, and I am glorified in them', and 'May the love wherewith Thou hast loved Me be in them and I in them', as John renders the texts). It is certainly worth observing that the assimilation of the nuptial and the

---

⁹ *The Living Flame of Love*, III.22.ff in the first redaction (Peers, vol. 3, pp. 71 ff), III.23 in the second (Peers, vol. 3, pp. 173 ff).
[10] Ibid. III.23 (first redaction), III.24 (second), pp. 72 and 173: 'Even so the angels have delight when they are fulfilling their desire in possession'.

filial in this way helps to destabilise the gender reference of the language; it is as if to express the element of desire, of eternal opening out on to the radical otherness, the *non aliud* otherness, of the divine persons, the simple filial language will not do the work. The Father–Word relation has to be 'eroticised' in order to make anything of the mutual dispossession involved in the relation; just as our adoption as children of God has to be read through the medium of the infinite desire of God for God. The strictly patriarchal aspect of the whole discourse – a reading of paternity and filiation in terms of origins or authority – is dissolved; even the normal way of expressing the erotic in a religious context, God as male and the soul as female, is confused and compromised by the shifting significance of the word 'beloved' in a passage like III.68 of the *Flame*.[11] While the word's primary reference is obviously to the divine Word, it is very much as if each person of the Trinity is in some sense the beloved, the recipient of the divine act of gift. God's giving of God to God, as received by the soul, is clearly the Word's eternal giving to the Father; but it is also a total surrender in love to the Spirit. To try to analyse all this in terms of the gender roles either of God and the soul or of the divine persons is not easy – far less easy, in fact, than it is in some of John's lyrics, which operate with a more direct erotic language for the relation of soul to Christ. It may well be important to re-read those lyrics with all this in mind, as a reminder that even the apparently simple structure of the poetry's images opens out to a far wider context of meaning in relation to the divine life.

It is in effect another kind of negative theologising about the Trinity that we see here. The relatively straightforward notion that we are incorporated into the eternal Word's relation to the eternal Source is fractured and reworked by way of the 'deliberate mistakes' of erotic imagery introduced into the picture. The trinitarian relations need more than a discourse of origins (paternity) to express them; between this canonical language and the uncanonical and unconventional language of divine desire, some of the narrower possible readings of what might be meant by 'Father' and 'Son' are being questioned. As Pseudo-Dionysius might

---

[11] III.78 in the second redaction. 'The soul . . . is giving God in God to God Himself . . . [I]t sees that, since He belongs to it, it may give and communicate Him to whomsoever it desires; and thus if gives Him to its Beloved, Who is very God that gave Himself to it' (Peers, pp. 101 and 204). In both redactions, the following section (69, 79) refers to Jn 17.10, Christ saying to the Father, 'All that is mine is thine and thine is mine'; the second redaction further complicates the picture by saying that the soul gives its self-gift to the Holy Spirit, 'that he may love himself therein'. The soul surrenders itself into the very excess of the divine life.

have said, this is 'not Father and Son as it is with us'.[12] And the impetus behind such reworking is in significant part the discovery of the objectless darkness at the centre of Christian prayer: how are we to understand *that* as the living of the relation between 'Father' and 'Son', or to connect that with the life of the Spirit?

The question raised at the very beginning of the *Flame* is what it means to think of our acts becoming God's (1.4). If the focal moment of advance in Christian prayer and living is the midnight of emptiness evoked in the *Ascent/Night*, is it possible to think *this* as God's act? In one sense, yes – the sense that involves us speaking, as John does, of the Spirit acting to purify our affections and attachments. But this is only the preliminary to the action of God that transfigures us; and that action is *experienced* as darkness, for the most part. The complexities of III.66ff. are, I believe, an attempt to see this darkness as God in action; as the growth of that other-directed, 'deflected' love that the relation of Father, Son and Spirit must exemplify. Thus, whatever the unsystematised language of either devotion or a simplistic theology may say, we must speak with great caution about how the distinct persons act or how we 'encounter' them. II.1 of the *Flame*, a celebrated passage, offers a trinitarian reading of the action of God upon the soul in terms of analysing the contact into three elements – the hand that touches, the touch itself as an event and the burn or wound caused by the touch. The act originates with the Father, the 'hand'; the 'touch' is the arousing of 'desire for eternal life' in the soul, and this is identified with the Son; the wound or burn is the Spirit. And the effect of this action overall is the changing of death into life, the transforming of the soul's substance into the fire of divine life. In II.6, John elaborates the way in which the wound is 'healed' by being reopened again and again by the divine touch, until all that remains is the 'wound of love'. The touch of God, the life of the Son, is 'infused' into the soul; and, although John does not here explicitly say that this infused divine life is to be identified with desire, in some sense, a later passage (III.66) certainly speaks of infused desire as what awakes in the inner caverns of the soul's life. The strength of this desire is what causes the intense pain that the soul experiences, bound as it is to the limited goods of the body (II.12): what is evoked is the experience of overwhelming longing, whose only satisfaction lies in its being deepened still further, a longing that is at once acutely painful because it is simply

---

[12] The allusion is to the famous final passage of the *Divine Names* (XIII.3, PG 3, 980D–981A): 'not oneness or threeness as it is with us'.

and literally impossible to imagine what would terminate such longing and supremely conscious of joy and power in the awareness that this is nothing other than the incomparable freedom of divine love itself.

Thus the action of God on the soul is a single *event* of encounter, irreducibly threefold in its constitution. When a hand touches an object, the actual organic thing that is the hand makes contact with another reality and in greater or lesser measure affects that other subject; so with the act of God. Appropriately, the Son is the concrete point of contact, the event of encounter – in the incarnation, in the sacraments, in the ordinary operations of grace in the Church which is his Body. But equally this contact is *abidingly* concrete in the form of longing, *eros* for the Kingdom, a fiery and energetic desire: this is what it is to be in touch with God. And this 'being in touch' is kept burning by the wounds deepened by the Spirit; as the Spirit constantly purges our untransfigured desires, the Spirit makes more and more room in us for the life of divine desire that is the Son. But the process is inevitably one in which what we will *experience* is absence and darkness. Our acts become God's in the process whereby we come to long and love with God's longing and loving; and that can only be realised in us through emptiness, since God desires no 'object' but God, no satisfaction except the eternal continuance of an outpouring into the other.

III

John of the Cross's doctrine of the Trinity is not a systematic picture by any means, and it is deliberately teasing in its extravagant use of the language of desire, so apparently inappropriate to the changeless and self-sufficient God in whom John undoubtedly believed. But his language is out to do two thing for us (at least). First, it challenges us to imagine a love that is certainly more 'like' desire than anything else we can conceive, and yet is wholly other-directed. It is thinkable as desire because only such a word, it seems, can carry the energy of a love that is not simply a static contemplation. The use of the word can also help us engage with the complex phenomenology of human desire. Girard's account of desire as 'mimetic' has become very familiar in recent years: I learn to desire by seeing the desire of others; and the danger of this imitative process is that I then conceive myself as competing with the other for what I have learned *from* the other to desire.[13] This rivalry in desire more and more distracts

---

[13] See particularly René Girard, *Things Hidden since the Foundation of the World* (London: 1987), pp. 7–10, 283–91.

me from the object and locks me into a destructive mutual hostility with the other: I look no longer at the object but at them. And what John of the Cross's scheme proposes is that we think of the love of Father, Son and Spirit in the divine life as a counter-model to all this. Here is love which is always focused on the sheer otherness *of* the other as object of desire, a love of pure gift or bestowal. So far from wanting to supplant or overcome the desire of the other, this love is in love with the actual loving or desiring of the other (as we have noted in Augustine's much-misunderstood analogies, divine love in the classical theological tradition loves the act of loving, loves its own replication or imaging in the other). James Alison, in a fine discussion of the Johannine language of unity between Jesus and the Father, shows how this spells out a mimesis without rivalry. 'The Other, the Father, is absolutely constitutive of who (Jesus) is. Yet, because there is no appropriation of identity over against the Other who forms him, the complete dependence on the Other rather than being a limitation or a source of diminishment is exactly what enables the creative flow of life bringing about life to be made manifest'.[14] The unity of Father and Son 'is one of mutual possession, or "indwelling", to use the term untainted by association with rivalistic interpenetration. The psychological understanding that permits such statements is exactly that adumbrated by J. M. Oughourlian when he shows how, for the triangular mimetic theory of desire, "the Other is consubstantial with the self's consciousness"'.[15] And what the trinitarian picture proposes is the question, 'What would that consubstantiality mean when separated decisively from competition?' As Alison goes on to say, 'desire' is an inadequate word because it is bound to suggest 'some sort of lack'; but even 'love' is weak when we are trying to think of the creative energy of divine life in this connection, especially as it overflows into the 'wider spiral' represented by the difference of the Spirit emerging from the difference of Father and Son: 'their interpenetration is productive of a form of possession of each of them which is not merely identical with either of them'.[16]

So it may yet be a revealing mistake to use here the language of desire, knowing its oddity; at the very least, it allows us to connect the nature of divine love with the angularities and failures of created love, without simply appealing to a crude analogy between divine and human 'interpersonal' relation. But it also helps to bring into focus the second

[14] James Alison, *The Joy of Being Wrong, Original Sin through Easter Eyes* (New York: 1998), p. 198.
[15] Ibid., p. 199. [16] Ibid., pp. 200–1.

major contribution of John of the Cross to a reconstruction of trinitarian imagination. The centre of all trinitarian discourse is the conviction for Christian believers that they stand where Jesus Christ stands and are related to the divine source of this life as he is related to it. John attempts to purge this of any lingering and sentimental assimilation of divine relation to human: to share Christ's relation to the Father is not to enjoy a supreme experience of emotional intimacy, but to be drawn into the profoundly elusive and alarming 'deflections' of love that constitute the life of the Trinity; it is to share in Jesus' confrontation of the divine absence, a confrontation endured and made sense of because it is sustained by the same act of divine self-giving that refused to stand still and become an object for contemplation. Jesus faced with the absence of the Father is also Jesus endowed with the resource to give himself so wholly to the Father that he is free to act for the Father in the world. In that action on behalf of the Father, he also renders himself absent as a simple terminus of piety; he is ascending to his Father and ours, as the Johannine Christ says to Mary Magdalene, assimilating his paradoxical presence to the presence of the Father in own ministry and suffering. He is with the community of faith not as the steady object of their attention and devotion, as an historical other in the past, but as or 'in' the Spirit, the self-giving live that is realised in the believer assimilated to Christ, the believer who then in turn is set free to act for Christ, in the name of Christ. Here again we may recall de Certeau's account of the process of revelatory origination as a set of interlocking absences, of reciprocal 'lack'. Coming to stand where Jesus stands, if that is considered as the fundamental goal of Christian practice, has, finally, little to do with reproducing a particular pattern of historical action, even if it is only through the particular historical narrative that any of these conceptions can be generated. It is to be 'deflected' towards the absence of any static divine object so that the divine life may be lived in us as subjects.

The whole pattern may be better grasped when expressed visually; and it is extraordinary how closely the structure of this negative trinitarian theology is echoed by that most familiar of classical visual representations of the Trinity, Andrei Rublev's icon of the hospitality of Abraham.[17] As with all Byzantine icons, the lines of perspective and focus converge upon the beholder: the picture defines a place for the beholder to stand. In

[17] Endlessly discussed in this context. For a good basic orientation, see Leonid Ouspensky and Vladimir Lossky, *The Meaning of Icons*, Crestwood, NY, 1982, pp. 200–5; there is a brilliant and nuanced discussion in Gavin D'Costa, *Sexing the Trinity. Gender, Culture and the Divine* (London: 2000), pp. 153–63.

Rublev's composition, the place to stand is very plainly indicated by the fact that we are faced with a table around which sit three figures, so that where we are is on the 'vacant' side of the table. What immediately confronts us is thus the central figure of the composition, the angel on the opposite side of the table; but this figure does not look back at the beholder but towards the figure on its right. This figure in turn does not directly return the gaze of the central angel but moves our own gaze towards the figure on our right as we look; this third figure does not appear to meet the gaze directly of either of the other two, but the lines of the composition draw us inexorably back to the central figure with whom we began. In short, the picture is a graphic representation of the deflection we have been considering in this chapter: no one of these figures is simply there for us to look at 'full face'. From our initial stance on the empty side of the table, we are continually drawn and redrawn in to the movement of the looks and gestures of the three towards each other. Interpretations vary as to which of the angels we should take for which trinitarian hypostasis – and in one sense it is obviously unimportant, perhaps even important that we should *not* be able to specify an answer to such a question. But there is a certain biblical and traditional aptness in the reading that sees the central figure (who is undoubtedly wearing the robes that are associated with Jesus in Byzantine art, the blue overmantle, ochre tunic and white or gold *laticlavium* over the right shoulder) as the Logos, whose gaze directs us to the Father on our left and thence to the Spirit, whose posture echoes closely that of the central figure and brings us back to it.

To describe our engagement with the icon in these terms is also to raise the question of where we ultimately are in relation to the trinitarian figures. It is true (as many sermons on this image will say) that we occupy our place at the vacant seat at the table; yet we do not sit still there, any more than the other figures sit in motionless isolation. We are, as I have said, drawn in and redrawn in to a movement. In such a context, to know myself would be to know myself *in* the movement of being displaced by or through the self-displacing love of the Trinity. What I now see in myself is the motion of the Father, the Son and the Spirit; myself as the 'site' where this eternal movement of dispossession is being enacted. This is hard to state with any clarity. It does not, for example, mean that awareness of God as an object somehow replaces awareness of myself; or that I see myself perfectly reproducing a pattern of divine life by my own decision or attainment. Judging from what contemplatives write about this, it seems to be more like the self-awareness of the musician in performance.

To be aware of myself *is* to be aware of the music I am performing; I don't hear that music as I might if I were listening to someone else playing or singing – not least because my sheer *physical* involvement is different when I am actually performing myself. I consent to something happening in or through my agency, and that consent requires the full resource of my skill and effort; but what happens is at another level nothing to do with my skill and effort. And how exactly *this* performance, at this time and place, will go is beyond any exact prediction or control.

I *think* this is something like what Christian contemplatives want to say about the awareness of themselves 'in' God – what John of the Cross means by saying (in II.30 of the *Living Flame*) that the natural 'operations' of the soul are, in the state of union with God, 'changed into movements of God', so that the chief faculties of the soul are now the understanding, the will, the memory and the delight of God himself. As Augustine had grasped, knowing myself is inseparable from knowing God; but this means that knowing myself is being aware of the process occurring in me of the self-dispossession of God in love.[18] Or, in plainer terms and terms far more familiar from another religious tradition, knowing myself without illusion is confronting emptiness, learning to shift away from the centre of my preoccupation the dramas of a solitary ego so that what simply *is* takes place in me. For the Buddhist, who would most naturally use such language, what *is* is not construed with reference to a divine activity; for the Christian, what most simply and fundamentally is is the action of the threefold divine life. But in each case, the truth that is sought about the self is necessarily inseparable from the emptying out of what we might regard as ordinary self-consciousness – not to replace it with an extraordinary consciousness, a consciousness of extraordinary objects, but to enter into a radical expectancy and receptivity, an unanxious awareness of my incomplete, even insubstantial, life – or rather the insubstantial nature of a life failing to seek its definition in that wholeness of reality which – for the Christian at any rate – is grounded in the eternal loving generation of otherness that is God's life. And this in turn suggests, as James Alison and other disciples of Girard have insisted, that the Christian narrative of Jesus, his Father and his friends directs us to a re-imagining of the self that is capable of freeing us from a fundamental commitment to violence. Like God, *I* cease to be an object or possible object in which desire can be once and for all terminated; I am freed

---

[18] For a fuller account, see Rowan Williams, 'The Paradoxes of Self-Knowledge in the *De trinitate*', in *Augustine:Presbyter Factus Sum*, ed. J. T. Lienhard, EC Muller and R. J. Teske (New York: 1993), pp. 121–34.

from the supposition that I must be the final answer to someone else's question, that I have the right to expect a full stream of undeflected desire coming to rest with me. What will be properly lovable in me is my lovingness, my reality turned towards an other, not my reality turned upon itself. This does not mean that I cannot be lovable until I *achieve* lovingness; this is not a matter of moral prescription and condition. It simply means that the degree to which I cease to be for myself a fixed quantity, a defined and defended ego, is the degree to which I am able to allow love to enter and make a difference. The movement of love is always already in action – I do not have to, indeed I cannot, earn it; but my freedom to recognise and receive it does depend on my imagination of myself. And, to borrow again from Alison's essay, we could say that the renewed imagination of the self was the appropriation by me of 'the creative imagination of Jesus'.

A structure such as this may help us avoid one of the more blatant errors that ethics and spirituality can fall into on the subject of selfless love. There is a way of talking about all this that suggests that there is something basically *wrong* with being a self in the first place – occupying a position, having a specific psychology and history. It finds dramatic expression in Simone Weil's dictum, 'To say "I" is to lie': the specificity of the self is something that always stands between God and the world's reality, so that, if God's love is to be 'released' fully into the world, the 'I' must be cancelled.[19] A more completely trinitarian account of self-dispossessing love would have to correct this: the problem does not lie in the mere fact of identity itself, of the reality of the person or agent, but in the fantasy of the person as a self-subsisting terminus of desire (its own or another's). To redefine the problem in terms of sheer identity is to say that peace, unity, reconciliation, even love, are really only masks of the absence of difference: all identity must be reduced to the eternal sameness of divine act. But the trinitarian pattern tells us that divine act is not an eternal sameness at all, but *relational* act; so that the challenge for creatures is not the abolition of difference and the cancellation of the subject, but the subject's growth into precisely that recognition of and enactment of the self's reality *in* the other that is the heart of the theological vision.

To think about the self in trinitarian perspective like this prompts some reflections on the subject of desire in the human context, given

[19] Simone Weil, *First and Last Notebooks*, tr. Richard Rees (London: 1970), p. 132, for 'To say "I"...' cf. her *Notebooks*, tr. A. Wills, London 1956, pp. 378ff. on how the presence of the conscious ego 'deprives' God of contact with what I encounter and what I encounter of contact with God.

the admittedly eccentric use of the term in relation to God. If in the divine life 'desire' has to be reimagined as love for the love of the other, the passion for an other to be fulfilled, desire in the human context that might be recognised as imitating or sharing in God's love will be precisely the desire that does not refer to other's good exclusively to myself. Desire can set free rather than possess and enslave; my satisfaction is in the freedom of the other to be involved in the same way with yet another, finding satisfaction in *their* liberation. This may sound bizarre when we remember that Christian theologies of eros emphasise with pretty universal consistency the imperative to faithful and exclusive erotic bonding. But the contradiction is only apparent. The covenant of erotic faithfulness in Christian practice is something of a paradox: when I promise exclusive fidelity to one other human being, I promise that my faithfulness will not be dependent on having my wants gratified at any given moment. I make a commitment that reflects divine grace to the extent that it declares itself independent of future 'performance'. That mutual promise frees, or should free, erotic activity from certain kinds of anxiety, the fear of failing to conform to the other's will or fantasy and inviting rejection. Desire is thus liberated at another level – not the quest for another (a more gratifying) partner, but the desire that sexual bonding itself so strangely adumbrates: desire for the other's good irrespective of the other's capacity to satisfy me, to meet my lack. The promise of love beyond gratification which is bound up in covenants of sexual love is what is nurtured and augmented by the covenant. And – again strangely for the eye of contemporary North Atlantic humanity – a similar process is at work in the life of vowed celibacy. The promise *not* to enter a covenant of mutual erotic faithfulness and not to engage in the search for gratification is a way of saying that I shall struggle to keep my sense of lack or need radically unconsoled; my desire to be desired by another is held, deferred or displaced, its difficulty acknowledged and explored, so that I may learn to be free from the longing to *make* another mine, and so free in turn to be a sign or 'space' of freedom in my relation with any particular other.

The point I am making, in response to the attitude of a Simone Weil, is that 'Godlike' desire does not grow without the facing and negotiating of need and lack as they are experienced in specific lives and specific relations; the vows of partnership or celibacy are means to challenge and expand, but not to cancel the erotic. It is this concrete self with all its history and its contingent 'givens' which is offered into the joy or fruition of the other, the gratuitous, non-functional excess of particularity that is my life, something shaped by factors well beyond the self-referential desire of a human other. It is that gratuitous and non-functional excess that I celebrate when erotic love is most fresh and free. The marriage vow itself is meant to be the strongest possible affirmation of this gratuity, the refusal once and for all to make love dependent on the satisfying of expectation. The monastic vow sets the gratuity of my being in the fact of God, refusing to let it be seen as simply the potential object of another's (self-referential) desire, and so assuring every other who is encountered that their gratuity and excess of being will be honoured here. Otherness and history are not a tragic fall from purity, but the context in which desire may grow to its 'Godlike' dimension, may grow, that is, beyond the longing for the other to reflect back my own identity. The created self, made in God's image, is unmistakeably and irreducibly erotic, and its desirousness is not something to be eradicated. To be as a created subject is to be a locus of desire; it is not a lie to say 'I' – unless that 'I' is trapped in the terms of functional and symmetrical gratifications, held back from the radical delight in the otherness of the other's desire that is rooted in the love of the Trinity.

IV

What this chapter has sought to explore is a negative theology of the trinitarian life that derives its negative character not from general and programmatic principles about the ineffability of the divine nature, but from the character of the relations enacted in the story of Jesus and thus also in the lives and life-patterns of believers. The apophatic is not simply a response to the perceived grammar of talking about God – though this is a significant element in apophatic usage and an appeal to the narrative and relational aspect of it should not blind us to these grammatical considerations. As we have seen, the development of a coherent language about the unknowability of the divine nature went originally hand-in-hand with a clarification of the distinctness of the hypostases. The more it became necessary to insist that the difference of the hypostases could not be assimilated to the sort of differences with which we are familiar, the clearer it became that the differentiation of Father, Son and Spirit had to be conceived in the strictest possible connection with the traditional set of negations about divine nature – that it does not admit of materiality, divisibility, degrees of completeness, varying levels of instantiation and so on. The fourth-century controversies turned in large measure on just this issue; the attraction of the theology of Nicaea's critics was that it was wholly clear about the impossibility of division or degree in the divine substance.[20] And the genius of Nicaea's defenders was to show that this very concern was better met by a theology that insisted upon the substantial equality of the three divine subsistents than by the restriction of indivisibility, impassibility, and so on to the person of the Father. Once it is clear that the divine indivisibility is the interweaving of otherness, not a kind of atomism, it becomes plain also – as fourth and fifth-century writers are fond of repeating – that both the unity and the plurality of the divine life are something other than 'cases' of the sorts of unity and plurality with which we are familiar; the classical expression of this point comes, of course, in Pseudo-Dionysius.[21]

Thus the use of negation to characterise the divine life expresses not simply the retreat of the finite mind before infinite reality – though it does at least that; it expresses the process of 'finding our way' within the life of the three divine agencies or subsistents. It is grounded in the endlessness of the movement from Son to Father, Father to Son, Father to Spirit and so on: the endlessness of self-bestowal, which never reaches a terminus, never exhausts the otherness of the other. Gregory of Nyssa's account of the whole contemplative movement into the divine centres upon this theme of endless *eros*, such that, as he says at the beginning of his *Life as Moses*, there is no *horos*, a word meaning equally 'limit' and 'definition', to the life of virtue.[22] But this insight needs further locating within the trinitarian framework outlined by St John of the Cross, to prevent it becoming no more than a particularly strong expression of the finite–infinite disparity. Trinitarian difference is both the difference of the uncontainable divine as such and the difference of the infinite 'circulation' of divine life between and among the three hypostases.

This reinforces one of the points most regularly and consistently made by modern Eastern Orthodox writers, perhaps most notably by Lossky. Apophatic theology is more than a conceptual move, because it is anchored in the reality of personal *kenosis*, divine and human.[23] Here is the final answer to the question posed at the beginning of this chapter about how we are, in negative theology, to avoid a polarising of inaccessible divine substance of nature and manifest persons. Apophatic observations about the divine nature are, as we have said, 'grammatical' remarks about the impossibility of specifying what it is that makes God to be God. Apophatic accounts of the trinitarian persons and their relations

[20] See Williams, *Arius*, pp. 215–29.   [21] See above, n.12.   [22] PG 44, 300D.
[23] Classically expressed in Vladimir Lossky, *The Mystical Theology of the Eastern Church* (London: 1957), chs. 2, 11 and 12.

are a way of expressing and evoking the particular theme of the end-lessness and non-possession of trinitarian relation, gift or love. The two dimensions of negative theology here do not represent two objects under discussion (nature and persons), but simply mark the two moments of recognising the radicality of divine difference that arise in the lived process of not only trying to speak consistently of God but trying to live coherently in the pattern of divine life as it is made concrete to us in the history of Jesus and made available to us in the common life of the Spirit-filled community.

7

The formation of mind: Trinity and understanding in Newman

Mark A. McIntosh

FLEEING APOPHASIS, AVOIDING THE TRINITY

The apparent anxiety driving Descartes' rush toward absolute certainty provoked one of his critics to remark: 'Your new method denigrates the traditional forms of argument, and instead grows pale with a new terror, the imaginary fear of the demon which it has conjured up. It fears it may be dreaming, it has doubts about whether it is mad.'[1] It is a curious if not surprising feature of the modern quest for clear and distinct ideas that the more decisively all ambiguity is shunned, the more intolerable, even fearsome, becomes every aspect of real mystery. If it cannot be exposed as specious reasoning or ridiculed as abstruse 'scholastic' wrangling, it comes to be reviled as a dangerous threat to human freedom and flourishing.[2] But, as Alciphron amiably reassures his friends in Berkeley's dialogue: 'Fear not: by all the rules of right reason, it is absolutely impossible that any mystery, and least of all the Trinity, should really be the object of man's faith.'[3]

---

[1] Quoted by Louis Dupré, *Passage to Modernity: An Essay in the Hermeneutics of Nature and Culture* (New Haven and London: Yale University Press, 1993), pp. 83–4.

[2] For wide-ranging but complementary studies of this early modern anxiety about mystery see Michael J. Buckley, *At the Origins of Modern Atheism* (New Haven and London: Yale University Press, 1987); Stephen Toulmin, *Cosmopolis: The Hidden Agenda of Modernity* (New York: Free Press, 1990); William C. Placher, *The Domestication of Transcendence: How Modern Thinking about God Went Wrong* (Louisville, KY: Westminster John Knox Press, 1996).

[3] George Berkeley, *Alciphron, or the Minute Philosopher*, Dialogue VII.8, ed. David Berman (London and New York: Routledge, 1993), p. 130. Cf. also VII.14, pp. 139–40: 'Thus much, upon the whole, may be said of all signs: that they do not always suggest ideas signified to the mind: that when they suggest ideas, they are not general abstract ideas: that they have other uses besides barely standing for and exhibiting ideas, such as raising proper emotions, producing certain dispositions or habits of mind, and directing our actions in pursuit of that happiness, which is the ultimate end and design, the primary spring and motive, that sets rational agents at work: that signs may imply or suggest the relations of things; which relations, habitudes or proportions, as they cannot be by us understood but by the help of signs, so being thereby expressed and confuted, they direct and enable us to act with regard to things.'

Alciphron's comfortable dismissal of mystery to the contrary notwith-standing, I shall argue here that the more real mystery is not only tolerated but actually lived into, the more religious certainty comes to light and truth becomes embodied in a human life. Bishop Berkeley himself was pointing in this direction (though at the time few seem to have grasped the significance of his suggestion). Berkeley's spokesman in the dialogue, Euphranor, responds to Alciphron by arguing that the words in which Christians speak of mystery ought not to be interpreted so positivistically, as though they simply, solely, and directly framed distinct ideas or could point directly at some reality. Rather, he proposes, it may be that such words are signs by which a life comes to be regulated and put into a right relationship with a reality that lies beyond any easy coining into intellectually manipulable concepts:

Whence it seems to follow that a man may believe the doctrine of the Trinity, if he finds it revealed in Holy Scripture that the Father, the Son, and the Holy Ghost, are God, and that there is but one God, although he doth not frame in his mind any abstract or distinct ideas of trinity, substance, or personality; provided that this doctrine of a Creator, Redeemer, and Sanctifier makes proper impressions on his mind, producing therein love, hope, gratitude, and obedience, and thereby becomes a lively operative principle, influencing his life and actions, agreeably to that notion of saving faith which is required in a Christian.[4]

The rationality of mystery, suggests Berkeley, is discovered not by some algorithm capable of reducing all language to either simple ideas or quantifiable things, but by a transformed life, a living apophasis in which the reality of divine mystery is known only as it becomes embodied in the slow and patient work of learning to live by grace.

But for this understanding of mystery to be recoverable in Western thought, something of a turning point would have to be reached: the point at which sceptical doubt about the capacity of reason has been deepened and stretched into a new appreciation for real mystery and a willingness to explore its meaning and significance – not by analysis into simple propositions but by the experiment of living. To arrive at such a new perspective would not be easy, for by the end of the seventeenth century disputes about the nature and validity of the doctrine of the

---

[4] Ibid. A little later, a somewhat 'enlightened' Alciphron replies: 'It seems, Euphranor, and you would persuade me into an opinion, that there is nothing so singularly absurd as we are apt to think in the belief of mysteries; and that a man need not renounce his reason to maintain his religion. But, if this were true, how comes it to pass that, in proportion as men abound in knowledge, they dwindle in faith?' (VII.11, p. 136).

Trinity – the paradigmatic mystery – had rendered trinitarian thought so antagonistic and wearisome, in the general climate of opinion, that the very mention of the Trinity seemed in danger of becoming (as it clearly was for Alciphron) a 'free thinker's' favorite bogey-man.[5]

Perhaps there was something instructive for Christian thought when Hume, in the *Dialogues Concerning Natural Religion*, contrived to make the dogmatist Demea an unwitting ally of the sceptical Philo against the erstwhile rationalist theologian Cleanthes. Though poor Demea realises too late the true spirit of Philo's agreement with him, Philo's earlier employment of Demea's views is suggestive: 'None but we mystics as you [Cleanthes] were pleased to call us, can account for this strange mixture of phenomena, by deriving it from attributes infinitely perfect but incomprehensible.'[6] As the supposedly assured results of rationalist theology are inexorably dismantled by Hume, it becomes clear that the sceptic is tellingly aware of how indigestible any real sense of divine incomprehensibility must be in Cleanthes' rationalist system. For Hume, it may be safe to say, this intractability simply leaves belief in God all the more obviously in doubt. But for a more religious mind, it might recall a way of speaking about and understanding God that seemed to have been lost among the deists and free-thinkers, a way of living in relationship with mystery that patiently exposes the mind to what it cannot grasp.

It may not be surprising that rationalist thought should have little room for the mystery of the Trinity, or that a more deeply sceptical turn of mind such as Philo's (and Hume's) should appropriate the incomprehensible itself as an acid solvent for complacent rationalist verities. But would I be warranted at all in thinking that there is some positive connection between a robustly trinitarian approach to God and apophaticism? I want to suggest that various examples of rationalist theology, whether of the Eunomians in the fourth century or of the deists in early modernity, ought to make us suspicious of a god whose philosophically pristine ineffability is so highly touted.

---

[5] For a somewhat picturesque account see John Redwood, *Reason, Ridicule and Religion: The Age of the Enlightenment in England 1660–1750* (London: Thames and Hudson, 1976); especially chap. 7, 'The Persons of the Trinity'. On the particular example of the trinitarian argument that developed between John Locke and Bishop Edward Stillingfleet, see Richard H. Popkin, 'The Philosophy of Bishop Stillingfleet', *Journal of the History of Philosophy* 9 (1971), pp. 303–19; William S. Babcock, 'A Changing of the Christian God: The Doctrine of the Trinity in the Seventeenth Century', *Interpretation* 45 (1991), pp. 133–46.

[6] David Hume, *Dialogues Concerning Natural Religion*, Part x, ed. Richard H. Popkin (Indianapolis and Cambridge: Hackett Publishing Company, 1980), p. 64.

Gregory of Nazianzus certainly argued that it was precisely his Eunomian opponents who had defined deity into a conveniently manipulable conceptualization: for, he says to them, you 'cannot even take the measure of yourself, and yet must busy yourself about what is above your nature, and gape at the illimitable'.[7] By contrast, Gregory proposed that the language for God (unbegotten and ingenerate) being used by the Eunomians was not in fact a simple idea that neatly *describes* the divine nature but rather a sign for the trinitarian relationship of the Father in respect of the Son and the Spirit. For Gregory, when we move forward on a trinitarian basis such language initiates us into a true apophasis, for it opens before us the truly incomprehensible abyss of the trinitarian life, the understanding of which is not discoverable as ideas we have about it but as the life we come to share within it.

And there is certainly an analogy in the case of early modern deism. Archbishop Tillotson's remote and chilly references to the doctrine of the Trinity hardly portend a new embrace of radical apophaticism but rather an extreme distaste for it. For Locke, the doctrine of the Trinity was either a foolish piece of mystification or else a pretended logical model that simply failed to make real sense.[8] Perhaps the dynamic at work here is what John Coulson, drawing on Coleridge, has called the difference between an analytic use of language and an older fiduciary use of language. The analytic language brought into being through the efforts of thinkers like Bacon and Hobbes, for the sake of the new philosophy, needed a complete one-to-one correspondence between word and idea or thing. But with religious language, like poetry, 'we are required to make a complex act of inference and assent, and we begin by taking *on trust* expressions which are usually in analogical, metaphorical, or symbolic form, and by acting out the claims they make'.[9] This life of being formed by the incarnate, embodied imagery of religion is in a very real sense apophatic, for it does not permit the language to be fixed into a noetic possession but trusts the language to lead one, by the very means of its incarnate imagery, into deeper and deeper communion with reality. It is

---

[7] Gregory of Nazianzus, *The Theological Orations* II.29, trans. Charles Gordon Browne and James Edward Swallow in *Christology of the Later Fathers*, ed. Edward Rochie Hardie (Philadelphia: Westminster Press), p. 157.

[8] Consider Locke's complaint that the very first principles of trinitarian thought were impossible to make sense of; I am supposed, Locke complains, 'to find two individuals, without any difference: but that, I find, is too subtle and sublime for my weak capacity' (quoted in Babcock, 'A Changing of the Christian God', p. 145).

[9] John Coulson, *Newman and the Common Tradition: A Study in the Language of Church and Society* (Oxford: Clarendon Press, 1970), p. 4.

not the encapsulation of reality but its promising deferral – for the sake
of a truer encounter beyond the reifying conceptual grasp of the knower.

John Henry Newman represents a particular case of this mutual implication of trinitarian and apophatic thought. What allows Newman to risk
a real exposure to apophasis is his inclination to root the deepest form of
apophasis not in a radical scepticism *tout court* but more particularly in the
Incarnate Son's yearning to know and do the Father's will, even from
within the deepest depths of human alienation from God. Newman's
apophatic tendency (if such it may be called) is thus recontextualised in
the trinitarian mission of the Son. It is not a bare or contentless apophasis, but an apophasis which is itself the super-expressivity of the infinite
relations of the divine Persons, and the incarnation of that relationality
in the broken and distorted language of a fallen world. The recovery of
negative theology and of a trinitarian habit of thought seem integrally
related in Newman.

INSENSIBILITY TO MYSTERY

It may be easiest to begin exploring these themes in Newman by noticing
first of all what he wants to overcome: an obtuse and clumsy insensibility
to the reality of mystery. This debility arises even when we think of
everyday features of life. For we are often in danger of stepping away from
the wholeness and mutifaceted nature of our own involvement with life's
details. We forget the sensitive network of encounters, impressions, and
feelings in which our own thoughts originally occurred. So, I believe, for
Newman we easily tend in later reflection to climb up into an abstract and
artificial judgement about things, a partial view that marches brusquely
forward as though everything had been decided but whose concrete
grounds in the congress of actual things and real life have been rendered
imperceptible and mute. The gravity of this problem is two-fold: first,
we fall into the habit of thinking that this abstract and explicit form of
reason is the true measure of reality; and then second, when, as it often
does, it is unable adequately to warrant on its own terms what we really
hold as true or even to notice the rich actuality of life in which we have
met truth in the first place, we are tempted to a despairing or else cynical
scepticism and a flight from the very reality in which the mind would
find its true enjoyment.

So in the last of the *University Sermons*, Newman pleads with his listeners,
first, not to mistake their rational constructions of reality for the thing
itself, but then also not to despair when they realise that their tools of

thought have been only that, no more. Our abstract reasonings in general, or even doctrinal formulations in particular, might be compared to mathematics:

Various methods or *calculi* have been adopted to embody those immutable principles and dispositions of which the [mathematical] science treats, which are really independent of any, yet cannot be contemplated or pursued without one or other of them. The first of these instruments of investigation employs the medium of extension; the second, that of number; the third, that of motion . . . They are, one and all, analyses, more or less perfect, of those necessary truths, for which we have not a name, of which we have no idea, except in the terms of such economical representations . . . They stand for real things, and we can reason with them, though they be but symbols, as if they were the things themselves, for which they stand . . . While they answer, we can use them just as if they were the realities which they represent, and without thinking of those realities; but at length our instrument of discovery issues in some great impossibility or contradiction, or what we call in religion, a mystery.[10]

Newman's argument is, as it were, a positively apophatic one. There is a utility to reasoning in general and to doctrinal reasoning in particular, but such forms of rationality are best employed not as ends but as means, as 'instruments of discovery' for exploring into an unimaginable depth of reality which the reason alone can barely even perceive let alone grasp.

It is for this reason that he is so impatient with the kind of self-satisfied, short-circuited way of thinking about religion which fails to recognise this 'economic' or regulative or analogical character of our language. Such interpretive flatness renders its exponents immune to a transforming encounter with divine reality; or else its mortally attenuated version of divinity inevitably disappoints and is rejected, often leaving potential believers mistakenly sure they have tried religion and found it wanting. Newman imagines the religiously insensible blundering around heaven itself: 'They would walk close to the throne of God; they would stupidly gaze at it; they would touch it; they would meddle with the holiest things; they would go on intruding and prying, not meaning anything wrong by it, but with a sort of brute curiosity.'[11] In this passage, Newman picks out the correlate of a merely analytic approach to religious thought, namely a reductionist approach to reality in general. If, in other words, language

---

[10] John Henry Newman, Sermon XV.38, 'The Theory of Developments in Religious Doctrine', *Fifteen Sermons Preached before the University of Oxford*, 3rd edn (Notre Dame, IN: University of Notre Dame Press, 1997), pp. 344–5.
[11] 'Christ Hidden from the World', *Parochial and Plain Sermons*, IV.16 (San Francisco: Ignatius Press, 1987), p. 883.

has ceased to conduct its speakers towards a deeper dimension of life and has now become merely opaque and univocal, then it will be increasingly difficult for people to conceive of reality itself as extending beyond the necessity of nature and on into mystery.

The 'intruding and prying' that Newman describes as a well-intentioned but 'brute curiosity' sounds very like the new approach to reality that Newman knew stemmed from the rise of modern science, and specifically from the anti-teleological thought fostered by Bacon. Newman is far from opposing science per se, but he is more than un-comfortable with the assumption that scientific patterns of rationality ought to be the world's sole approach to truth – even the basis for a religious apprehension of reality. Newman quotes Bacon as approving Democritus as against Aristotle because the former 'never meddled with final causes'.

Lord Bacon gives us both the fact and the reason for it. Physical philosophers are ever inquiring *whence* things are, not *why*; referring them to nature, not to mind; and thus they tend to make a system a substitute for God . . . The study of Nature, when religious feeling is away, leads the mind, rightly or wrongly, to acquiesce in the atheistic theory, as the simplest and easiest. It is but parallel to that tendency in anatomical studies, which no one will deny, to solve all the phenomena of the human frame into material elements and powers, and to dispense with the soul. To those who are conscious of matter, but not conscious of mind, it seems more rational to refer all things to one origin, such as they know, than to assume the existence of a second origin such as they know not . . . If we come to [nature] with the assumption that it is a creation, we shall study it with awe; if assuming it to be a system, with mere curiosity.[12]

Newman was to make a very similar point years later in *The Idea of a University;* namely that while science is a crucial part of the circle of knowledge, neither it nor its methods can operate in persistent isolation from religion; for in such cases the native human desire to understand and to know is deprived of that larger vision which alone prevents it from degenerating into an omnivorously reductionistic curiosity.[13]

In the latter case, warns Newman, such thinkers 'conceive that they profess just *the* truth which makes all things easy. They have their one idea or their favourite notion, which occurs to them on every occasion. They

[12] 'The Tamworth Reading Room', *Essays and Sketches*, vol. II (Westport, CT: Greenwood Press, 1970), pp. 208–10.
[13] *The Idea of a University Defined and Illustrated*, ed. Martin J. Svaglic (Notre Dame: University of Notre Dame Press, 1982); see especially University Teaching, Discourse II, 'Theology as a Branch of Knowledge.'

have their one or two topics, which they are continually obtruding, with a sort of pedantry.'[14] What is most noteworthy here is Newman's diagnosis that such minds, who have 'clear and decisive explanations always ready of the sacred mysteries of Faith', edge over time towards inflexibility and, above all, isolation: 'Narrow minds have no power of throwing themselves into the minds of others.'[15] It is this deformation of the person, this incapacity for sympathy and relationship that strikes Newman as the most serious issue. In his view, personal formation is the foundation for truthful religious knowledge. That is because religious knowledge itself seems most capable of advancing truthfully in persons whose personal training and habits of mind enable them to be profoundly and honestly present to God, listening and sensitive to the reality of the other. In the absence of such a personhood, religious knowers become 'proud, bashful, fastidious, and reserved', their particular moral character rendering them stiff and remote from the living encounter with the personal truth who is God: 'it is because they do not look out of themselves, because they do not look through and beyond their own minds to their Maker, but are engrossed in notions of what is due to themselves, to their own dignity and their own consistency'.[16]

PERSONAL FORMATION FOR RELIGIOUS KNOWING

Newman's comment above about the difficulty of not being able to look *through* one's own mind to the Maker suggests how entangled, in his view, are the two dimensions of our question. For it isn't at all simply a matter of how the subject knows an object, but much more concretely, how the divine reality (the object) itself shapes and forms the mind of the subject who draws near seeking understanding. Newman's analysis, in other words, of the problem of modern insensibility to mystery leads him to the conclusion that there must be some practice of apprehending religious reality which modern rationalism has overlooked. And this has meant that rationalism, oblivious to the role that this practice and formation of the mind plays in giving a truthful vision to faith, has tended therefore to see religious belief as merely a weak or uncritical form of reason. We must now explore this practice of personal formation, with its underlying ground in trinitarian apophasis.

---

[14] *University Sermons*, 'Wisdom as Contrasted with Faith and with Bigotry', p. 306.
[15] Ibid., pp. 306, 307.
[16] *The Idea of a University*, University Teaching, Discourse VIII, 'Knowledge Viewed in Relation to Religion', p. 146.

We can see Newman reflecting on this problem about the mental habits appropriate to religious knowing in some of his comments on John Locke in the *Grammar of Assent*. It is characteristic that Newman prefaces his argument with the personal observation that he has 'so high a respect both for the character and the ability of Locke' that he feels 'no pleasure in considering him in the light of an opponent' of his own long cherished ideas.[17] But nonetheless, Newman is quite sure that something has gone badly astray somewhere between Locke's admission, on the one hand, that sometimes 'probabilities' rise to the level of complete assurance, and on the other hand, Locke's warning against ever 'entertaining any proposition with greater assurance than the proofs it is built on will warrant'.[18] With apparent reluctance, Newman concludes that Locke's logical inconsistency here is the symptom of an unreal and narrowly theoretical view of the human mind. 'Instead of going by the testimony of psychological facts, and thereby determining our constitutive faculties and our proper condition, and being content with the mind as God has made it, [Locke] would form men as he thinks they ought to be formed, into something better and higher.'[19] It is interesting not only that Newman feels he is being truer to the empirical reality of human beings than is Locke, but also that his reading of human capacities is more able than Locke's to find consistent room for the *limitations* of the mind – limitations which in Newman's view have a very important and positive role. For while he criticises Locke's misguided design to 'form' the human mind into 'something better and higher' than God has made it, Newman designedly uses this same term, thus hinting very definitely that what is at stake here is a quite different approach to mental *formation*.

But what kind of formation of mind could find a useful role for the *absence* of knowledge? For Newman this is really a question about epistemological culture, about the habits and practices by which we almost instinctively try to understand something. Consider, first, a negative example in which an inadequate formation of 'religious understanding' short-circuits what is, in Newman's view, an essential feature of healthy religious knowing. When Newman considers what it would mean for a university *not* to teach theology as a distinct discipline, he wonders whether the partisans of such an approach really do mean the same

---

[17] *An Essay in Aid of a Grammar of Assent* (Notre Dame: University of Notre Dame Press, 1979), pp. 137–8.

[18] Ibid. Newman is quoting Locke, *An Essay Concerning Human Understanding*, Book IV, chaps. xvi, 'Of the Degrees of Assent', and xix, 'Of Enthusiasm'.

[19] Newman, *A Grammar of Assent*, p. 139.

thing as he does when they talk about 'God'. If God is powerful or skilful, 'just so far forth as the telescope shows power, and the microscope shows skill' then we are really only talking about 'Nature with a divine glow upon it'.[20] In such a case, says Newman, he can quite understand why it would be a waste of time to include theology among the university disciplines, because we would be talking about a discipline of knowledge whose capacity for astonished wonder had been rationally circumscribed to become a mere affectation, at best a pious emotional response to what is entirely graspable, manipulable, and determined by all the other branches of knowledge. It would be 'just as we talk of the *philosophy* or the *romance* of history, or the *poetry* of childhood, or the picturesque, or the sentimental, or the humorous, or any other abstract quality, which the genius or the caprice of the individual, or the fashion of the day, or the consent of the world, recognizes in any set of objects which are subjected to its contemplation'.[21] In such a culture of knowledge there is no real room for the radically new or the other or the incomprehensible; everything is massively clear, explicable, quantifiably appreciable. Most significantly, the personal formation inherent to such a culture would be that of the religious genius, the exquisitely cultivated appreciator of the sublime. This kind of formation does *not* really have a use for the ability to encounter the unknowable.

By contrast, Newman is envisioning a different kind of formation. Whereas a rationalist religion may be based on 'evidences', such evidences are flat, all their meaning is on the surface; they have nothing luminously unknowable about them and elicit no personal commitment in the process of knowing. Newman has in mind a process of formation in which real knowledge is gained only by a willingness to go on pursuing what cannot be grasped, by a humble attention to what cannot be reduced to simple facts or distinct ideas, and by 'that instinctive apprehension of the Omnipresence of God and His unwearied and minute Providence which holiness and love create within' the one who desires to understand.[22] It is this intuitive sense of divine presence that informs the religious sensibility and makes it an instrument of knowledge. But there must be, in Newman's view, some structure or process whereby the forming of this moral and religious sensibility takes place, a patterning which knits knowledge together into wisdom, and shows the relationship of many impressions to one coherent whole. Apart from that concern

---

[20] *Idea of a University*, pp. 28–9.   [21] Ibid., p. 29.
[22] *University Sermons*, 'The Nature of Faith in Relation to Reason', p. 214.

for the whole, the religious mind as easily degenerates into superstition, prejudice and bigotry, as into rationalism or indifference.[23] An 'instinctive apprehension of the Omnipresence of God' must be sustained by a formation in holiness that liberates the mind, leaving it sensitive to the overwhelming reality of the divine mystery and thus freeing it from the temptation to reduce this sense of God to partial, one-sided bigotry on the one hand or pale, rationalist, abstractions on the other.

There is reason to think that Newman was far from being out of step with his age in his concern that the formative power of mystery not be reified. Edward Sillem, in his analysis of the sources of Newman's philosophical views, quotes from the *Discourses on Painting and the Fine Arts* delivered by Sir Joshua Reynolds before the Royal Academy in 1786. What is especially intriguing from our point of view is that Reynold's language foreshadows Newman's in two ways: it speaks of the formation of a habitual reason or faculty of judgement that works with the whole of a person's experience of life, and it connects that formation process particularly to the apprehension of visible forms and expressions, and to the impressions they make upon the mind. Half a century later, we see Newman working towards a parallel insight, namely that the wholeness of real wisdom often leads us to a perception we cannot adequately explain on simple rational grounds, precisely because our vision has been shaped by countless impressions made upon us throughout the course of life, and particularly by those impression-making sacramental forms of the Christian life which draw us into a participatory process of knowing.

So, for example, Reynolds writes:

there is in the commerce of life, as in art, a sagacity which is far from being contradictory to right reason, and is superior to any occasional exercise of that faculty; which supersedes it; and does not wait for the slow progress of deduction, but goes at once, by what appears a kind of intuition, to the conclusion. A man endowed with this faculty, feels and acknowledges the truth, though it is not always in his power, perhaps, to give a reason for it; because he cannot recollect and bring before him all the materials that gave birth to his opinion ... This impression is the result of the accumulated experience of our whole life, and has been collected we do not always know how or when. But this mass of collective observation, however acquired, ought to prevail over that reason, which however powerfully exerted on any particular occasion, will probably comprehend but a partial view of the subject ... If we were obliged to enter into a theoretical

---

[23] See *University Sermons* XII, 'Love the Safeguard of Faith against Superstition', and XIV, 'Wisdom as Contrasted with Faith and with Bigotry.'

deliberation on every occasion, before we act, life would be at a stand, and art would be impracticable.[24]

In Reynolds' view, the formation process for this faculty of perception is cumulative and existential; it shapes the personal character in ways that give one the capacity for intuitive insights beyond the more pristinely deductive process of analytical reason. And this means that such a faculty of habitual or intuitive perception will have to accept in humility its inadequate 'knowledge', its inability to justify its insights on purely rational and discursive grounds. Indeed, Reynolds warns his listeners that if they attempt to pin down 'by a cold consideration' the impressions which great things produce upon the mind, they will lose the very possibility of that greatness being infused into their own art; the artist will be tempted to 'reconsider and correct' the very ideas that had inspired him, 'till the whole matter is reduced to a commonplace invention'.[25]

What is so striking in Newman is the degree to which this kind of approach is transposed into moral, spiritual and theological terms. For the impression which converse with God has upon us is unveiled, of course, not in a painting or statue but a life of holiness and loving attentiveness to the ever greater concreteness of God's life. And yet the aesthetic and spiritual patterns of formation are parallel. Just as overmuch 'cold consideration' tempts the artist to reduce concrete originality to a merely 'commonplace invention', so too a believer may be tempted to reduce the spiritual life to pious good manners or a merely notional acceptance of religious propositions.

In a sermon on the 'Moral Effects of Communion with God', Newman suggests that the words and acts of the church's life of prayer initiate believers into a converse with the Kingdom of God, and that in countless untold ways this shapes the believer's spiritual sensibilities, awakens and heightens many moral qualities which might otherwise have lain dormant or grown distorted. One who prays habitually 'is no longer what he was before; gradually, imperceptibly to himself, he has imbibed a new set of ideas, and become imbued with fresh principles ... As speech is the organ of human society, and the means of human civilization, so is prayer the instrument of divine fellowship and divine training'.[26] Again like Reynolds, Newman suggests that if one attempts to reduce every

[24] Sir Joshua Reynolds, *Discourses on Painting and the Fine Arts*, 1768; quoted in *The Philosophical Notebook of John Henry Newman*, vol. 1, *General Introduction to the Study of Newman's Philosophy*. ed. Edward Sillem (New York: Humanities Press, 1969), pp. 208–9.
[25] Ibid., p. 209.
[26] Newman, *Parochial and Plain Sermons*, IV.15, pp. 871–2.

insight or inspiration that emerges from this formation to a purely rational basis, then the living reality of the insight will be lost. In such a case, 'the next world is not a reality to him; it only exists in his mind in the form of certain conclusions from certain reasonings. It is but an inference; and never can be more, never can be present to his mind, until he acts, instead of arguing.'[27]

Here we begin to see the crucial paradox at work: namely that the only possible presence of the divine reality to the human mind is that of an absence, an eluding of the grasp of purely rational inference and argument. And this presence, in Newman's view, becomes available only to the one who begins to *act*, to live concretely in converse with the divine life. So there is a crucial dialectical relationship between the cataphatic and the apophatic, between the concrete form by which the person comes to know God and the surpassing of all conceptual knowledge as the same person acts more and more within the very patterns and converse of God's life.

From his studies of the Fathers, especially of Alexandria and Cappadocia, Newman had certainly been exposed to this dialectical paradox of cataphatic and apophatic, word and silence, and to the way in which it comes to be embodied in the dynamic of a lived spiritual journey.[28] Hans Urs von Balthasar comments on this same existential dialectic in Gregory of Nyssa, remarking that for the great Cappadocian the representations of God in the cosmos become empty or dead if they are reified into simple rational concepts; the signs of God are only truly cataphatic, truly expressive of God, if they transport the beholder beyond themselves to the very abyss of apophasis: the vertiginous awareness of the infinite richness of divine life. If the soul learns not to foreclose the signifying power of the sacramental sign but rather is drawn into a never-ending journey by means of it, then the cataphatic and the apophatic are most truly themselves, truly in a dialectical relationship that gathers momentum within the believer's life. Balthasar usefully highlights a distinction in Gregory's thought between the cataphatic *content* of a divine sign and the apophatic *movement* that is aroused by the sign. The 'vision' or growth in understanding is, importantly, not identified with an intellectual grasp of the sign per se but with the transforming action and movement in pursuit of its ever-receding divine surplus of meaning.[29]

---

[27] Ibid., p. 872.

[28] For a classic study of this theme in Newman, see Charles Frederick Harrold, 'Newman and the Alexandrian Platonists', *Modern Philology*, 37/3 (February 1940), pp. 279–91.

[29] Hans Urs von Balthasar, *Presence and Thought: Essay on the Religious Philosophy of Gregory of Nyssa*, trans. Mark Sebanc (San Francisco: Ignatius Press, 1995), e.g., pp. 98–9.

We often see Newman making a similar distinction, most famously perhaps in his *Apologia* account of how 'carried away' he was by the 'broad philosophy' of Alexandria:

Room was made for the anticipation of further and deeper disclosures, of truths still under the veil of the letter, and in their season to be revealed. The visible world still remains without its divine interpretation; Holy Church in her sacraments and her hierarchical appointments, will remain, even to the end of the world, after all but a symbol of those heavenly facts which fill eternity. Her mysteries are but the expressions in human language of truths to which the human mind is unequal.[30]

But while the mysteries of holy church may only be expressions 'of truths to which the human mind is unequal', they are clearly nonetheless, in Newman's view, the divinely appointed means for forming the mind and drawing it into that converse with eternity which alone can illuminate the mind with truth. The church's sacramental life becomes, in Newman's reading, the matrix for this dynamic dialectic of cataphatic and apophatic, for the soul's awakening and arousal to a pursuit of truth in the highest sense.

We can see at least preliminarily three fundamental aspects to this sacramental dialectic of formation. The first is that Christ is mysteriously present to believers through the concrete forms and practices of the church's life. The second is that the minds and hearts of believers are transformed by their participation in these habits of worship, service, and teaching, and this transformation is consummated by the power of the Holy Spirit knitting believers more and more completely into the grace and ministry of Christ. And finally the truth of God and the reality of believers' own vocation are mutually disclosed in this process, but in a way which sustains in believers an availability of spirit and a longing movement towards the infinity of divine truth. In other words, the personal formation of mind envisioned by Newman has a fundamentally trinitarian matrix. The deepest kind of knowing and understanding of reality consists, for Newman, in being drawn by the Holy Spirit into the mission of the Incarnate Word and in coming to share in his relationship with the Father.

In respect of the first point, this is no more than Newman's own particular formulation of Christianity's basic sacramental theology, namely that the church's life is a way of living into the mystery of Christ's presence. 'The Ministry and Sacraments, the bodily presence of Bishop and

---

[30] Newman, *Apologia Pro Vita Sua*, ed. Martin J. Svaglic (Oxford: Oxford University Press, 1967), p. 37.

people, are given us as keys and spells, by which we bring ourselves into the presence of the great company of Saints', says Newman, suggesting how by participation in the church's life one enters into the life of Christ's Body.[31] Newman argues throughout his sermons that the life of the church is a process of fitting believers for heaven. And this is especially true of the sacraments: 'In these is manifested in greater or less degree, according to the measure of each, that Incarnate Saviour, who is one day to be our Judge, and who is enabling us to bear His presence then, by imparting it to us in measure now.'[32] The transforming presence of Christ is sensed by believers in a way that roots them in the saving action of Christ on their behalf: 'We recollect a hand laid upon our heads, and surely it had the print of nails in it, and resembled His who with a touch gave sight to the blind and raised the dead. Or we have been eating and drinking; and it was not a dream surely, that One fed us from His wounded side, and renewed our nature by the heavenly meat He gave.'[33] Newman's language in this and similar passages seems evocative of a believer's confusion in the presence of a consolation quite beyond the ability of the mind to calculate or control.

And that is suggestive of the second feature of this formation process, namely the Spirit's role in forming and renewing the life of believers. The sacramental economy of the Christian life is the concrete and objective framework within which believers encounter and are formed by the presence of Christ. The Holy Spirit works within this process to draw believers through the sacramental forms and into a living participation in that reality which the signs betoken. The church's 'sacraments are the instruments which the Holy Ghost uses' to realise and effect in believers the new life opened before them by Christ.[34] It is a life that progresses by way of the cataphatic, the shaping impression of the forms and images of the sacramental economy. These external signs of Christ's ministry form believers into a new body, a new pattern of life, which is animated by the Holy Spirit who fills each and every member with the mind of Christ. And it is this latter indwelling by the Spirit that draws believers on towards the apophatic journey into ever deeper trinitarian relationality.

Observing this process of formation is quite central to the epistemological concerns of this essay. For my argument has been all along that far from seeking to evade the sceptical (even Humean) critique of rationalist thought, Newman has found a way of deepening it. He has extended

[31] Newman, *Parochial and Plain Sermons*, IV.11, p. 835.
[32] Ibid., V.1, p. 956.   [33] Ibid., p. 957.   [34] Ibid., III.16, p. 620.

it down into an even more profound critique of rationalism by opening up that sceptical dissatisfaction into the endlessly yearning apophasis of trinitarian life. Indeed the formation of mind, for Newman, takes place precisely as one is rooted more and more deeply by the Spirit into the life of Christ.

We can begin to see the apophatic consequences of this move in regard to the third element of Newman's framework, namely, a way of knowing that is structured by the ever more of Christ's own mission as the Word of the Father. Needless to say, such an organic and developmental vision of knowing truth would be highly consistent with Newman's usual lines of thought. His regular concern is for the 'realizing' of the mind, for the patient training up into actuality of what was by nature merely provisional in our capacity to know and understand truth. And in Newman's view this process requires humility in the face of what we cannot know, and a wisdom that frees us from the urge to commodify truth into the coinage of our own rational certainties. This is true even at the most elemental level in our natural pursuit of knowledge, as Newman points out in the *Grammar of Assent*:

Instead of devising, what cannot be, some sufficient science of reasoning which may compel certitude in concrete conclusions, [we are left] to confess that there is no ultimate test of truth besides the testimony borne to truth by the mind itself, and that this phenomenon, perplexing as we may find it, is a normal and inevitable characteristic of the mental constitution of a being like man on a stage such as the world. His progress is a living growth, not a mechanism.[35]

And in Newman's view, this humble reliance on 'the testimony borne to truth by the mind itself' is not a liability, but is a sign of the crucial importance of the mind's proper and healthy formation and of its necessary and indeed salvific reliance upon communion with God. Later in the same passage we can in fact see that Newman very characteristically presses his observation about the normal and natural limits of human knowing and the significance of the mind's formation – to the point of recognising the divine matrix of human knowing. As an undeniable marker of our need for communion with God, says Newman, we see how difficult it is to understand the highest and most religious truths. This is in order

that the very discipline inflicted on our minds in finding Him, may mould them into due devotion to Him when He is found. 'Verily Thou art a hidden God,

35 *Grammar of Assent*, chap. 9.1, p. 275.

the God of Israel, the Saviour,' is the very law of His dealings with us. Certainly we need a clue into the labyrinth which is to lead us to Him; and who among us can hope to seize upon the true starting-points of thought for that enterprise, and upon all of them, who is to understand their right direction, to follow them out to their just limits, and duly to estimate, adjust, and combine the various reasonings in which they issue, so as safely to arrive at what it is worth any labour to secure, without a special illumination from Himself?[36]

The particular language Newman adopts here (direction, follow, esti-mate) is noteworthy: it is the language of practical pathfinding, and speaks of a kind of habitual knowledge or skill only available to someone long practised and experienced in the task. And as we have seen, Newman has a very definite sense of how this practical skill, which is nonetheless a 'special illumination', is received and activated by the mind, for it is none other than – at least in its most complete form – the event of the Spirit realising in us the mind of Christ, a mind well habituated to the vast hiddenness of God.

It is very much as if the skill and pathfinding knowledge of Christ, the pioneer of faith, were to become available to the believer. By the Holy Spirit, believers have access to Christ's approach to reality: 'you must use His influences, His operations, not as your own (God forbid!), not as you would use your own mind or your own limbs, irreverently, but as His presence in you. All your knowledge is from Him; all good thoughts are from Him; all power to pray is from Him.'[37] Newman's warning not to mistake the Incarnate Word's mystical presence and understanding for the believer's own merely confirms how complete, in his view, the identification of the believer's mind with Christ's must be.

But Newman is not implying here that there is a kind of vague or amorphous religious tinge given to human understanding. Rather the power and wisdom that come to shape the believer's mind are formed very concretely by the historical pattern, the earthly formation process, so to speak, of Jesus' own mission. 'What was actually done by Christ in the flesh' during his earthly ministry is 'really wrought in us'.[38]

Or to express the same great truth in other words; Christ Himself vouchsafes to repeat in each of us in figure and mystery all that He did and suffered in the flesh. He is formed in us, born in us, suffers in us, rises again in us, lives in us; and this not by a succession of events, but all at once: for He comes to us as a Spirit, all dying, all rising again, all living . . . His whole economy in all its parts is ever in us all at once.[39]

[36] Ibid., p. 276.   [37] *Parochial and Plain Sermons*, v.10, p. 1034.
[38] Ibid., p. 1038.   [39] Ibid., p. 1039.

Newman delineates this mystical indwelling of Christ in the believer quite carefully in terms of the most crucial, identifying patterns of Christ's mission, in terms of the events that mark and shape him as the one he is. Christ's vision of reality is not just in general terms 'divine', it is a vision of reality in terms of the paschal mystery, of the Word's infinite relationship to the Father in the Spirit, a relationship wrought out in the terms of a broken human world.

PARTICIPATING IN TRINITARIAN APOPHASIS

So far I've been arguing that the sacramental economy of personal formation is itself, in Newman's view, the extension of the Incarnation, and that the moral and spiritual formation of the mind is rooted through Christ in an ever deepening participation in the trinitarian life. But what kind of knowing, what kind of formation of mind, would this lead to? Let me try to answer this question in two ways. First by drawing some final conclusions regarding Newman's notion of knowing – in particular his view that the kind of knowing we come to through personal formation is a moral and spiritual wisdom, a practical discernment or *phronêsis* (to use the term he adopts from Aristotle) and not a general metaphysical clairvoyance. It is, in other words, the kind of knowing that judges rightly about the fitness and truthfulness of actions and ideas. And second, I want to expand the sense in which this discerning quality of mind is itself sustained by an apophatic journey into the ever greater mystery of God's trinitarian self-giving.

I have already argued above that the mind's capacity to know is, for Newman, shaped most definitively within the trinitarian framework of the church's life. Moreover, this is hardly the place to rehearse the extensive literature on Newman's teaching about *phronêsis* and the illative sense (the term he deploys in the *Grammar* to refer to our capacity to judge truly).[40] What I want is merely to give a sense of how a mind formed within this trinitarian pattern of life might in fact discern what is true and know what is right. I'm arguing, in other words, that the various notions of discernment and the illative sense that we find throughout

---

[40] For three thoughtful and concise discussions of Newman's epistemology (among very many), see Joseph Dunne, *Back to the Rough Ground: Practical Judgment and the Lure of Technique* (Notre Dame: University of Notre Dame Press, 1997), chap. 1; Andrew Louth, *Discerning the Mystery: An Essay on the Nature of Theology* (Oxford: Oxford University Press, 1983), chap. 6; Mary Katherine Tillman, 'Economies of Reason: Newman and the *Phronesis* Tradition', essay in *Discourse and Context: An Interdisciplinary Study of John Henry Newman*, ed. Gerard Magill (Carbondale, Illinois: Southern Illinois University Press, 1993).

Newman's work are best understood in terms of their trinitarian matrix in his thought.

Nothing could be clearer in Newman than the link between one's moral and spiritual growth and the capacity to know truly. And, as we have seen, this link is grounded in the believer's growth into the mind of Christ. This shapes the process of knowing and discernment in important ways. In the last of the University Sermons, Newman had argued that while 'the Christian mind' certainly 'reasons out a series of dogmatic statements', it cannot do this simply by treating the doctrines merely as 'logical propositions'; rather such a mind must reason 'as being itself enlightened and (as if) inhabited by that sacred impression which is prior to them, which acts as a regulating principle, ever present, upon the reasoning, and without which no has a warrant to reason at all'.[41] Newman is saying here that the living reality in question so impresses itself upon the mind and patterns its thoughts as to provide a kind of intuitive vision and discernment which alone can properly regulate the deliberations of reason.

By the time of the *Grammar of Assent*, Newman had been able to work out a kind of taxonomy for this power of discernment. Starting from a provisional sense of the divine, humanity in the image of God is led either to the realisation of this image in a fully sensitive and perceptive conscience or else to the degeneration of this conscience to the level of a stifled whisper. Whether this sensitivity to God's will 'grows brighter and stronger, or, on the other hand, is dimmed, distorted, or obliterated, depends on each of us individually'.[42] Intriguingly, Newman supposes that the more frequently people ignore or act against this apprehension of God, the more it 'may become almost indistinguishable from an inferential acceptance of the great truth, or may dwindle into a mere notion of their intellect'.[43] This is an inverse variation on Hobbes' view of the imagination as but a 'decaying' sense of reason; for Newman is here suggesting that in certain cases the operation of deductive reason itself may be but a decaying remainder of the deeper and truer intuition of the religious imagination!

As Newman goes on to chart the course of 'a mind thus carefully formed upon the basis of its natural conscience', he observes a steadily increasing sensitivity to the divine presence and activity in all things. Newman says that a mind so formed is able to arrive at a 'theology of

---

[41] Newman, *University Sermons*, 'The Theory of Developments in Religious Doctrine', p. 334.
[42] *Grammar*, 5.1, p. 105.   [43] Ibid., p. 106.

the religious imagination' which 'has a living hold on truths which are really to be found in the world, though they are not upon the surface . . . It interprets what it sees around it by this previous inward teaching, as the true key of that maze of vast complicated disorder; and thus it gains a more and more consistent and luminous vision of God from the most unpromising materials.'[44] This rather beautiful passage highlights the vital connection between the capacity to interpret reality truly and the capacity to intuit the presence of God in all things; indeed for Newman these two capacities converge to a single apex.

When men begin all their works with the thought of God, acting for His sake, and to fulfil His will, when they ask His blessing on themselves and their life, pray to Him for the objects they desire, and see Him in the event, whether it be according to their prayers or not, they will find everything that happens tend to confirm them in the truths about Him which live in their imagination, varied and unearthly as those truths may be. Then they are brought into His presence as that of a Living Person, and are able to hold converse with Him, and that with a directness and simplicity . . . so that it is doubtful whether we realize the company of our fellow-men with greater keenness that these favoured minds are able to contemplate and adore the Unseen, Incomprehensible Creator.[45]

Here we can see more clearly than ever how for Newman right discernment is the organic growth within a human person of the mind of Christ; for discernment seems to be modelled upon and grounded in Christ's own desire to act for the Father in all things, to interpret the will of the Father in all things, and to remain through all things in 'converse with Him'.

That this is in fact the case can be seen from Newman's University Sermon of 1832 entitled 'Personal Influence, The Means of Propagating the Truth'. Here he had already imagined what the personal formation of a 'Teacher of the Truth' would be like, and as he sketches the training of such a person, it becomes clear that he has been describing Jesus' own life. Intriguingly, Newman allows for a developmental process of formation: each period of personal growth brings with it new tests, new occasions to discern truth by listening for God's will in situations of increasing complexity. 'In him the knowledge and power of acting rightly have kept pace with the enlargement of his duties, and his inward convictions of Truth with successive temptations opening upon him from without to wander from it.'[46] The capacity to apprehend the truth, Newman suggests, is only truly realisable within a steady desire to hear

44 Ibid.   45 Ibid., pp. 106 7.   46 *University Sermons*, p. 80.

and serve the Source of all truth. It is this desire that the Teacher must plant in the heart. 'It is not a mere set of opinions that he has to promulgate, which may lodge on the surface of the mind; but he is to be an instrument in changing (as Scripture speaks) the heart, and modelling all men after one exemplar; making them like himself, or rather like One above himself, who is the beginning of a new creation.'[47] And to make others like himself is for Christ also to plunge them into the same human incomprehension that he faced, but more importantly, it is to conduct them toward that ineffable converse with the Father which is the very life of the Incarnate Son.

This is in fact the final piece of our picture, the piece which must to an extent always remain beyond our grasp. For if a proper human understanding of the truth of all things is grounded ultimately in Christ's personal sensitivity to God's will in all things, it is also an understanding of truth that always remains open towards the incomprehensible mystery of divine self-sharing. Time and again Newman contrasts the inexplicable condescension and incomprehensibly loving humility of God in Christ and in the saints with the banal, utilitarian perspective of human nature turned away from God. There is enough vestigial religion in public opinion to prevent most people from expressing 'their repugnance to the doctrine' of voluntary self-giving, says Newman, 'but you see what they really think of Christ, by the tone which they adopt towards those who in their measure follow Him'.[48] Newman then acidly ventriloquises the world's observations: 'Here is a lady of birth; she might be useful at home, she might marry well, she might be an ornament to society, she might give her countenance to religious objects, and she has perversely left us all; she has cut off her hair, and put on a coarse garment, and is washing the feet of the poor.'[49]

Exactly the same kind of uncomprehending obtuseness, says Newman, obtrudes in the very manner in which the world attempts to reason about Christian doctrine. As perhaps the most famous example, he points to the way in which the worldly mind attempts and fails to make sense of the Incarnation, precisely because it stands outside the living reality of the Son's relationship with the Father, and so perceives only an argument, apparently quite illogical, about how the Creator could also be a creature. By contrast, says Newman, 'how different is the state of those who have

---

[47] Ibid., pp. 86–7.
[48] *Discourses Addressed to Mixed Congregations* (London: Burns and Oates, 1881), Discourse xv, 'The Infinitude of the Divine Attributes', p. 313.
[49] Ibid., p. 314.

been duly initiated into the mysteries of the kingdom of heaven!'[50] Those who have begun to share precisely in the mystery of the Incarnate Son's life, in his relationship with the Father, have the key to enter into the meaning of the doctrine:

We are able indeed to continue the idea of a Son into that of a servant, though the descent were infinite, and, to our reason, incomprehensible; but when we merely speak first of God, then of man, we seem to change the Nature without preserving the Person. In truth, His Divine Sonship is that portion of the sacred doctrine on which the mind is providentially intended to rest throughout, and so to preserve for itself His identity unbroken.[51]

It would seem to the merely rational inquirer that the clearest and simplest approach would yield the most adequate answers; God is supposed also to be human; but these are mutually exclusive terms, and so the doctrine is irrational. The paradox is that the more one participates in mystery, the more permeable one's thought is to the incomprehensibility of the trinitarian life, the more one is able to grasp or at least be grasped by the truth. Newman's point is that as believers come to share in the mystery of the Incarnate Son, they find themselves beginning to understand his humility and self-giving love from within, to recognise that it embodies and echoes in fragile human terms the infinite and incomprehensible self-giving of the eternal Son.

Newman's analysis of human knowing leads him to suspect an underlying cause for both rationalism on one side and bigotry and superstition on the other. Small-mindedness in all its forms stems from a refusal to remain available to mystery – above all to the ground of mystery, the incomprehensible love which is God's infinite existence. The sheer prodigality of God's giving is overwhelming to the mind. Christ, says Newman, made his whole life 'a free offering to His Father, not as forcing His acceptance of it. From beginning to the end it was in the highest sense a voluntary work; and this is what is so overpowering to the mind.'[52] The problem, Newman believes, is that this divine extravagance is fundamental to reality, and if we persist in trying to evade it we distort our perspective about everything. The absolute self-giving of Christ

suggests to us, as by a specimen, the infinitude of God. We all confess that He is infinite . . . but, we ask, what is infinity? . . . the outward exhibition of infinitude is mystery; and the mysteries of nature and of grace are nothing else than

[50] *Parochial and Plain Sermons*, III.12, p. 581.   [51] Ibid., pp. 586–7.
[52] *Discourses to Mixed Congregations*, XV, p. 309.

the mode in which His infinitude encounters us and is brought home to our minds. Men confess that He is infinite, yet they start and object, as soon as His infinitude comes in contact with their imagination and acts upon their reason. They cannot bear the fullness, the superabundance, the inexhaustible flowing forth, and 'vehement rushing' and encompassing flood of the divine attributes. They restrain and limit them to their own comprehension, they measure them by their own standard, they fashion them by their own model.[53]

It is just this intolerance for mystery with which we began, and here we see Newman explaining why it is so injurious to the human mind. The reality of the universe encounters us ceaselessly with this 'outward exhibition of infinitude', and if human rationality has no room for the apophasis set loose by such an 'inexhaustible flowing forth', then humankind will inevitably, and defectively, fall to measuring reality by a false scale. Participation within the mystery of the Incarnate Son's infinite self-giving is, in Newman's view, the crucial formation of healthy human minds, lending them the moral wisdom and, above all, the tolerance for mystery that constitute right judgement.

It may seem surprising to allot John Henry Newman a prominent place in the history of apophatic thought. But I have tried to show how Newman's concern for the right course of human understanding led him to a new engagement with the mystery of the Trinity – not simply as a doctrine to be itemised but as a way of thinking about the real, as a matrix for the formation of human mindfulness. And it was from that perspective, I believe, that Newman was able to rediscover the indispensable function of an apophatic trajectory. He saw the importance of grounding all human knowing within the eternal trinitarian converse of God's own infinite knowing and loving of God. This rediscovered apophasis functions regulatively for Newman in every act of mind, shaping its habits of interpretation, preserving it from shrinking the real to quantifiable dimensions, and sustaining that suppleness of thought which springs from wonder at the superabundance of God's life.

---

[53] Ibid., pp. 310-11.

8

In the daylight forever?: language and silence

Graham Ward

The title of this chapter deliberately echoes the title of an early volume by George Steiner, also called *Language and Silence*.[1] There is no essay in the volume with that title, but there are several essays devoted to various forms of association between language and silence; essays which witness to the varieties of silence. In 'Retreat from the Word', for example, Steiner treats the crisis in literacy in the middle years of the twentieth century. It is a crisis in which language and reality have become divorced, where, in a world in which mathematics map the profundities of what is real, the world of words has shrunk. In the 'retreat from the authority and range of verbal language'[2] we are heading towards a tawdry banality, a silence into which civilisation will slide and perish. In 'Night Words' he treats this increasing banality with respect to the 'new pornographers'[3] who parade the vital privacies of sexual experience, taking away the words that were spoken in the night to shout them from midmorning rooftops. In the commercialisation of sex, Steiner observes, lies the kenosis of the Word (capital letter), the impoverishment of Logos itself. And in a selection of six essays, organised under the heading 'Language out of Darkness', Steiner treats what is evidently, as for Adorno, the root of the traumatising autism: the death-camps and the ethnic cleansing of Nazi Germany. The silence grows palpable: 'The language will no longer grow and freshen. It will no longer perform . . . its two principal functions: the conveyance of humane order which we call law, and the communication of the quick of the human spirit we call grace.'[4] So, among those writers who remained in Germany (when so many others left), Gottfried Benn

---

[1] 'In the Daylight Forever' comes from a popular song which topped the charts in 1998 by the all-girl group B*witched. The song takes up a theme reoccurring in many forms in contemporary culture, life after death, the concept of a heaven totally divorced from the earth in which the predominant experience is of light, harmony, union and self-fulfilment.
[2] *Language and Silence* (London: Faber 1967), p. 40.
[3] Ibid., p. 98. [4] Ibid., p. 124.

'withdrew first into obscurity of style, then into silence'.[5] And on the very eve of barbarism Schönberg has Moses cry: 'O word, thou word that I lack.' German is no longer a language in which to write creatively. First Adorno's famous aphorism 'There is no poetry after Auschwitz', and then the suicidal silences of Paul Celan, Sylvia Plath and Primo Levi appear as refrains through the volume. The silence distends from German to English, from Italian to French as Steiner charts the slide from *Bildung* to bathos, from the tragedy's catharsis to the babbling of the absurd.

It is the election of silence by those most able to articulate that disturbs him most. He explores this election in another essay in the volume, 'Silence and the Poet' with respect to Hölderlin and Rimbaud. And in doing so he invokes seemingly less nihilistic silences. 'Seemingly', because Steiner is aware that Hölderlin's 'quiet madness' may both be read as 'a negation of his poetry' or 'the word's surpassing of itself, for its realisation not in another medium but in that which is its echoing antithesis and defining negation, silence'.[6] Hölderlin's silence is either the descent into Babel or the consummation of the word. Steiner enquires further into the silence of the sublime, the frozen silences of the magic mountain. At eighteen, Rimbaud published *Une saison en enfer*, then put away his pen and embarked on a short-lived career selling arms in Sudan. He had achieved the perfect. There was nothing more that could be said. As Steiner points out, 'In much modern poetry silence represents the claims of the ideal.'[7] Words dissolve into the purer notation of music; leaving the verbal behind is a positive spiritual act, cognisant of transcendence, trembling on the neon edge of immediate relation. Steiner writes: '[I]t is decisively the fact that language does have frontiers, that it borders on three other modes of statement – light, music, and silence – that gives proof of a transcendent presence in the fabric of the world. It is just because we can go no further, because speech so marvellously fails us, that we experience the certitude of a divine meaning surpassing and enfolding ours. What lies behind man's word is eloquent of God.'[8]

Silence, in Steiner's work, is more ambivalent than the rich densities of meaning in words themselves. But two dominant and antithetical modes are evident: the silent bankruptcy of language as rhetoric which veils the void, or the silent horizons of the transcendent. Beyond language is either nihilistic despair or divine plenitude. Either way, words, the condition for the possibility of communication, have become unhinged from the world, taking on a rhetorical affectivity that seduces rather than

---

[5] Ibid., p. 128.   [6] Ibid., p. 67.   [7] Ibid., p. 68.   [8] Ibid., pp. 58–9.

educates. Words are unhinged also from the divine, for 'the categories of God are not parallel or commensurate to those of man'.[9] Mathematics and music become both threat and promise. On the one hand, they threaten literacy since it is language that has 'so far, in history, . . . been the vessel of human grace and the prime carrier of civilisation', while, on the other, music and mathematics 'are "languages" other than languages. Purer, perhaps'.[10]

What I wish to do in this essay is revisit this topic of language and silence and submit Steiner's deliberations to a genealogical critique. For what does Steiner presuppose, and leave unquestioned, about the nature and operation of language in order to produce his spacings for the relationships between words and silence, words and the Word? And whence come these presuppositions? Our understandings of the nature and operation of language (and therefore our spacings of the relationship between language and silence, language and the divine) are culturally and temporally specific. With regards to cultural specificity, scholars of comparative linguistics from Humboldt, Sapir, Whorf (and the more contemporary examinations of the relationship between translation and colonialism) have come to see that different languages encode different symbolic world-views – different construals of time, space, objects, subjects and their connectedness. Moreover, within any cultural evaluation of a language, attention can be given to one part of speech over another, transforming the way the operation of language is understood. An understanding of language as dominated by the role of the verb, rather than the noun, the preposition or the conjunction, expresses and produces a world-view quite different from the construal of language dominated by nomenclature. With regards to the diachronic development of language, it is not only that early English differs from Shakespearean English, Mediaeval French from contemporary French, but even our theories about the nature and operation of language change. The act and function of naming are conceived differently in other historical epochs. The relationship between words and the world in the work of Gregory of Nyssa, John Locke, John McDowell and Jacques Derrida differ considerably. With respect to the language of mysticism, Frederick J. Streng has pointed out that 'different assumptions about the function of language contribute to different interpretations of the soteriological significance found in different sorts of mystical awareness'.[11] He observes, concerning the assertions of certain mystics, that 'the key function of such

[9] Ibid., p. 159.   [10] Ibid., p. 132.
[11] Frederick J. Streng, 'Language and Mystical Awareness', in Steven Katz (ed.), *Mysticism and Philosophical Analysis* (Oxford: Oxford University Press), p. 141.

claims is to release the individual from attachment to the assumption that words have a one-to-one correspondence with separate entities in either ideal or physical experience'.[12] If Steiner represents (and sums up) a dominant western European perspective on the relationship between language and silence – a perspective which he views as developing from the seventeenth century and reaping its first fruits in the nineteenth century *avant-garde* and the twentieth-century crisis of representation – then a genealogical account of this position would unlock other possibilities for the nature and operation of language. From these possibilities we can begin to construct new filiations between language and silence.

ON THE SUBLIME AND THE KITSCH

I suggest Steiner's construal of language and silence is caught between two faces of modernity, both of which have a theological heritage: the kitsch and the sublime. These two aesthetic categories have a structural relationship to other binaries constructing the modern world-view: body/mind, secular/sacred, immanent/transcendent, particular/universal, public/private, subjective/objective, female/male. We will examine the category of the sublime first.

The experience of the sublime is an encounter with the ineffable, the silence of the unpresentable. It is the entry into the white margins beyond words. Take, for example, the final line of Keats' sonnet 'On First Looking into Chapman's Homer': Cortez straddling the Atlantic and Pacific, gazing out upon immeasurable distances 'silent on a peak in Darien'. The sublime marks the limit, end and rupture of the rational order; it remains what Kant termed *unerklärlich*. Jean-François Lyotard, reworking the Kantian sublime, suggests 'There are no sublime objects, but only sublime feelings.'[13] Objects dissolve into the immediacy of experience. The feeling is one of grasping the present, one of universal validity, of unlimited freedom. Nothing can prepare for its coming; it arrives as a surprising event which suspends consciousness. I have written about this elsewhere and do not intend to rehearse that analysis.[14] Furthermore, John Milbank has also delineated how the sublime functions as modernity's transcendent and leads directly to the neo-Romantic

---

[12] Ibid., p. 150.

[13] *Lessons on the Analytic of the Sublime*, tr. Elizabeth Rottenberg (Stanford: Stanford University Press, 1994), p. 182.

[14] See 'The Ontological Scandal' in Grace Jantzen (ed.) special issue of *John Ryland's Bulletin on Representation, Gender and Religion*, vol. 80, no. 3 (Autumn 1998), pp. 235–52.

pursuit by certain poststructural thinkers of aporia, rupture, the impossible, the unpresentable, and the irrational.[15] What is important here is to bring out certain emphases with respect to language and silence. These emphases are: (a) the centrality of feeling or experience which displaces consciousness, language, knowledge and reason; (b) the aspiration towards an immediacy beyond, better than and determinative of mediation – presence beyond and outside representation; (c) the perceiving subject, and the objective spectacle which overwhelms both seeing and subjectivity; (d) a dislocational event that suspends and denigrates a certain conception of time and space (as both measurable and regular); (e) the constitution of incommensurate orders – the immanent and the transcendent which renders difference and alterity as fixed and external positions; (f) the foregrounding of the arbitrary – both in terms of the rupturing, unpredictable experience and the relation between the linguistic sign and the world it represents.

These emphases have a theological heritage. In fact, the development of the sublime from Burke to Philippe Lacoue Labarthe is the rendering into secular aesthetics of erstwhile theological concerns. These concerns were most prominently evident in new existential understandings of revelation – legitimating early Protestant biblicalism – and the development of what Michel de Certeau has termed 'the science of mystics'.[16]

For Certeau, the cry of the mystic (or the possessed) in the sixteenth and seventeenth centuries was the tearing apart of the social symbolic in an attempt to find another tongue, a more authentic tongue, with which to speak. This tongue would allow the voice of the other to be heard. This ecstatic cry ruptures the routine and quotidian, incising across the surface of the world a testimony to the ineffable distinctiveness of the God beyond being. Revelation links an ecstatic non-knowing, an abyssal silence, with words. The violence and violation of the mystic event is subsequently rehearsed in what Certeau terms a 'manner of speaking' (suggesting a connection between the verbal excesses of mysticism and the visual excesses of Mannerism). As the mystic operates as translator of an ultimate alterity, difference is produced by subjecting the everyday use of language to a linguistic torturing. The manner of speaking is likened to circumcision, to cutting away at the flesh of word to make manifest the spiritual. Words are shattered and semantic units split. Commenting

---

[15] 'Sublimity: the Modern Transcendent', in Paul Heelas, ed., *Religion, Modernity and Postmodernity* (Oxford: Blackwell, 1998), pp. 258–84.
[16] *The Mystic Fable: Volume One the Sixteenth and Seventeenth Centuries*, tr. Michael B. Smith (Chicago: University of Chicago Press, 1992).

upon Diego de Jesus' Introduction to the *Obras espirituales* of John of
the Cross, Certeau writes about the 'process of fabrication' in which
'mystic phrases' were constructed: 'It was characterised both by a *shift
of subject* within the meaning space circumscribed with words and by
a *technical manipulation* of these words in order to mark the new way in
which they were being used. In short, it was a practice of detachment. It
denatured language: it distanced it from the function that strove after an
imitation of things. It undid the coherence of signification, insinuating
into each semantic unit wily and "senseless" shifts of interplay.'[17] And so
the adjective 'mystic' deflects attention from the noun it qualifies, from
that which the noun represents. In doing so, the signified is erased in
favour of the signifier. This is the paradoxical structure of the mystical
manner of speaking: the transportation beyond language (which is the
content of what is spoken) in fact opacifies the sign, giving weight to
its materiality. In pointing towards an outside, to that which exceeds
language it 'produces nothing more in language than the effects relative
to what is not in language'.[18] What remains paramount is the primacy
of experience itself: the experience of transcendence is translated into
the affectivity of rhetoric, the pyrotechnic spectacle of the verbal. The
staging of the transcendent imitates the excesses of ecstasy. The very
linguistic excesses here point the way towards the obverse side of the
sublime – the kitsch. For with this notion of the sublime we are on our
way to the commodification of language and the wholesale production
of spectacle.

   Certeau provides a genealogy for this mystic science and, in part,
this genealogy too is theological. Following de Lubac (and in agreement with Balthasar and, more recently, Eric Alliez, John Milbank and
Catherine Pickstock), Ockhamist linguistics is very clearly to blame.[19]
Nominalism deontologised words. It fostered a metaphysics of linguistic
atomism which was subsequently encouraged by the break up of Latin
as a *lingua franca* and the development of vernacular languages. It established the founding dualisms of modernity: epistemology/ontology,
word/thing. The dominant role of the verb in Mediaeval Latin – which
was related to Christology for Christ was God's verb – was dethroned in
favour of the noun. God is now encountered on the far side of language
and knowledge.

---

[17] Ibid., pp. 140–1.   [18] Ibid., p. 144.
[19] See here P. T. Geach, 'Nominalism' in *Logic Matters* (Oxford: Blackwell, 1972), pp. 289–301, for
   an earlier account of Occamist linguistics and the heresy they foster.

I will not rehearse here what has now become so much an intellectual commonplace that the ground is well prepared for revisionist studies of Scotus and Ockham. What is interesting is the way Certeau relates this displacement of the ontological and the increasing questions about whether and how language refers, to a shift in ecclesial practice and politics towards 'strategies of the visible'. He notes, again following in the footsteps of de Lubac: 'After the middle of the twelfth century, the expression [*corpus mysticum*] no longer designated the Eucharist, as it had previously, but the Church.'[20] The Church, as the social body of Christ, begins to make its hidden (*mysticus*) sacramental body visible. In this move to the specular – the origin of which Certeau locates at the Third Lateran Council (1179), and so prior to the work of Ockham (making the nominalist deontologising of language a product of an earlier theological shift) – the Eucharist 'constituted a focal point at which mystical reality became identified with visible meaning . . . Moreover, it consolidated clerical power . . . In this instance the sign was the presence it designated . . . This Eucharistic "body" was the "sacrament" of the institution, the visible instituting of what the institution was meant to become.'[21] The Eucharist becomes the first in a developing line of objects fully present to themselves. Eucharistic real presence prepares the ground for empiricism.[22] The Eucharist announces a univocity of being which is the basic presupposition of the natural sciences. But simultaneously, and paradoxically, it also produces equivocity.[23] For the Church's 'strategies of the visible' – which included professionalising the clergy and drawing the secrets of secular life into its confessional and juridical spaces – 'transformed the very practice of knowledge and signs'.[24] In doing so it established a hierarchical disassociation between the mystical and the visible, presence and representation. The paradox again: the desire and move towards greater transparency produces an increasing opacity. It is a paradox that will endlessly push apart communion and

---

[20] *The Mystic Fable*, p. 82.   [21] Ibid., p. 86.

[22] See my *Cities of God* (London: Routledge, 2000), pp. 156–74 for a genealogy of 'presence'.

[23] Theologians now began to articulate the doctrine of analogy in terms of univocity and equivocity (rather than Aristotelian paronomy). Later, with Cajetan, they manufacture a more technical vocabulary (*analogia attributionis, analogia proportionalis, intrinseca, extrinsica* etc.) employed even by seventeenth century Protestants like Quenstedt and, in the twentieth century, by Karl Barth. Is not this whole discussion of analogy set up by and reproductive of the concerns of nominalism? Was it now that an older thinking about *allegoria* – which emphasises the role of the verb (of temporality) – recedes, only to return in quite a different guise with the Stoicism and Gnostic dualisms of the Baroque?

[24] *The Mystic Fable*, p. 89.

communication, installing a gap, an absence, or a lack to be overcome. The simplicity and purity yearned for generates representational excess; mystical science requires lexical excess.

The kitsch now announces itself, and announces itself first in an *ecclesia* developing its theatricality and spectacle. The kitsch arises in a culture of excess. Unlike the sublime, the kitsch proclaims that the other side of language is not transcendental meaningfulness, but meaninglessness. The sign is not a sign *of* anything but simply the fabrication of something. Hence, Steiner's ambivalent 'silence' – the silence that can be eloquent of God can also, simultaneously, be a silence of futility and banality. The silence of full presence can also be the silence of unredeemable absence; the silence of plenitude can also be the silence of the void.

The German dramatist Wedekind wrote, in 1917, that 'Kitsch is the contemporary form of the Gothic, Rococo, Baroque.'[25] What comes to be a dominant cultural form, a pseudoart, in the late nineteenth and twentieth centuries because of techniques for mass production and professional marketing, has its roots in the metaphysics and cultural forms of former epochs. Kitsch is the exultation of ornamentation for its own sake, of superficiality, of ephemerality. Like the camp it flaunts the glitter and the glamour of its surfaces. It is eclectic and vulgar. Tocqueville, on his first visit to New York, observed how what he saw as marble temples and palaces along the shoreline turned out, on closer inspection, to be made of 'whitewashed brick . . . [and] columns of painted wood'.[26] More recently, Jean Baudrillard has commented on Las Vegas that its buildings are straight from film-sets; they aspire to the weightlessness and insubstantiality of theatrical scenery, backed as they are by the desert at the foot of the Sangre de Cristo Mountains. Kitsch announces that though the sign is bankrupt, such emptiness can be entertaining, diverting the gaze away from the desert itself. The kitsch is unashamed idolatry. For Baudrillard simulacrum now embraces its own manufacture, creating an ethos fostering the contemporary production and promotion of cyberspaces and virtual realities, soft ontologies (Vattimo) and hyperrealisms (Eco). For Baudrillard (and other para-Marxists like Fredric Jameson and David Harvey) the production of kitsch objects typifies late-capitalism. For capitalism after the mid 1970s, when America came off the gold standard, is characterised by the self-conscious exaltation of the

---

[25] Quoted in Matei Calinescu, *Five Faces of Modernity* (Bloomington: Indiana University Press, 1977), p. 225.

[26] *Democracy in America*, ed. J. P. Mayer and Max Lerner, tr. George Lawrence (New York, 1966), p. 61.

alienation and reification of consumer products. In a world-view which proclaims that pleasures are evanescent and to be seized as they present themselves, kitsch offers instant and easy enjoyments that are temporary and faddish. It shares borders with decadence and hedonism, but, more significant for the ideas being examined in this essay, it glories in aesthetic inadequacy. The kitsch signals the failure of the aesthetic to express, substituting spectacle and ostentation for 'the real thing'; it glories in the suggestion of wealth. Kitsch is the art-form of the haughty, the brash, and the confident.

Wedekind perceptively recognises the Rococo and Baroque as the predecessors of kitsch. Certeau would add Mannerism also: 'The *Meniera*, an elaboration of language upon itself, the subtle and sumptuous effects of which illustrated indefinite capacities, was exalted. This expressionism was made up of artefacts that exorcised the referential and set in movement a space shattered into contrasting fragments. In paintings, the passions depicted portray mainly a passion of forms and colours subjected to the delicious tortures of an art.'[27] What Certeau does not do is explore the association between the turn of the Church towards strategies of visibility and the multiplication of 'artefacts that exorcised the referential' which characterised Counter-Reformation culture. For it is the Church that first fostered the ethos of the kitsch and hence, even today, it is the gory presentations of the sacred heart, the Lourdes water in plastic bottles with blue celluloid caps of the Virgin, and the fat yellow candles burning before the plaster saints which most clearly typify the celebration of the superficial.[28] Kitsch draws close to bathos. The most profound is suddenly conceived as expensive vulgarity: high-art as depictions of a can of Campbell's soup; the barley-sugar twists and tasselled marble drapes of the ornate baldacchino by Bernini in St Peter's.

The Baroque announces the secularisation of perception and visibility out of which the modern engagement with the spectacle that Guy Debord so dramatically portrays emerges. 'The spectacle is the nightmare of imprisoned modern society which ultimately expresses nothing more than its desire to sleep.'[29] The spectacle, not religion, is the contemporary

---

[27] *The Mystic Fable*, p. 141.

[28] See here Baz Lurhmann's *Romeo and Juliet* where Juliet's deathbed scene takes place on a raised dais in the centre of a Cathedral, surrounding with thousands of burning candles and approached by an aisle illuminated by a dozen or so large blue neon crosses. Or witness Francis Ford Coppola's *Bram Stoker's Dracula* which portrays scenes of licking the blood from the side of the Count as if he were Christ. In fact, the vampire genre is a kitsch presentation of theological motifs – particularly Christology and the Eucharist.

[29] No. 21.

opiate of the people and the Baroque, with its exaggerated attention to surfaces, first gave it expression.[30] It was the triumph of that rendering of the invisible visible which Certeau describes as occurring at the end of the sixteenth century; the invisible concerned the divine (the gasps of ecstasy on Bellini's Teresa and the blessed Ludovico Albertoni), the infinite darknesses of Copernicus' universe (as felt and feared by Pascal in *Pensées*) and the passions of the soul (in Rembrandt's depiction of Bathsheba or Jan Six). The secularisation of the visible is coupled with a new appeal to the immediate. John Rupert Martin speaks of the 'sense of presence imparted by the greatest portraits of the seventeenth century . . . Here is no barrier between the subject and the observer'.[31] This attention to the presence of things leads to their reification, their glorification. We are on the road to the market fetishism that marks both advanced consumerism and the kitsch. The Baroque announces a certain 'in your face' triumphalism, with its voluptuous forms, its expressive energies and its monumentality. The multifigured scenes (many of them Scriptural or based on the lives of the saints) of Carracci and Rubens bespeak what Stephen Calloway terms a culture of enthusiasm for excess. Calloway reminds us, in a way that directly associates the Baroque with the kitsch, that 'baroque' was a derogatory term for the 'extravagant and whimsical, grotesque, and even coarse and vulgar'.[32] There is self-conscious theatricality here, a passionate rhetoric of gestures,[33] and an erotic candour all brought to the depthless surface of the work itself. Christine Buci-Glucksmann speaks of the Baroque 'erotics of nothing'. In the derangement of appearances, the enchantment of illusion, the overembodied universe of the Baroque 'this "nothing of being" changes into an infinity of ecstatic delight . . . a plethora of forms'.[34] She continues: 'As it becomes impossible to determine finitude and appearances in

---

[30] It is important to note that I am not condemning all Baroque art as kitsch. The Baroque is far more nuanced than that. It gave us Rembrandt, Poussin and La Tour. I am drawing attention to a certain logic of the Baroque, a logic of secularised visibility that helped to produce the world modernity sees, investigates, assumed to be there as the 'given' state of things.

[31] John Rupert Martin, *Baroque* (London: Allen Lane, 1977), p. 91.

[32] *Baroque, Baroque: The Culture of Excess* (London: Phaidon, 1994), p. 7. Calloway goes on to point out how the Baroque emerges in the Romantic period, as the Byronic (ironic and sardonic) side of the sublime (p. 12). The book as a whole treats the twentieth century return to Baroque aesthetics and, in particular, examines 'The Great Baroque Revival 1980s and 90s' (pp. 182–232), where the postmodern films of Greenaway and Jarman, the *haut couture* of Lacroix and Galliano and the superrealist images of Pierre and Gilles conflate the categories of the sublime, the kitsch, the opulent, the decadent and the macabre.

[33] Martin, *Baroque*, p. 86.

[34] Christine Buci-Glucksmann, *Baroque Reason: The Aesthetics of Modernity*, tr. Patrick Camiller (London: Sage, 1994), p. 130.

relation to any identity or reference, any essence or substance, we are left with an infinite regress towards a point that is always slipping away, a pure otherness of figure . . . The baroque signifier proliferates beyond every-thing signified, placing language in excess of corporeality . . . baroque reason brings into play the *infinite materiality* of images and bodies.'[35] We are close here to Baudrillard's simulacra, to the glorification of surface, the exaltation of the superficial, the surrender to the first devouring look and the ephemeral which is characteristic of the kitsch. Illusion conscious of itself, conscious of its own staging, seeks only to be sensational, not meaningful, spectacular not significant. On the other side of the *tromp d'oeil* visions of eternity lies caricature, 'born at the same moment as Baroque art itself',[36] after Annibale Carracci.

That the Church continued its commitment to such visibility is evident in the decoration of chapels and monuments, the number of votive pictures, paintings from Scripture, baldacchino, altarpieces, statues of saints, the designing of churches and the patronage of Popes. Italy was the first centre for Baroque sensibility, particularly between the pontifi-cates of Sextus V (1585–90) and Paul V (1604–21). 'Having renounced the dreams of temporal hegemony that had haunted some of the Renaissance pontiffs, the new popes transferred the will to power to a spir-itual empire, whose grandeur must now be reflected by Rome.'[37] Artists were encouraged 'to elaborate that "oratorical" style which was natural to the programme of apologetics and propaganda allotted by the Council of Trent to religious art'.[38] Baroque sensibility displayed a theatrical ex-ercise of secular power; papal power as sovereign power. The Council of Trent and the publication of Loyola's *Spiritual Exercises* are viewed as two of the foremost influences on the development of the Baroque. But in giving herself over to the triumph of the visible, to the phantasmago-ria of worldly goods, the Church sublates any theology of the sign to an aesthetics, and any theology of time to the serial stuttering of the present.

Mimesis in modernity moves between these two poles – the sublime and the kitsch – both of which de-create by insisting upon the inad-equacy of signification in the very process of signifying. The sublime and the kitsch are mirror reflections of each other, each producing depthlessness, each denigrating the body as such and materiality as such. For both require the disintegration (and proclaim the fundamen-tal illusion) of time and space. That which lies beyond can be either

---

[35] Ibid., pp. 134–9.   [36] Martin, *Baroque*, p. 99.
[37] Germain Bazin, *Baroque and Rococo* tr. J. Griffin (London: Thames and Hudson, 1964), p. 11.
[38] Ibid.

theistically or atheistically interpreted; it can either be plenitude or void. As Steven Katz observes: 'Though two or more experiences are said to be "ineffable", the term "ineffable" can logically fit many disjunctive and incomparable experiences. That is to say, an atheist can feel a sense of dread at the absurdity of the cosmos which he labels ineffable, while the theist can experience God in a way that he also insists is ineffable.'[39] The relationship that binds and yet polarises the sublime and the kitsch is the same relationship that binds and yet polarises theism and atheism. The paradoxical ambivalence of Steiner's observations on the relationship of language to silence shares this same logic. His position is a rehearsal of an implicitly gnostic understanding of language which has dominated western European culture for centuries, and which Christianity helped to disseminate. But the subsequent emphasis upon the poverty of language issues from viewing signification as descriptive: the signs name that which lies outside the signs and they have established themselves as names through social convention. Katz's points to how both the theist and the atheist 'label'.

To some extent, the move from modernity to postmodernity has only accelerated the development of such an understanding. The attention given by certain poststructural thinkers to what Ricoeur terms 'the aporetics of discourse', to hiatuses of one sort or another, to ontological ruptures and epistemological breaks, to broken middles and what Foucault calls 'eventalisation' are all in line with mimesis in modernity. Significantly, Certeau himself, although aware of the theological genealogy of contemporary accounts of signification and aware of alternative theological accounts in the tradition, continues the same gnostic trajectory. At the end of *The Mystic Fable*, he rejects the frank espousal of nihilism evident in the mystic nomad, Jean de Labadie – who embraces darkness, loss and journeys, like Cain, into endless exile. Labadie 'no longer has anything to "say" but the "lie" of an image', he tells us. 'Labadie has led us to the edge of a shore where there is nothing, formally, but the

---

[39] Stephen Katz, 'Language, Epistemology and Mysticism,' in (ed.), *Mysticism and Philosophical Analysis*, p. 48. Katz himself is making a different point. The essay argues for the complexity of comparing 'ineffable' when used by Christian, Sufi, Tao, Buddhist and Hindu mystics. The same term is covered quite different ontological realities. His work has countered the construal of mystics having unmediated experience of an ultimate reality, by insisting that 'there is no evidence that there is any "given" which can be disclosed without the imposition of the mediating conditions of the knower. All "givens" are also the product of the processes of "choosing", "shaping", and "receiving"' (p. 59). Experiences are determined by cultural conditions and religious beliefs. I would make the same claim but wish to push further than Katz, who remains within a Kantian epistemological framework and finally accepts there is an 'out there', 'ontological claims that lie beneath and are necessary correlates of language' (p. 52). Katz's view of the nature and operation of language is still playing out word/object dualisms.

relation between defiance and loss. That "excess" marks a boundary. We must return to the "finite" place, the body, which *mystics* or the mystic "infinitizes", and let Labadie pass by.'[40] Certeau rejects the way that his fellow countryman, Jean Baudrillard, welcomes. But, despite the rejection and the insistence on a return to the body and the finite – return to a doctrine of creation – he repeatedly wishes to explore '*la rupture instauratrice*'. Furthermore, in two works which cover the period of his most prolific production '*Comme une goutte d'eau dans la mer*' written in 1973 and '*Extase blanche*' written in 1983, he appeals to the transcendentalism of the sublime; he repeats the journey towards erasure. The only difference between Labadie's journey and Certeau's is the employment of daylight rather than darkness. Certeau enters that 'daylight forever' that is still being rehearsed today:

> Here is what the final bedazzlement would be: an absorption of objects and subjects in the act of seeing. No violence, only the unfolding of presence. Neither the fold nor hole. Nothing hidden and thus nothing visible. A light without limits, without difference; neuter, in a sense, and continuous. It is only possible to speak of it in relation to our cherished activities, which are utterly annihilated there. There is no more reading where signs no longer are removed from and deprived of what they indicate. There is no more interpretation if no secret sustains and summons it. There are no more words if no absence founds the waiting that they articulate. Our works are gently engulfed in this silent ecstasy. Without disaster and without noise, simply having become futile, our world . . . ends.[41]

This is, as the sublime and the kitsch are, the apotheosis of spectacle. It produces, affirms and operates within the parameters of modernity's dualisms (with their unequal valorisations): presence/absence, language/silence, mediation/immediacy, inside the created world order/ beyond in the divine order, here/there, immanence/transcendence, experience/representation of experience, object/word. The self and the subject–object relations which are ultimately engulfed are all products of Cartesianism.

RETURN TO ALLEGORY[42] AND THE MYSTICAL SENSE

Not all poststructuralists follow Certeau's trajectory. Some adamantly critique these dualisms as they stake out the metaphysical boundaries of

---

[40] *The Mystic Fable*, p. 293.

[41] See 'White Ecstasy' trs. Frederick Christian Bauerschmidt and Catriona Hanley in Graham Ward (ed.), *The Postmodern God*, (Oxford: Blackwell, 1997), p. 157.

[42] One of the important questions to raise here concerns the history of allegoresis. For this 'return' to allegory (by Paul de Man, for example) issues from a re-evaluation of allegory in Baudelaire

modernity (and postmodernity). Some poststructural thought offers ways of rethinking the nature and operation of language in a manner which attempts to rewrite the relationship between language and silence. In particular, we will look at the quite different projects of Jacques Derrida and Michel Serres with respect to their appreciation of allegory.

The work of both thinkers issues from Saussure's understanding of the nature and operation of language. As I have argued elsewhere, Saussure's thinking develops within a broadly Kantian framework.[43] His concern lies not with the relationship between word and the world it may or may not hook up to. His concern is not then with demonstrating or denigrating any correspondence view of language. His attention is drawn to a system of associations and differentials within any speech act. As such he is concerned with the signifier/signified relationship (how names signify), not with the *economy* of the signifier (the movement of the signifier with respect to any textual field). Though Saussure is attentive to both the synchronic and the diachronic aspects of language, it is the synchronic, the time-frozen moment of a speech act, which structuralism attended to. With Derrida's work the emphasis is on the *economy* of the signifier – the fact that the signification of any word is caught up in the forward pull of the signifiers that follow it. This establishes an endemic deferral of meaning within language. Signs then are not only caught up in nets of identities and differences, they are part of economies of deferral. This observation is axiomatic for Derrida's understanding of *différance*, the dissemination of meaning and the supplementary nature of the sign.

This poststructural move, then, turns its attention towards temporality, what Paul de Man, in developing his understanding of allegory, called 'the rhetorics of time'.[44] The rhetorics of time critique movements beyond language and putative engagements with either the presence or the absence of meaning inferred to lie ultimately on the other side of words. For Derrida, encounters with presence and absence necessitate illegitimate transcendental moves towards atemporality. His poststructural emphasis upon the rhetorics of time forestalls and questions the possibility of such a move. To the freeze-framing attention paid to names/labels is added an attention to verbs, to economies, to deferrals, withdrawals,

and Benjamin. Benjamin, in particular, is aware of the investment in allegory by Baroque poetics. But Baroque poetics, as I have pointed out, disseminate the paradox of the sign as sublime and/or kitsch. How then does Baroque allegory differ from the poststructural allegoresis of Derrida?

[43] Graham Ward, *Barth, Derrida and The Language of Theology* (Cambridge: Cambridge University Press, 1995), pp. 200–6.

[44] See *Blindness and Insight: Essays in the Rhetoric of Contemporary Criticism* (London: Methuen, 1983), pp. 187–228.

tracings, practices, teleologies and eschatologies. Derrida's examination of the 'middle-voice' with respect to *différance* illustrates this.

All discourse is haunted, for Derrida, by this other scene – that which frames language, that which exceeds and keeps its signification from being finalised. And the finalisation of meaning – its accomplishment as a perfected act of communication – is the fantasy that language dreams. But language is established through iteration, and iteration is the very principle which forstalls language ever being able simply to say. *Différance*, dissemination and supplementarity constitute deconstruction (and *de construction*) of meaning. All discourse, therefore, performs for Derrida the allegory of *différance*. Allegory names that continual negotiation with what is other and outside the text. In this negotiation language deconstructs its own saying in the same way that allegorical discourse is always inhabited by another sense, another meaning. Saying one thing in terms of another is frequently how allegory is defined. Saying is always deconstructive because is operates in terms of semantic slippage and deferral, in terms of not-saying. In this all acts of communication betray a similarity to negative theology – they all, in saying, perform an act of not-saying. Both allegory and negative theology, then, are self-consciously deconstructive; they are discourses in which the mimetic economy is conscious of itself. As discourses they perform the kenosis of meaning that *différance* announces. The near-neighbour of this duo is irony.

There are important differences between the way in which deconstruction operates in these three modes of speaking: allegory, negative theology and irony. In allegory and negative theology, the shifting of sense is semantically constructive – although in distinct ways. In negative theology one sense is subverted in order to facilitate a higher sense, it serves and supports the possibility of this higher sense. In negative theology this hierarchy of senses, effecting a semantic displacement, is fundamental and theologically informed. In allegory one sense folds into another sense without displacement. The boundaries of where one sense becomes another are impossible to locate because simultaneous senses occupy the same discursive space without priority. Irony is closer to the discourse of negative theology in that it subverts and establishes a hierarchy of sense. But here the subversion is semantically destructive: one sense is undermined by another. The displacement here is violent; whereas in the discourse of negative theology the displacement is 'natural' because in accord with a theological ordinance.

What is important to recognise in these distinct operations of deconstruction is that difference in allegorical discourse is not made substantive or structural; the 'other' sense (and which is the 'other sense' is precisely put into question in allegorical discourse) is never separated off or isolated. The other or different sense has no existence independent of the saying itself. We cannot pass beyond the saying. There is no beyond. The other lives within, is known only within, the familiar. Difference in allegory does not announce a metaphysical or theological apartheid – which is what a hierarchically arranged dualism announces. Difference, the other sense, is intrinsic to and makes possible the significance of any more obvious sense. The movement of sense continually shifts – one coming into focus here, another there. The abstract nouns of the seven deadly sins in *Piers Ploughman* get tied in to the more concrete predications of Langland's description of *Accidia*, as in: 'Thanne come Sleuthe al bislabered, with two slymy eizen.'[45] Both subjects and predicates are brought into the wider discursive play of the narrative, performing and producing a temporality encoded in the verbs.[46] The reader is a pilgrim in a tropological land, walking as through a dream where the seeming substantiality of this or that, of here or there, can at any moment become something, or be suggestive of something, else. 'How easy is a bush supposed a bear.' Allegory is translocational, transpositional, transfigurative, transcorporeal: allegory makes possible the statement 'This is my body.'

We are coming closer now to the rub of the matter. Negative theology is what Certeau termed 'a manner of speaking'. Irony and allegory – and *différance* – announce ways of viewing the world or, in theological terms, they are implicated in doctrines of creation. All three discourses are practices – that is, someone is acting in a certain way when speaking about God negatively, in being ironic or reading the world allegorically. That action is a statement about the way in which the world of that subject is meaningful. The action constructs, affirms and expresses the perspective of both a particular subject and the communities in which that subject is involved. So, for example, allegory and irony, like deconstruction, 'is inseparable from a general questioning of *tekhnē*',[47] not just a questioning of technical reasoning. Irony points to dislocations, calling

---

[45] J. A. W. Bennett (ed.), *Piers Ploughman* (Oxford: Clarendon Press, 1972), Passus v, line 392.

[46] P. T. Geach in both his essay 'Nominalism' and *Reference and Generality: An Examination of Some Medieval and Modern Theories* (Ithaca: Cornell University Press, 1962) emphasises the adverse effects of the two-name theory of nominalism, pointing to how any act of naming is dependent upon the language system requiring both name and verb. Allegory's attention to time and, therefore, the verb effects a relationality between names. Allegory does not eclipse naming in favour of the verb; rather it suspends reference (that to which the name points).

[47] *Memoires for Paul de Man*, trs. Cecile Lindsay *et al.* (New York: Columbia University Press, 1989), p. 16.

into account the world as *commedia*. It unweaves the safety and seduc-
tions of synecdoche – the part as the whole – suggesting an ambiguous
world-view in which tragedy and serendipitous chance are all too possible. Allegory performs not only the suspension of proper names, but
the suspension of the material itself. It dissolves the line between name
and thing and any assumption that the world is a static state, upon the
basis of which knowledge of things through the transparency of words
is believable. In allegory the act of naming escapes, because the names
are excessive to, a metaphysical essentialism which establishes the law
of identification. It emphasises that we see 'as'. It announces that we
read continually; we have to because we see 'as'. We read the world;
a world in which phenomena are time-bound and so never the same
from one moment to the next. Creation, in allegory, is a work that is
still proceeding; and inseparable from that proceeding is the meaning of
and in the world, which is also ongoing and incomplete. The deferral
of meaning in *différance* allows us to witness transferential relations between phenomena given in time. Derrida asks, 'is there a proper story
for this thing [deconstruction]? I think it consists only of transference,
and a thinking through of transference, in all the sense that this word ac-
quires in more than one language, and first of all that of the transference
between language'.[48] Allegory, like deconstruction, is the performance
of transference. Situated within an allegorical reading – and reading is
always itself transferential and a situating of ourselves with respect to
that transferential process – we perform transference. Not that we are
transferred from here to there – which appears to be the logic of the
mystical discourse in the seventeenth century (if Certeau is right). For to
be transferred from here to there would again require the law of identification – that I already possess certain knowledge of who I am, where
I am and where there 'is'. In allegory I am given over to the process of
transference where the other continually arrives and translates the sense.
And in translating the sense I am myself translated, losing the stabilities
of being able to identify, losing the meaningfulness of ascent or descent,
inside or outside.

Allegory, like *différance*, installs the quasi-transcendent.[49] This quasi-
transcendent refuses the dualism of immanence and transcendence,

[48] Ibid., pp. 14–5.
[49] It is exactly at this point that I would differ slightly in my understanding of Derrida's work (and
therefore his importance for theological thinking) from John Milbank and Catherine Pickstock.
Both of them view Derrida as nihilistic because both read him as constructing (in the wake of
Kant) a transcendental argument in which that which makes the drift of signs possible is a choatic
flux in which difference and differentiating rule. Thus, deconstruction viewed as a transcendental

forestalling the dualisms of absence and presence, mediation and immediacy, phenomenal and noumenal, body and spirit. Luce Irigaray, herself attempting to sublate these dualisms, speaks oxymoronically of a 'sensible transcendent', practising the linguistic hysteria of the mystics (*mysteria*, she will call it).[50] But elsewhere she will employ the metaphor of incarnation to make the same point. It is, ultimately, an enquiry into the nature of incarnationalism that our rethinking of the relationship between language and silence will conduct us, as we will see. Derrida will speak of a certain kenosis – without apparently realising that kenosis can only be understood theologically in terms of Christ. '"God" "is" the name of this bottomless collapse, of this endless desertification of language. But the trace of this negative operation is inscribed *in* and *on* and *as* the *event* (what *comes*, what there is and which is always singular, what finds in this kenosis the most decisive condition of its coming or its upsurging).'[51]

Derrida here is examining the apophatic writings of Angelus Silesius. His language, miming Silesius', is freighted with negativity: 'bottomless collapse', 'endless desertification'. In fact, for those wanting to take up Derrida's work as a therapeutic tool for examining theological discourse, Derrida's explicit writings on negative theology may not be the most productive place for investigation. For he takes up and mimes the negativity in a way which needs to be counter-balanced by his accounts of deconstruction as the 'promise' and the 'yes, yes'. Derrida's discourse on and within negative theology can too easily be dismissed as nihilistic if attention is only paid to the constantive statements that can be extracted from this work. Respect for the very brio of the discourse – its abrasiveness, its elusiveness, the rhetorics of its polyphonic performance – is necessary.

schema turns Derrida into a dualist and a gnostic. There have been attempts, by theologians, to make deconstruction a new linguistic turn in a Kantian idealism – witness Mark C. Taylor and John Caputo. And in a recent discussion with Derrida, Derrida himself claims with respect to Levinas that he is trying to out transcendentalise Levinas. Nevertheless I still wish to argue for a distinction between a trancendentalism and a quasi-transcendentalism. *Différance* is not *difference*, not the hypostasis of *différence*. Early in his work Derrida spoke of *archi-différance*, but emphasised that it was not an origin as such. He quickly dropped the term in favour of increasing attention to time, economy and how the *aporia* that *différance* installs is never grasped (much less experienced as such). It is time which installs deferral and with deferral *différance* – but *différance*, like the 'other' in allegory, is always another aspect of the same, an aspect issuing from the excess of what is said. Hence Derrida's wrestling with the 'unheard of analogy' in Levinas' work bears witness to an exploration which refuses univocity, equivocity and the stasis of naming, giving due weight to time, to the verb. *Différance*, I am suggesting, names an ongoing *analogia temporalis* – or allegory. I think this saves Derrida from being a transcendental nihilist *à la* Nietzsche and Heidegger.
[50] *Speculum of the Other Woman*, tr. Gillian C. Gill (Ithaca: Cornell University Press, 1985), pp. 243–364.
[51] *On the Name*, ed. Thomas Dutoit, trs. David Wood, John P. Leavey, Jr, and Ian McLeod (Stanford: Stanford University Press, 1995), pp. 55–6.

For example, there is a staging of at least two voices in his essay 'Sauf le nom' (since the voices are not named, only several pronominal interjections of 'I' located, the voices cannot be numbered). One voice corrects, sometimes questions, sometimes develops the thought of the voice preceding it. So that where statements suggest a passing 'over to the other edge'[52] into a total alterity or an absolute outside, other statements insist that the 'event remains at once *in* and *on* language, then, within and at the surface'.[53] That is, there is no pure outside. The outside is already operating within. And in the movement to absolute surrender there is a recognition that 'everything would remain intact . . . after the passage of a *via negativa*'.[54] So, while rehearsing Silesius' 'bottomless collapse', what Derrida points to in this essay is the way the 'collapse' never comes. The edge of the absolutely external is never crossed. So we never fully make that passage into the desert. We never have access to the abyss as such. Language can never complete the kenotic process. The desertification is a form of playing within God, not a movement over the edge into that which is wholly other. 'Negative theology then can only present itself as one of the most playful forms of the creature's participation in this divine play.'[55] The other in *différance* is quasi-transcendental and that is why it is inscribed 'in and on and as' the event of writing, finding in the surrender of fixed and stable reference 'the most decisive condition for its coming and its upsurging'.

What Derrida draws us towards here is a thinking about language in terms of creation and participation. He does not use the metaphor of incarnation, but the economy of discourse transgresses construals of inside and outside, immanent and transcendent, in a way analogous to the Christian understanding of the incarnate Word and the God who is not simply *for us*, but also *with us* and working *through us*. Conceived in this way, kenosis becomes the allegory of deconstruction while deconstruction becomes the allegory of all signifying economies. We are picking up here the theological provenance of allegory, a provenance older that the theological genealogy traced behind Steiner's language and silence polarity. We can read again, and in a different way, the relationship between language and silence.

Before examining the importance of this theological genealogy, with the assistance of the work of Michel Serres, let me just draw out two sets of consequences of this thinking: first with respect to how it counters the construal of language and silence as represented in Steiner's work;

---

[52] Ibid., p. 70.   [53] Ibid., p. 58.   [54] Ibid., p. 74.   [55] Ibid., p. 75.

secondly with respect to the theological implications of rejecting Steiner's model of the relationship between language and silence.

For Steiner, as we saw, it is axiomatic that language is inadequate. But Derrida's work calls this into question. For from whence can one announce that the words employed are inadequate? For who can calibrate the degrees of adequacy and inadequacy?[56] Inadequate to what? The logic of linguistic adequation is concomitant with a correspondence theory of language – where the words are *equal* to that to which they refer. It is a requirement of such thinking that a subject position of the I, from which the identities and essences of both word and things can be assessed, is self-transparent. Adequation is an evaluative term implying judgement and requiring knowledge of the true state of things. It has to come from a position outside the linguistic matrix. It demands a view from no where. As Aquinas realised, only God understands the world literally. But, unlike Steiner's concept of language, Derrida's account of *différance* construes language not as simply denotative – accounting for what is there – but as connotative also, and participating in a dynamic unfolding.

Secondly, for Steiner, it is axiomatic that silence lies on the other side of language. Derrida will also call this into question. As there is no pure outside, and therefore no experience of the outside as such, there is no transcending of language into the silences and daylight beyond words. Derrida emphasises that there is aporia; there is ambiguity or metaphoricity which prevents language from strictly being denotational, and so prevents language from being the transparent medium for identities and identification. This aporia remains irreducible. But he stresses that it is 'Aporia, rather than antimony . . . insofar as it is neither an "apparent or illusory" antimony, nor a dialectisable contradiction in the Hegelian or Marxist sense, nor even a "transcendental illusion in a dialectic of the Kantian type", but instead an interminable experience.'[57] He goes on to say that there is no experience of aporia as such: '*the aporia can never simply be endured as such.* The ultimate aporia is the impossibility of the

---

[56] It is important to note that this does not only apply to theological language. Because of the *diastema* between creation and the uncreated God, theological discourse exemplifies linguistic inadequacy. But, for Derrida, no proper name is identical to that which it names; not just the name 'God'. To use Aquinas' term – which he employed to argue that God was not indeed a proper name or could be properly named – all naming is 'appellative': an appeal for a knowledge that has not yet arrived. Thomas' teaching on analogy concerns not adequacy but appropriateness – the grammar for that which is appropriate arising for the articles of the Faith. Even so, human creatures cannot ever know the degrees of appropriateness, only that, on the basis of what God has revealed about God's self – set in the articles of the faith – certain statements and descriptions (like 'God is three people') are ungrammatical.

[57] *Aporias*, tr. Thomas Dutoit (Stanford: Stanford University Press, 1993), p. 16.

aporia *as such*. The reservoir of this statement seems to me incalculable.'[58]
It is in this sense that one has to understand Derrida's infamous statement '*il n'y a pas de hors texte*'. We have to rethink, then, the relationship
between language and silence in a way that recognises silence as integral
to communication; silence *as* a form of communication.

For Derrida, as there is always a rhetoric of aporia, there will also be a
rhetoric of silence. Silence becomes analogous to the blank margins of a
page, the space beneath the vaulting of a Cathedral, or a musical interval.
The margin frames and focuses the text. The empty spaces here establish
a certain tension between the arrangement of the letters, the words and
the syntax into a communication and the empty margins which create a
space for the cessation of intellection. It is a space for/of breathing. The
margins, therefore, articulate, possibly at a somatic level, a certain rest,
a certain Sabbath, a space for the activities of prayer and meditation. In
silence a rest is written into the fabric of creation. There is articulation
through this rhythm and in this rhythm. And every poet knows how
to take advantage of the rhythm of the margins and make it part of
the poem through enjambment, line length, and the spatial dynamics
of the typesetting. The margins are not silent as such. The silence is
architectured and integral to the speaking or the phrasing. Think of the
interval between the first and second opening phrase of Beethoven's Fifth
symphony. The hiatus is in continuity with, and therefore part of, the
larger musical composition. This is not a silence, an emptiness beyond
communication. As every musician knows a highly important aspect of
musicianship is calibrated according to the phrasing. Even the sublime
moment in Keats's sonnet 'On First Looking into Chapman's Homer'
is architectured. On this account of language and silence there are no
gaps or ruptures or top-down revelations as such. With respect to the
discourse of negative theology, there are not then 'fissures opened by our
language' that are not simultaneously bound and constructed by that
language. To accept the independent existence of the fissures as such is
to become blind to one's own use of metaphor. There is aporia and there
is the constant negotiation of aporia through supplementation. There is
quasi-transcendence.

What are the implications for this for a theological account of the relationship between language and silence? Derrida is no theologian, and
when he employs theological vocabulary (like kenosis, like the Word) he
does not think them through with any theological sophistication. We will

---

[58] Ibid., p. 78.

return to this. Hence the Word is related to logocentrism (the full, realised presence of meaning) and the transcendental signifier which sta-
bilises and gives identity to all things. Derrida shows little understanding
of the relationship of the Word to the Triune Godhead and creation. He
show little understanding of 'presence' as it is understood theologically.
He reads presence as modernity read presence – as immediate, direct
truth, as self-authenticating meaning, as the full realisation in this moment of time (the now) of identity. Derrida does not understand presence
as grace. He does not understand the mediatorial operation of the Word
and the Spirit within creation, a creation which is not finished, and a
Word which is not yet complete. The presence of God in grace is not the
violence of the moment – but the unfolding of the divine maintenance
and sustenance of the world. Taking the incarnation seriously is not being
translated out of the world into immediate contact with God; it is recognising the movement of God in what has been gifted for us in the world.
Incarnation cannot admit the inadequacy of mediation and representation; for it is itself implicated as the divine sanctioning of mediation and
representation. To accept the antimony of language and silence theologically would implicate us in gnosticism. The contemporary desire for
the 'daylight forever', like Certeau's desire for 'white ecstacy', is gnostic.

   Christian theological anthropology begins with human beings *made
in the image of* and, as such, the creators and purveyors of image-making.
Christ is, the incarnation of the Word of God is, a quasi-transcendental
as such. Derrida writes about what 'takes place, what comes to pass
with the aporia'[59] of *différance*: 'the absolute *arrivant* does not yet have
a name or an identity. It is not an invader or an occupier, nor is it a
coloniser, even if it can also become one . . . Since the *arrivant* does not
have an identity yet, its place of arrival is also de-identified: one does
not yet know or one no longer knows which is the country, the place, the
nation, the family, the language, and the home in general that welcomes
the absolute *arrivant* . . . It even exceeds the order of any *determinable*
promise . . . because . . . the absolute *arrivant* makes possible everything
to which I have just said it cannot be reduced, starting with the humanity
of man.'[60] It is not simply that Christ is *différance* or Christ names *différance*
or Christ and the operation of the Spirit inform the economy of *différance*.
But if we wish to read the relationship between language and silence
theologically after Derrida then we have to begin by acknowledging
that Christ is neither a proper name that we know how to employ
(and know what we mean by employing it) nor an identity we can

---

[59] Ibid., p. 32.   [60] Ibid., pp. 34 5.

delineate and turn into a template. Aquinas again: 'God is not known to us in His nature, but is made known to us from His operations or effects ... This name God is an appellative name, and not a proper name'.[61]

Without denigrating the function of naming, and yet avoiding the errors of nominalism, *différance* names an operation, a quasi-transcendental allegory that continually draws Derrida back to a theological discourse. But it is a discourse always framed by the metaphysics of presence/absence; by an agenda established by the modernity that Derrida wishes to deconstruct. Theologically discourse is never examined in terms of its own logic. This is where we need to return to the theological genealogy of Derrida's construal of allegory and recognise why only a theological account of allegory can move us beyond the problematics (and the gnosticisms) of modernity. We can do this with respect to the contemporary angelology of Michel Serres.

Serres, like Irigaray, recognises the contemporary retrieval of the Mediaeval. 'Is it not true that in this age of sophisticated technical apparatus we still frequently turn to the Middle Ages in search of our images and secrets?' Irigaray asks.[62] Serres informs Bruno Latour that 'we are living today (and even more so in the United States than in Europe) closer to the middle ages than to the salons of the Age of Enlightenment'.[63] Serres' book, *Angels: A Modern Myth*, most fully details the connections between the late twentieth century's semiotic turn, advanced communications and the incarnationalism of the middle ages. This constellation of connections is framed by a reflection on angels as not only message-bearers but the incarnation of the tidings that they bear. The evil angels are the angels who draw attention to themselves above and beyond the giving of the message; the good angels are given over to/as the communication.

Today the City is a chattering, language-filled, puritan, message-bearing, advertisement-laden thing ... the power, the capacity, the speed and the shortcomings of angels haunt this City.

Throughout the whole world, all the networks are crying out about the hunger, are screaming a thirst for incarnation, in a situation where the body is horribly lacking. But at last, the Good News, the Messiah, the message, is flesh, immanent, which saves itself, in and out of itself.[64]

---

61 *Summa Theologiae* 1a q13 a8 9.
62 *Sexes and Genealogies*, tr. Gillian C. Gill (New York: Columbia University Press, 1993), p. 58.
63 *Conversations on Science, Culture and Time*, tr. Roxanne Lapidus (Michigan: University of Michigan Press, 1995), p. 25.
64 *Angels: A Modern Myth*, tr. Francis Cowper (Paris: Flammarion, 1993), p. 285.

Creation is conceived by Serres as message-bearing, as doxological, so
that psalms rise up from the shores and the rocks.[65] Everything exists in complex intercommunication, a profound relationality. What all
these messages suggest is a reign of angels announcing a new birth,
'the birth of the Messiah, who makes flesh divine and incarnates love'.[66]
We live in, and inseparable from, this continual interchange, this universal mediation which God opens up and establishes. Commenting upon
the Annunciation, Serres writes: 'It is God, covering the scene with his
bright shadow. Beneath the appearance and the image of an interaction
between two people, it all takes place as if God was face to face with
God: in potency on the angel's side; in act and end of meaning in the
woman's womb. Our physical eyes of flesh see Mary and Gabriel, but
faith contemplates, in spirit, the apparition facing the incarnation.'[67]
This double seeing – by faith and by our 'physical eyes' – is fundamental
to the re-enchanted world Serres is portraying. This is the focus of his
allegorical vision in which the world is 'fluid, fluent, even fluctuating,
[and] is becoming increasingly volatile'.[68] Interpretation is intrinsic to
living in such a world; it is fostered and fosters the ongoing transformation through communication. (Hermes is the forerunner of the angels).[69]
In such a world it is not only creation which speaks (for example, the con-
veying of messages by waves) but mechanical and technological objects
are almost endowed with the same qualities as human beings, for they
change things, they transform relationships: 'To consider them as objects
derives from the basic contempt that we still have for human labour.'[70]
With Serres labour becomes labouring, as in the creative bringing to
birth of a incarnate love in and through the interdependence and intercommunication of all things.

   Although unlike Derrida in emphatically announcing a Messianic
telos to world history (lending a soteriology and eschatology to a project
concerning our contemporary network society), Serres, like Derrida, defines a quasi-transcendence. Incarnation is the coming to be, the fleshing,
of this quasi-transcendence. His angelology invokes a system of immanent meaning: 'So are angels still pantheist? Certainly they are, because
by the fact that they pass everywhere and occupy all space, they enable
divinity to be seen at all points.'[71] And in a world where all physical forces
are also spiritual, where all things express intelligence,[72] a neopaganism
is all too possible. And yet Serres confuses the lines between immanence

---

[65] Ibid., p. 267.   [66] Ibid., p. 185.   [67] Ibid., p. 111.   [68] Ibid., p. 44.
[69] Ibid., p. 45.   [70] Ibid., p. 48.   [71] Ibid., pp. 91–2.   [72] Ibid., pp. 295–6.

and transcendence, for all is informed by, because all things mediate, a Word which forever exceeds the system of intercommunication itself. 'When we go sunbathing . . . who can say whether we are immersing our bodies in the sun itself, of which the light is part, or whether our bodies are being exposed to intermediary rays issuing from the mass of the sun and coming across through space to reach us? The infinite distancing of a transcendent God necessitates the existence of angels or radiating transmitters; whereas immanence can do without them.'[73] So the final hymn of the volume is to the All High. For, as Serres explains, glory must finally be accorded to God alone if there is to be peace on earth. For such a glory is forever out of our reach and so uncommodifiable.[74]

Now evidently, for the Christian theologian, despite Serres' attention to the incarnate Word, the transcendent God, and the divine *energia* which opens up this space of mediation and interpretation, his work cries out for a doctrine of the Trinity. But Serres' thinking points to, and begins to sketch, the theological framework that Derrida eludes to and plays with, but cannot elaborate. In doing so Serres retrieves the Mediaeval world picture that Certeau describes as prevalent before the metaphysics and linguistics of nominalism began to dominate; when all things drew their significance from the space within the incarnate Word. For Certeau, explicitly referring to Augustine, this world picture is characterised by an appreciation of *allegoria facti*, in which '*signa naturalia* escaped human codifications of meaning. It was therefore necessary to learn how to "interpret" them on the basis of an intelligence that ascended to the divine will, then descended towards its inscriptions in the opacity of "natural" things. They were the province of a "spiritual" or divine hermeneutics.'[75] *Allegoria facti* was founded upon three conditions, what Certeau names *allegoria theologicae* (where all things are understood from God's point of view, the God who spoke all things into being), *allegoria historiae* (where all *in factis* symbolism is inscribed within chronology) and *allegoria in factis* (where analogies exist between things themselves, like water and the Spirit). As Certeau notes: 'These three conditions for the *allegoria facti* (which depended on the status of theology, a certain conception of time, and a specific metaphysics) became less and less conceivable in the fourteenth and fifteenth centuries.'[76]

Without this theological frame for allegory – without retrieving, for Derrida's *différance*, the theological genealogy of the account of language it circumscribes – then the semiosis of meaning installed by allegory, while

---

[73] Ibid., p. 107.   [74] Ibid., p. 288.   [75] *The Mystic Fable*, p. 92.   [76] Ibid., p. 93.

deconstructing the binarisms of language and silence (the metaphysics of dualism and the theologies of gnosticism), will forever rehearse (and therefore require) them. And then Derrida is doomed, like Sisyphus, to repeat the same deconstructive gestures, endlessly and unproductively – which questions whether there is an 'economy' of *différance* at all.[77] With this theological frame, we can reaffirm an incarnational world view. And the quasi-transcendence, that delights in mediation and recognises silence as integral to the communication of the Word, no longer waits for the daylight forever (as sublime plenitude or kitsch void), but allows creation's daylight and darkness to constitute a rhythm in the redemption being wrought in Christ.

[77] This raises the question of whether the poststructural retrieval of allegory is the continuation and apotheosis of modernity's own investment in allegory? In *Origin of German Tragic Drama* (tr. John Osborne, London: New Left Books, 1977) Benjamin characterised Baroque allegory as fixated on mourning, melancholy and death: 'the allegorisation of the physis can only by carried through in all its vigour in respect of the corpse' (p. 218). Derridean allegory continues this characterisation. He concludes his essay 'Mnemosyne' with an account of allegorical metonymy (which could act as a synonym for *différance*) as 'a logic or an a-logic of which we can no longer say that it belongs to mourning in the current sense of the term, but which regulates (sometimes like mourning in the strict sense, but always like mourning in the sense of general possibility) all our relations with the other *as other* . . . Our "own" mortality is not dissociated from, but rather conditions this rhetoric of faithful memory . . . ' (*Mémoires for Paul de Man*, p. 39).

9

Apophasis and the Shoah: where was Jesus Christ at Auschwitz?

David F. Ford

George Steiner in his recent autobiography recalls his friendship with Donald MacKinnon and says:

> There could, for Donald, be no justifiable future for Christianity so long as Christian theology and practice had not faced up to, had not internalized lucidly, its seminal role in the millennial torments of Judaism and in the Holocaust. Primarily, this signified coming to terms with the horror of Golgotha, a horror unredeemed – this was Donald's compulsive instinct – by the putative wonder of resurrection or by any promise of celestial reparation.[1]

Steiner also writes of MacKinnon 'trying to "think" Auschwitz and Golgotha as implicated in some interrelated finality'.[2]

Golgotha and Auschwitz are also connected by Rabbi Dr Nicholas de Lange in his 1997 Cardinal Bea Memorial Lecture, in which he presses the question which I have included in my title, 'Where was Jesus Christ at Auschwitz?',[3] and de Lange is himself drawing on what his own teacher, Ignaz Maybaum, said on this theme.[4]

Both Jesus Christ and the Holocaust (or Shoah, as I will refer to it) invite thought about 'silence and the word', and I will explore the theme with special reference to one text by Anne Michaels related to the Shoah, and another on Christology by Dietrich Bonhoeffer.

SILENCE AND THE WORD IN *FUGITIVE PIECES*

Anne Michaels is a poet–novelist who steeped herself in the history and eyewitness testimony of the Shoah during the writing of her novel,

---

[1] George Steiner, *Errata. An Examined Life* (New Haven and London: Yale University Press, 1997), p. 152.
[2] Ibid.
[3] Nicholas de Lange, 'Jesus and Auschwitz', in *New Blackfriars*, vol. 78, no. 917/918 pp. 308–16.
[4] See Ignaz Maybaum, *The Face of God After Auschwitz* (Amsterdam: Polek and Van Gennep, 1965).

Fugitive Pieces.[5] What emerges is a somewhat fragmented yet often profound work on the Shoah. It has something of the impact of Solzhenitsyn's novels about the Gulag Archipelago. Anne Michaels does not combine her fictional skill with Solzhenitsyn's personal testimony, and her main authorial standpoint is that of the generation after the survivors; but this helps her into a more penetrating and self-aware appreciation of the levels and complexities of the language and silence of testimony, of the significance of time for memory, and of the subtle interrelations of evil, beauty, goodness and truth. In both of them the complementarity of history and fiction is instructive: neither the Gulag nor the Shoah can be done adequate justice to in 'straight' history.[6] There is also a fascinating question about the optimum time for matured testimony to 'epoch-making events'. There is a period at some distance from the events – when the first shock, surprise and even speechlessness has been come through, and when there has been time for meaning to have been distilled into a combination of testimony with wisdom – yet before the last eyewitnesses have died: that is the period, soon to end, in which we live now. It may therefore be the best time for producing classic testimonies to the Shoah in various genres and media.

Fugitive Pieces is largely about Jakob Beer, who when he was seven was in hiding behind the wall of the room where his parents were murdered during a Nazi action, and his older sister Bella disappeared. He was rescued by Athos, a Greek geologist and archaeologist, who hides him in his own home on a Greek island during the war and later emigrates with Jakob to Canada. Jakob becomes a poet who writes about the Shoah, and he also edits Athos' posthumous work, *Bearing False Witness*, about the Nazi falsification of archaeological evidence. There is a complex interweaving of testimonies by and to Jakob and to the Shoah, covering three generations, and this allows for fascinating interrelationships of time, memory, language and truth to be explored. And again and again there is the theme of silence.

The book is like a phenomenology of silence in various forms.[7] It describes the silence of the room after the traumatic event of the action, of a parent's apartment after his death; more metaphorical silences after a marriage fails ('And then the world fell silent' – p. 139) and after the

---

[5] Anne Michaels, *Fugitive Pieces* (London: Bloomsbury, 1998). She underlines this by acknowledging her principal sources at the end of the book.

[6] Cf. Paul Ricoeur, *Time and Narrative*, volume 3 (Chicago: University of Chicago Press, 1988), chapter 8, 'The Interweaving of Fiction and History', especially on 'epoch-making events'.

[7] I am grateful to Rachel Muers for her research in progress on silence from which I have learnt much, not least her survey of the phenomenological literature.

Shoah itself; and the 'ghastly silence' (p. 285) when the sound of the waves stops in Hawaii before an earthquake. There are silences of absence, of overwhelming grief, of a past that has been erased, of lack of news, of response to emptiness and to plenitude, of sleep, of lack of forgiveness because the one who could forgive has gone, and of long intervals between notes as a child tries to play a piano piece without making mistakes.

In Ben's family, where the parents survived the camps but the father could not talk of it,

[t]he code of silence became more complex as I grew older. There were more and more things to keep from my father. The secrets between my mother and me were a conspiracy. What was our greatest insurrection? My mother was determined to impress upon me the absolute, inviolate necessity of pleasure . . . Loss is an edge; it swelled everything for my mother, and drained everything from my father. Because of this, I thought my mother was stronger. But now I see it was a clue: what my father had experienced was that much less bearable. (p. 223)

The father has a special relationship with his daughter-in-law, who respects his silence, broaching the rich theme of reserve:

What I had mistaken for confidentiality from my father was simply the relief of a man who realizes he won't have to give up his silence. It's the ease Naomi's grace encourages in everyone. She will honour privacy to the end. (p. 249)

Ben only discovers after his parents' death that he had had a brother and sister who died in the Shoah:

I'll never know whether the two names on back of my father's photograph, if they had ever been spoken, would have filled the silence of my parents' apartment. (p. 280)

Perhaps at the heart of the novel's sensitivity to 'silence and the word' is its treatment of testimony to the Shoah. The awesome task of giving testimony is traced from many angles:

I began to understand how here, alone, in the red and yellow of poppies and broom, you had felt safe enough to begin *Groundwork* [Beer's first volume of poetry on the Shoah]. How you descended into horror slowly, as divers descend, with will and method. How, as you dropped deeper, the silence pounded. (p. 266)

Truth grows gradually in us, like a musician who plays a piece again and again until suddenly he hears it for the first time. (p. 251)

Grief requires time. If a chip of stone radiates its self [the previous page was about radiocarbons and rock magnetism], its breath, so long, how stubborn might be the soul. If sound waves carry on to infinity, where are their screams now? I imagine them somewhere in the galaxy, moving forever towards the psalms. (p. 54)

I listened to these dark shapes as if they were black spaces in music, a musician learning the silences of a piece. I felt this was my truth. That my life could not be stored in any language but only in silence; the moment I looked into the room [where his parents lay murdered] and took in only what was visible, not vanished. The moment I failed to see Bella had disappeared. But I did not know how to seek by way of silence. So I lived a breath apart, a touch-typist who holds his hands above the keys slightly in the wrong place, the words coming out meaningless, garbled. Bella and I only inches apart, the wall between us. I thought of writing poems this way, in code, every letter askew, so that loss would wreck the language, become the language.

If one could isolate that space, that damaged chromosome in words, in an image, then perhaps one could restore order by naming. Otherwise history is only a tangle of wires ...

English was a sonar, a microscope, through which I listened and observed, waiting to capture elusive meanings buried in facts. I wanted a line in a poem to be the hollow ney of the dervish orchestra whose plaintive wail is a call to God. But all I achieved was awkward shrieking. Not even the pure shriek of a reed in the rain. (pp. 112–13)

The content of the testimony has an utter realism which again and again rings true as it evokes well-known elements of the Shoah: sheer terror; children killed wantonly, playfully; starvation; humiliation; the brutality of an action beginning with beating on doors; torture; forced marches; prisoners exhuming thousands of rotting corpses; 'those who breathed deep and suffocated' (p. 139); the scholars of Lublin sobbing as they 'watched their holy and beloved books thrown out of the second-storey window of the Talmudic Academy and burned' as a military band played and soldiers sang (p. 138); and the devastation of so much ordinary life:

That they were torn from mistakes they had no chance to fix; everything unfinished. All the sins of love without detail, detail without love. The regret of having spoken, of having run out of time to speak. Of hoarding oneself. Of turning one's back too often in favour of sleep.

I tried to imagine their physical needs, the indignity of human needs grown so extreme they equal your longing for wife, child, sister, parent, friend. But truthfully I couldn't even begin to imagine the trauma of their hearts, of being taken in the middle of their lives. Those with young children. Or those newly in love, wrenched from that state of grace. Or those who had lived invisibly, who were never known. (p. 147)

For all the vividness, it is a realism which conveys not just the inexpressibility of the Shoah but its pressure to find new forms of inexpressibility, more adequate forms of silence. Beer's life is dedicated to witnessing to the Shoah in poetry, but we are only given (p. 268) a two-line fragment of his poetry – and that is not directly about the Shoah. So the novel surrounds with words the crucial testimony which is never made explicit – and which, of course, only exists in a fictional oeuvre. It evokes chasms of silence of many sorts in survivors, families, victims, perpetrators, nations, genres. It also describes a life dedicated to a discipline of words inextricable from a discipline of silence. There is a simultaneity of word and silence embodied in Jakob Beer's life and work, testified to by himself and others, and all related to (though not by any means reducible to) the Shoah.

RESONANCES WITH ANNE MICHAELS: SILENCE AND THE WORD IN BONHOEFFER'S *CHRISTOLOGY*

At this point the startling opening of Bonhoeffer's *Christology* is apposite:

Teaching about Christ begins in silence. 'Be silent, for that is the absolute' (Kierkegaard). This has nothing to do with mystical silence which, in its absence of words, is, nevertheless, the soul secretly chattering away to itself. The church's silence is silence before the Word. In proclaiming the Word, the church must fall silent before the inexpressible: Let what cannot be spoken be worshipped in silence (Cyril of Alexandria). The spoken Word is the inexpressible: that which cannot be spoken is the Word. It must be spoken, it is the great battle cry of the church (Luther). The church utters it in the world, yet it still remains the inexpressible. To speak of Christ means to keep silent; to be silent about Christ means to speak. The proclamation of Christ is the church speaking from a proper silence.

We are concerned here with the meaning of this proclamation. Its content is revealed only in the proclamation itself. To speak of Christ, then, will be to speak within the context of the silence of the church. We must study christology in the humble silence of the worshipping community. Prayer is to be silent and to cry out at the same time, before God in the presence of his Word. We have come together as a community to study Christ, God's Word. We have not met in church, but in the lecture room. We have academic work to do.[8]

The simultaneity of silence and crying out, understood in the context of prayer 'before God in the presence of his Word' leads into Bonhoeffer's basic Christological principle: the priority of the 'Who?'

[8] Dietrich Bonhoeffer, *Christology* (London and New York: Collins, 1971), p. 27.

question. Thought about Christ is continually in danger of being captured by 'How?' questions, trying to understand how Jesus Christ fits into our frameworks, disciplines and classifications, how he can be understood in causal terms or in coherence with other ideas, how incarnation might be possible, how the history of Jesus might be proved, and so on. At the heart of Christology is the perception that the appropriate framing question is the one addressed to Jesus Christ in prayer: 'Who are you?'[9] The answer (in brief – Bonhoeffer spends most of the lectures expanding on it) is: the historical (*geschichtliche*), crucified and risen Jesus Christ who is God and human for us. There is an asymmetrical simultaneity of life, death and resurrection in this person who is hiddenly present, mediated through word, sacrament and community.

Intrinsic to this interrogative encounter is silence:

> 'Who are you?' asks Pilate. Jesus is silent. Man cannot wait for the dangerous answer. The Logos cannot endure the Anti-Logos. It knows that one of them must die. So it kills the person of whom it is asked.[10]

The silence of the Word who is killed is the key to Christian silence, and the risen Christ is always simultaneously the crucified one. It is the silence of this particular person, who both speaks and is silent as incarnate, crucified and risen. The simultaneity of silence and word is here defined through the simultaneity of the life, death and resurrection of Jesus Christ.

And there is a further *simul*: the question we address to Christ, 'Who are you?' is reversed as we are addressed by him: 'Who are *you*?' – 'The Christological question "Who?" is finally formulated only where this reversed question is also heard.'[11]

The resonances between the simultaneities of Michaels and Bonhoeffer should be clear. Bonhoeffer, as is appropriate for his lecture genre, conceptualises the key issue of the priority of the 'Who?' question, while Michaels' novel conveys it through narrative. By the end of *Fugitive Pieces* she has portrayed silence as constitutive in the identities of her key characters. The 'How' questions have not been ignored – how to 'seek by way of silence', how to cope with the silence of absence and death, how to describe and interpret the forms and codes of silence, how language relates to silence, how silence is part of the 'descent into horror'. Indeed, Michaels gives these a significance which might invite into opening up Bonhoeffer's theology to such questions more than he does. Especially on questions to do with language he has little to say. But

---

[9] Ibid., pp. 28ff.   [10] Ibid., pp. 33–4.   [11] Ibid., p. 34.

Michaels does implicitly follow Bonhoeffer's priority of the 'Who?' while doing so polyphonically through a range of characters.[12]

But does Michaels have anything resembling the *simul* of Bonhoeffer's incarnation, crucifixion and resurrection? I have already described her realism about the horror of the Shoah, analogous to that of the crucifixion. The novel is also pervaded by what might be read as an incarnational realism, savouring ordinariness, physicality, the life of the senses, the natural world, pleasure, human relationships, without any hint of dualism or dichotomy as regards what is 'spiritual'.

But there is also a clear indication that the horror of the Shoah does not have the last word. This third dimension of her realism is signalled by the occurrence, without any loss of the other two dimensions, and in close (often inextricable) relationship with them, of words such as truth, goodness, beauty, dignity, gratitude, grace, revelation, faith, trust, hope, singing, poetry and, above all, love.

In the Golleschau quarry, stone-carriers were forced to haul huge blocks of limestone endlessly, from one mound to another and back again. During the torture, they carried their lives in their hands. The insane task was not futile only in the sense that faith is not futile.

A camp inmate looked up at the stars and suddenly remembered that they'd once seemed beautiful to him. This memory of beauty was accompanied by a bizarre stab of gratitude. When I first read this I couldn't imagine it. But later I felt I understood. Sometimes the body experiences a revelation because it has abandoned every other possibility. (p. 53)

Irony as scissors, a divining rod, always pointing in two directions. If the evil act can't be erased, then neither can the good. It's as accurate a measure as any of a society: what is the smallest act of kindness that is considered heroic? In those days, to be moral required no more than the slightest flicker of movement – a micrometre – of eyes looking away or blinking, while a running man crossed a field. And those who gave water or bread! They entered a realm higher than the angels' simply by remaining in the human mire. (p. 162)

Yet it is also clear that the simultaneity of these realisms is not symmetry. They are not in balance. There is far more than survival in the aftermath of the Shoah; nor is it a matter of reaffirming natural and social life as if there had been no cataclysm.

Since his death, I've come to respect my father's caches of food around the house as evidence of his ingenuity, his self-perception. *It's not a person's depth you must discover, but their ascent. Find their path from depth to ascent.* (pp. 249–50)

---

[12] For polyphony as a hermeneutical key to Bonhoeffer's theology see David F. Ford, *Self and Salvation: Being Transformed* (Cambridge: Cambridge University Press, 1999), chapter 10.

To remain with the dead is to abandon them.
All the years I felt Bella entreating me, filled with her loneliness, I was mistaken. I have misunderstood her signals. Like other ghosts, she whispers; not for me to join her, but so that, when I'm close enough, she can push me back into the world. (p. 170)

The hope is not only personal; there are hints of it even on the meta-narrative level of history:

Athos's backward glance gave me a backward hope. Redemption through cataclysm; what had once been transformed might be transformed again. (p. 101)

But the primary level of this realism of hope and redemption is the face to face. Perhaps the climactic moment in the novel is Jakob Beer's discovery of the joy of love with his second wife Michaela. The key image for it is taken from a story of a Polish painter born ten years before the war who said at the party where Jakob met Michaela: 'All my life . . . I've asked myself one question: How can you hate all you have come from and not hate yourself?' (p. 184) He had bought himself tubes of bright yellow paint but could not bring himself to use them.

The first morning I woke to Michaela – my head on the small of her back, her heels like two islands under the blanket – I knew that this was my first experience of the colour yellow. (p. 184)

Your poems from those few years with Michaela, poems of a man who feels, for the first time, a future. Your words and your life no longer separate, after *decades of hiding in your skin* . . .

> *Is there a woman who will slowly undress*
> *my spirit, bring my body to belief*
> (pp. 267–8)

There are obviously immense differences between the testimony of Bonhoeffer to Jesus Christ and that of Anne Michaels to the Shoah and the fictional Jakob Beer, but their structures of simultaneous, asymmetrical, multiple realisms, to which silence and speech are intrinsic, and which are embodied in particular persons, are sufficiently analogous to be mutually illuminating and interrogating.

Perhaps the most penetrating question suggested by Michaels about Bonhoeffer's concept of silence is whether he allows silence a full simultaneity with speech beyond the crucifixion. For Michaels, the horror of the Shoah does not have the last word, but nor does it have the last silence:

there is a further rich phenomenology of silence beyond it – analogies of 'the colour yellow' at the heart of the silences of love. Silence for Bonhoeffer retains the sense of a limit-concept, and its pivotal event is the crucifixion. It is never developed as a habitable medium which is as important to communication and to joy in God as are words. His dismissal of mystical silence as 'the soul secretly chattering away to itself' no doubt has relevance to some practices; but the silence of many mystics could also be heard as an other-oriented adoration which takes seriously Bonhoeffer's own principle of the simultaneity of word and silence, and which allows for the ultimacy of silence as well as word.

BEYOND RESONANCES: WHERE WAS JESUS CHRIST
AT AUSCHWITZ?

Resonances such as those between Bonhoeffer and Michaels are not sufficient answer to the hard questions posed earlier by MacKinnon and de Lange. Those questions call for theology which grapples both with what MacKinnon calls 'the millennial torments of Judaism' during the past two thousand years, and with de Lange's challenge to Christians about the presence of Jesus Christ in Auschwitz. They are vast topics, and I will offer just one theological approach to each question.[13]

The Gentile sub-plot: a non-supersessionist Christian theology

The first approach will be dealt with very briefly, because, while I see it as a minimal essential requirement for Christian theology which takes MacKinnon's point seriously, yet for my purposes here it is the framework for answering my title question rather than the central issue, and I have also discussed it elsewhere.[14] This is the issue of supersessionism.

Supersessionism sees the church as superseding the Jews as the people of God. This can be accompanied by active hatred and attacks on Jews for their role in killing Christ and rejecting the Christian message, or it can encourage attempts to convert them, or it can be neutral or even benignly tolerant towards them; but the key point is that the theology of supersessionism opens the way for writing the Jews out of any positive role in the 'divine economy' of history. A contemporary way of putting it might be that Judaism is an anachronism in the Christian metanarrative:

[13] What follows is complementary with my article, 'A Messiah for the Third Millennium' in *Modern Theology* vol. 16, no.1 January, 2000 pp. 75–90, and there is some overlap.
[14] See 'A Messiah for the Third Millennium'.

Jews have no good future unless they become Christians. Supersessionism is an answer to 'How?' questions such as: How are Christians to account for the continuing existence of Judaism, and how are they to legitimate themselves theologically? It theologically silences contemporary Jews; or they are regarded as 'noise' over against the Christian Word. Auschwitz can be seen as a secularised attempt to fulfil the supersessionist meta-narrative, the logic of which is that there is no place for Judaism. There are, of course, many complicating factors (such as the fact that the Nazi racial anti-semitism eliminated converted Jews too), and I would not want to overstress the religious genesis of Nazism. Being an exceptional event does not mean that it must have had one exceptional cause. But even if many other indictments are issued – against, for example, racism, militarism, nationalism, bureaucracy and 'scientism' – the terrible truth for Christians is that the logic of their theology had fatal affinities with Nazi ideology.

One common way of approaching this has been through Romans 9–11, that agonised wrestling by Paul about the salvation of his people. One key element in a non-supersessionist theology is clear there: Gentile Christians are 'grafted in' to a heritage which remains that of the Jews – there is no second covenant, no cancelling. This is of the utmost importance, since it is precisely this that the church, when it became largely Gentile, often denied, whether explicitly or implicitly. The unsurpassable horizon of history remains that of God and the Jews. The main plot of the metanarrative is to do with God and the people of God. The grafting in of Gentiles, while embracing far greater numbers, is in fact a sub-plot. Eugene Rogers, following on from George Lindbeck's contention that both the church and Israel should be regarded as types, not of Christ, but of 'the people of God in fellowship with God at the end of time',[15] makes a convincing case for the contribution of an 'anagogical' interpretation of scripture, reading it in the light of the eschatological community as Paul does in Romans 9–11. He reads the plot as a Jewish one oriented towards consummation, with Gentile redemption a sub-plot. God's faithfulness to the covenant with Israel is permanent. There 'are not two stories, much less two covenants, but two ways the Spirit excites gratitude for the blessings of Abraham in the readers of the bible, who in this too can become sources of mutual blessing'.[16]

---

[15] Eugene F. Rogers, Jr, 'Supplementing Barth on Jews and Gender: Identifying God by Anagogy and the Spirit' in *Modern Theology*, vol. 14, no. 1 January 1998, p. 63.

[16] Ibid. p. 64. It is worth remembering that many Gentiles are not Christians. There are major implications, beyond the scope of this article, of non-supersessionist Christian theology for Christian theology in relation to others besides Jews.

That can be supported and developed in many ways,[17] but for now the important point is that if, in common Jewish and Christian terminology, the hope is for the coming of the Kingdom of God, yet there are likely to be enormous differences between the two (and, of course, within each) about the 'Who?' questions regarding God, the Messiah, and Jesus Christ as inaugurator of the Kingdom of God. The newness seen by Christians in Jesus Christ can fill their horizon and supersede the previous plot. Paul in Romans chapters 9–11 is resisting just this temptation. Is it possible to sustain a non-supersessionist account of the person of Jesus Christ? De Lange's question about Jesus Christ at Auschwitz, which can be seen as a horrendous consummation of Christian supersessionism, goes to the heart of the matter.

Where was Jesus Christ at Auschwitz?

In agreement with Ignaz Maybaum, Nicholas de Lange[18] sees the Shoah as the third *Churban* – the others being the Babylonian exile and the Roman destruction of the Temple in 70 AD. He calls it a twentieth-century Calvary and reads the Gospels as post-Holocaust literature, with the cross being a symbol or allegory of the Shoah. He speaks of Jewish wrestling with the question: 'Where was God at Auschwitz?' and throws out a challenge:

We have reached the point now, I believe, where we cannot engage in meaningful dialogue with any Christian who has not similarly confronted the question: 'Where was Jesus Christ at Auschwitz?'[19]

He sharpens this by a series of disturbing quotations from Dietrich Bonhoeffer, Martin Niemöller and Jürgen Moltmann,[20] and a vivid evocation of the crucified Jesus as the persecutor of his own people:

It is painful to contemplate the thought of those pierced hands dripping with the spilt blood of so many innocent victims.[21]

A Christian response to that cannot treat the crucifixion of Jesus as nothing but symbol or allegory; but nor can it treat Auschwitz as illustrating or symbolising the crucifixion. MacKinnon saw them as implicated in

---

[17] For my own way, see 'A Messiah for the Millennium'.
[18] Nicholas de Lange, 'Jesus Christ and Auschwitz'.   [19] Ibid., p. 309.
[20] In conversation with me (April 1999) Professor Moltmann has rejected Dr de Lange's interpretation of his position.
[21] Ibid., p. 311.

some 'interrelated finality', and it is one which does not permit overviews or integrations. How think them together in Christian theology?

Bonhoeffer's approach to the 'Where?' question is as follows:

If we look for the place of Christ, we are looking for the structure of the 'Where?' within that of the 'Who?'[22]

His further specification of the 'Where' within the 'Who' is:

'Where does he stand?' He stands *pro me*. He stands in my place, where I should stand and cannot.[23]

What if 'my place' is facing Auschwitz? How might Jesus Christ face Auschwitz? – In compassion; in judgement; in anguish; in silence; in death? Facing Auschwitz leads deeper into all the simultaneities discussed earlier: life, death and resurrection; speech and silence in many modes; radical questioning which is at the same time reversed onto ourselves. Above all, the Shoah stretches the conceivability of the *simul* of death and resurrection to breaking-point – a horror, in Steiner's phrase about MacKinnon, 'unredeemed . . . by the putative wonder of resurrection or by any promise of celestial reparation'. Is it possible to think the resurrection without in some sense leaving the horror of the death behind?

But note: these are 'How?' questions. At the heart of an answer to de Lange in line with Bonhoeffer is the basic testimony: however he might be there, or conceived to be there, the hidden, incomprehensible reality which is trusted in is that this person *is* there, facing Auschwitz. That is where a Christian response starts, with this 'Who'. There are then two massive questions: how does the response go on after starting like this? And is this not the ultimate in triumphalist supersessionism, a Christian subsumption and takeover of the Shoah?

A theology of Jesus Christ facing Auschwitz

There are already hints above at the lines of development of a theology of Jesus Christ facing Auschwitz. It is a theology of interrogative faith before the face of one who was a baby, ate, drank, taught, proclaimed the Kingdom of God, was transfigured, prayed in Gethsemane, was kissed by Judas, was arrested, tried, flogged, crucified, rose from the dead and ascended; and is looked to in hope for the world. It is simultaneously

[22] Ibid., p. 61.   [23] Ibid.

interrogative faith before the faces of the victims, of the perpetrators, of the silent and speaking witnesses, and of others. What it means to face Auschwitz in this sense can be entered into through testimonies, fiction such as *Fugitive Pieces*, and many other media and genres. Interrogative faith is stretched in study, imagination and feeling to do justice to the Shoah and to God in relation to it. But above all faith is exercised in practical response before one who is believed both to take radical responsibility for the world, to the point of death, and also to call others into comparable responsibility. It is the content of that responsibility that is most urgent for the Church and its theology after Auschwitz.

To be before this face that has witnessed Auschwitz is to be summoned to face Auschwitz in his spirit and to accept responsibility for such things not happening again. It is also, however, to accompany such Auschwitz-centred responsibilities (as MacKinnon, de Lange and Bonhoeffer all do) with interrogative faith in the full flourishing of creation in the Kingdom of God. The asymmetrical simultaneity of life, death and resurrection which, in the light of faith in the resurrection, allows trust that Auschwitz is not the last word (or the last silence) about human flourishing, works asymmetrically (and simultaneously) in the other direction too, seeing crucifixion and resurrection in the service of the message and realisation of the Kingdom of God. The desire for the Kingdom of God above all else is, perhaps, the point of deepest convergence between Jews and Christians – and there are analogous though perhaps lesser convergences in relation to many other faiths and worldviews.

Yet that still leaves the second question about whether the priority of the 'Who?' question addressed to Jesus Christ is a form of Christian supersessionism.

The face of the Messiah

How might this theology of the face of Christ avoid being dominating, triumphalist, exclusivist, supersessionist and other bad things? Christian theology has often been rightly subject to such accusations and suspicions. Yet the face and facing of Jesus Christ also holds the possibility of an alternative which helps Christian theology to be both radically self-critical in facing its own past and present and also dialogical with others. What follows is just a set of headlines for what this might be like.[24]

The very idea of facing can be seen as resistant to totalising overviews and syntheses. This particular face can be seen as challenging Christian

[24] For a fuller theology of the face of Christ, see David F. Ford, *Self and Salvation* (Cambridge: Cambridge University Press, 1999).

(and other) ideologies of domination and coercive practices. It is the face of one who is silent, who listens to cries, who is self-effacing, suffers violence, and dies. Its reality can represent a continual critique of power in the interests of the weak and suffering, an ethic of gentleness and being for others, and forms of communication that have the crucifixion as their central criterion and dialogue as their central practice. To face Jesus Christ means learning to be responsible before him, learning to be judged by him, to look on others as he looks on them, to have 'the mind of Christ', to be vigilant, and to speak and be silent in his Spirit.

It is also to be open to radical surprise. Christians have no overview of how Jesus Christ relates to other Christians or even themselves, let alone to Jews, Muslims, Hindus, agnostics, atheists, and so on. We trust that he relates in ways that are good beyond anything we or they can imagine. But what about Jews who reject him as Messiah and await the true Messiah? Neither Jews nor Christians can claim a total overview. Both affirm in radical ways that the category of 'surprise' is inseparable from eschatology. If anything is clear from Jesus' own teaching about God's future it is that those who are most confident that they have it worked out are likely to be most surprised. This above all is the place for reserve, for an agnostic yet expectant silence which is open to the unexpected. It is a silence to be filled with the prayer, vigilance and service which are the practical forms of anticipating the good surprise of welcome by the Messiah who is now met with incognito in responding to others.

LEARNING NEW SPEECH AND SILENCE

In his 'Thoughts on the Day of the Baptism of Dietrich Wilhelm Rüdiger Bethge' written in May 1944 in Tegel Prison, Dietrich Bonhoeffer concludes on a prophetic note about language and silence. He says:

Reconciliation and redemption, regeneration and the Holy Spirit, love of our enemies, cross and resurrection, life in Christ and Christian discipleship – all these things are so difficult and so remote that we hardly venture any more to speak of them. In the traditional words and acts we suspect that there may be something quite new and revolutionary, though we cannot as yet grasp or express it. That is our own fault. Our church, which has been fighting in these years only for its self-preservation, as though that were an end in itself, is incapable of taking the word of reconciliation and redemption to mankind and the world. Our earlier words are therefore bound to lose their force and cease, and our being Christians today will be limited to two things: prayer and righteous action among men. All Christian thinking, speaking, and organizing must be born anew out of this prayer and action . . . It will be a new language, perhaps quite non-religious, but liberating and redeeming – as was Jesus' language; it will shock people and yet overcome them by its power; it will be the language of a new righteousness and truth, proclaiming God's peace with men and the coming of his kingdom . . . Till then the Christian cause will be a silent and hidden affair, but there will be those who pray and do right and wait for God's own time . . .[25]

There is something in that of Anne Michaels' 'seeking by way of silence' in the aftermath of trauma which has left a 'damaged chromosome in words'. It is analogous to her attempt to 'find [a] path from depth to ascent'.

How might such seeking proceed? Again, Bonhoeffer seems to seek new words rather than new silences, whereas she seeks new silences too. Bonhoeffer's concept of silence is rooted in the crucifixion and a constraining reserve which is to be overcome by the gift of new words. Together they suggest the need for a new ascesis of language and silence, disciplined by facing the Shoah and, in Bonhoeffer's case, by a new appraisal both of modernity and of the self-discrediting of Christianity during this period. They are united in the crucial importance of 'righteous action' in the ascesis, and in finding speech and silence inextricable from the rest of our ethics. There are only hints of worship in Michaels:

If sound waves carry on to infinity, where are their screams now? I imagine them somewhere in the galaxy, moving forever towards the psalms. (p. 54; cf. p. 195)

Bonhoeffer makes prayer central, and it is linked to the 'discipline of the secret' (*disciplina arcani*) of early Christian eucharistic practice. I understand him to mean by this secret the hidden reality of the crucified and risen Jesus Christ.[26] Eberhard Bethge has written that in the *arcanum* Christ takes everyone who really encounters him and turns them around to face other people and the world.[27] Prayer is the place where the priority of the 'Who?' question is sustained above all, and also the *simul* of speech and silence. In the growing number of Jewish and Christian liturgies focused on the Shoah, one striking feature is that same interweaving of words and silence.[28] To hear testimonies of victims and survivors and to be silent before them and before God as Jews and as

[25] Dietrich Bonhoeffer, *Letters and Papers from Prison*, ed. Eberhard Bethge (London: SCM, 1971) pp. 299f.

[26] David F. Ford, *Self and Salvation*, p. 263.

[27] Eberhard Bethge, *Dietrich Bonhoeffer: Theologian, Christian, Contemporary* (London and New York: Collins, 1977) p. 787.

[28] See Marcia Sachs Littell (ed.), *Liturgies on the Holocaust. An Interfaith Anthology* (Lewiston and Queenston: Edwin Mellen, 1986).

Christians (with some liturgies created for joint Jewish–Christian worship): that is to learn, or at least to seek and desire, new speech and new silence. And Michaels invokes Muslim worship in an image of desire and failure which somehow draws us deeper into the mystery:

English was a sonar, a microscope, through which I listened and observed, waiting to capture elusive meanings buried in facts. I wanted a line in a poem to be the hollow ney of the dervish orchestra whose plaintive wail is a call to God. But all I achieved was awkward shrieking. Not even the pure shriek of a reed in the rain. (pp. 112–13)

Soundings: towards a theological poetics of silence

Oliver Davies

For all the variety of content and diversity of approach evident in the preceding chapters, a common theme runs through them all: negation, variously conceived, is not to be seen as an adjunct to conventional Christian affirmations but rather as an integral element in their expressive power. Apophasis not only distinguishes Christian speech from ordinary human speech acts, setting the limit of what can be said about God, but also signals the sense that Christian speech is grounded at its origins in a Trinitarian dynamic, or even discourse, whose provenance is revelatory. This distinction is a crucial one, for it marks the point at which Christian apophasis as a semiotic phenomenon is overtaken by its dynamic as pragmatic language use. In other words, the need to negate in Christian apophatic discourse is not grounded in a recognition of the limits of language and expression as such, or at least not in that alone. Rather, it is shaped within particular liturgical communities who are called to give verbal expression to a specific intervention of God in history. Apophasis in this sense articulates the human response to a divine communicative presence, and it is burdened as much by an excess of presence as it is by an endemic sense of absence. If the latter is in a way the 'shadow' of expressivity, where language meets its own natural limits, then the former is the density of meaning and expression, conceivable as darkness, which is the measure of a truly divine act of communication. Christian apophasis then is about divine–human communication and relation, and is foundationally celebratory.

Silence is a complex term, which resonates richly within the liturgical and theological contexts of Christian tradition, and is also diversely and creatively significant for quite different times and places. As Graham Ward has argued, it is a kind of 'rhetoric', a paradoxical figure of speech, which crosses boundaries more easily than words may do, setting up new intensities of meaning.[1] My intention here is to reflect upon silence as a

[1] See above, p. 178 9.

distinctively religious sign, in terms both of the Judaeo-Christian tradition, and of secular postmodernism, in the hope that silence investigated in this way may become an instrument for furthering dialogue between the Church and the world, and between Christianity and other world religions.

But in order to undertake this task we shall have to observe a number of distinctions which exhaust the resources of the English word. I must ask the reader therefore to accompany me in this task of thinking silence principally through the Russian and Hebrew languages, with a little Greek. Only in this way will something of the extraordinary richness of silence as a sacred term come into view. We must begin then with a fundamental distinction, which will remain with us throughout. This is the difference between silence as the absence of noise and silence as the cessation of speech. The former I shall designate by the Russian word *tishina*, where *tishina* denotes the silence of the forest, or of the tundra, and carries with it some sense of the English word 'stillness'. The latter I shall call *molchanie*, which denotes silence maintained by someone who speaks.[2] The former then is a silence which speech breaks, while the latter is a silence of speech. Thus a conversation in the Russian forest will banish silence as *tishina*, but create the possibility of silence as *molchanie*. These two silences are constantly in tension, which is a topic to which we shall return, and their relation can be a richly ambiguous one. Thus if our two Russian peasants fall silent, we may read that silence either as the cessation of conversation and restoration of *tishina* or alternatively as *molchanie*, and the continuation of their conversation by means of silence. In the latter case there are further ambiguities, since *molchanie* may be aggressive ('an angry silence'), a refusal of some kind ('a stubborn silence'), or indeed it may be compliant ('silent acknowledgement') or reflective ('a pause for thought'). The silence may be awkward and embarrassed, in which we strive for speech, or it may be an easeful lull, a resting upon the mutuality of relation with no need – for the moment – of speech. The latter would mark the triumph of Gricean implicature over utterance: the overwhelming of speech by shared meanings. Or again the silence, *molchanie*, may be maintained only by the one partner, who cannot find words that are adequate to the intensity of their feeling, entailing for the interlocutor an attentive waiting upon the other to speak ('a pregnant silence'). In any case, the expressivity of *molchanie*, which is

[2] These are common terms in the Russian language, but there is an interesting discussion of them by Mikhail Bakhtin in his 'From Notes made in 1970–1', in *Speech Genres and other Late Essays*, trans. Vern W. McGee, (Austin: University of Texas Press, 1986), pp. 133–4.

determined by its contexts, is almost as varied as the expressivity of speech itself.[3]

In our distinction between silence as *molchanie* and *tishina*, the question is whether silence is the refusal to speak or the ground which makes speech as such possible. And it is here that the religious dimensions of silence begin to take shape, for is there not something primal – divine almost – about *tishina*: the silence of the forest? Like a black character on the white page, speech is in itself differentiation from silence. If speech orders and bestows world, as a multiple and intersecting complex of linguistically structured realities, then world itself is only to be thought against a generally unthematised background of silence, without which the word, which is difference from silence, cannot be. The Judaeo-Christian tradition affirms the unity of word and world: that creation is to be thought first and foremost as divine speech. And so we shall have to add to our assertion that in the beginning was the word, in the beginning was the divine *fiat*, the further affirmation that before the beginning there was the silence which allowed the word to be formed and heard. That silence we identify with God, who is eternal and infinite, and who, as silence, is the primordial and generative ground, enabling God's own and subsequently all human speech.

If we begin with silence therefore, as indeed we must, then the speech that breaks it is revelation. This is not simply noise, nor is it pure disclosure, but in some important sense it is a distinctively personal revelation, since from words we can infer the speakers who use them. Words, even divine words, are creative performance of the self in relation to others. Language intrinsically implies the indexicality of reference and address, and thus of speech agency, in terms of the one who speaks, of those who are spoken to, and that which is spoken of. Speech as sound then presupposes a differentiation from silence which is the result of a personal act of will. If the first sound is the uttering of the word, as in Judaeo-Christian cosmology, then we have to reckon with a God who speaks and accordingly *chooses* to speak. The emergence of word and world is not accidental but is the fertile consequence of a motion of the divine person and will; and is revelation.

The transcendent, unoriginate and infinite God who is one with the silence, who is the silence, chooses to break that silence by speaking. But God's speaking is in some sense identical with God himself; it is

3 For a survey of the different ways in which silence communicates, see Adam Jaworski, *The Power of Silence. Social and Pragmatic Perspectives* (London: Sage Publications, 1993) and *Silence. Interdisciplinary Perspectives* (Mouton de Gruyter: Berlin and New York, 1997).

self-reproduction through a creative act of the will: language mediating
the power and presence of God as God's word goes forth, creating the
world (by reference – the divine optatives)[4] and creating us as persons
(by address – the divine blessings and imperatives).[5] Therefore God is
both in the silence and in the speech, present both in the sameness and
in the differentiation. But God's presence in speech is not the same as
that in silence, for in speech he is both present to himself and present to
us and to the world. Language implies not just the speaker, but also
that which is spoken of, and the one who is spoken to; language is in its
essence communal. And so we can argue that if silence is God in himself,
then the divine speech, the *fiat*, is God in a differential relation with
himself, as silence, and in a creative relation with the world, which the
fiat summons into existence. As beings who are called into existence by
the divine speech act, through address (and who are thus in God's image
in that we too are speech agents), the parameters of our own existence
are determined by our speech relation with God. This must be thought
of as an answering relation of speech in some way, a creative human
response to the originary speech of God: as praise, credal affirmation,
witness, song, words that are 'useful for building up' (Eph. 4:29), poetry,
theology and prayer.

The divine *tishina* in itself has a powerful religious significance, tending
towards the *fascinans* and *tremendum*. This is the 'silence of the universe'
which so frightened Pascal.[6] It is the unbounded silence that is the ground
of existence itself. But if God chooses to break that silence and speak to us,
then we must note a second sense in which silence can take on religious
meaning. There is now the possibility of a divine *molchanie*. If God can
choose to speak with us and to us, he can also choose to refrain from
doing so. He can be silent in those communicative and expressive senses
which we noted in human *molchanie*, coming about between our Russian
peasants. And indeed, the exploration of diverse forms of divine *molchanie*
is a particularly rich seam in the Old Testament narratives of God and
his people. God's silence is by and large viewed as being extraordinarily
threatening to Israel: 'Why do you keep silent and punish us so severely?'
asks Isaiah (Isa. 64:12: *ḥāšāh*). In Ps. 83:1 it is seen as a divine refusal to
destroy the enemies of Israel (*ḥāreš*; cf. Ps. 109:1: *ḥāreš*). The Psalmist
therefore pleads with God not to 'remain silent' (Ps. 35:22: *ḥāreš*) and
far away, for if God is silent, then he may die (Ps. 28:1: *ḥāreš* and *ḥāšāh*;
39:13 [12]: *ḥāreš*). But elsewhere, it is the Psalmist's triumphant praise

[4] Gen. 1:3–26. [5] Gen. 1:28–9.
[6] Ph. Sellier, ed., *Pascal. Pensées* (Paris: Bordas, 1991), p. 256.

that God in fact 'comes and does not keep silence', judging the earth in righteousness (Ps. 50:3: *ḥārēš*). The verbs for maintaining silence that are used here are *ḥāšāh* (חָשָׁה) and *ḥārēš* (חָרֵשׁ) (the latter is preferred), and commentators note that *ḥārēš* emphasises 'active, intentional silence'.[7] In the first two examples given above, it is linked with the verbs *āpaq* and *šāqaṭ* respectively, which are suggestive of self-restraint or inactivity. But if the effect of God's silence is the punishment and destruction of his people, then the response of the people is a reciprocal silence. Jeremiah proclaims to Israel: 'You also, O Madmen, shall be brought to silence; the sword shall pursue you' (Jer. 48:2: *dāmam*). The Egyptians too, as Moses recalls, were reduced to silence: 'Terror and dread fell upon them; by the might of your arm they became still [silent] as stone' (Exod. 15:16: *dāmam*). A whole series of images use the verbal form *dāmam* (רָּמַם), which allows a fertile ambivalence between 'silence' and 'stillness', between being rendered 'dumb' and 'numb' by God's powerful action (e.g. Lev. 10:3; Isa. 23:2; Jer. 6:2; 47:5; Ezek. 24:17; 27:32). In such cases then, silence as *dāmam* is linked with extreme states of emotional shock. When God is silent (*ḥārēš*), then the people too are silenced (*dāmam*).

But there are also more affirmative aspects to the human silence conveyed by the word *dāmam* and its cognates. It is the appropriate response also to expectations of God's positive action in the world, in particular to his self-communication through speech. The Psalmist awaits God's coming: 'For God alone my soul waits in silence' (Ps. 62:1: *dūmīyyāh*; cf. Ps. 4:4: *dāmam*). In Lamentations we are told that 'it is good that one should wait quietly for the salvation of the Lord' (3:26: *dūmāh*), and that 'to sit alone in silence' is attended by hope (3:28: *dāmam*). Repeatedly Israel is urged to maintain silence as a prelude to hearing the word of God, though the word used in each of the following examples approximates to the English 'hush!' (*has*) (Deut. 27:9; Zeph. 1:7; Zech. 2:13). For the psalmist his own silence is likewise an important theme, but in the use of *dāmam* it suggests a state of being overwhelmed by God's power, rather than a defiant refusal of speech. The initiative therefore lies with God: 'You have turned my mourning into dancing; you have taken off my sackcloth and clothed me with joy, so that my soul may praise you and not be silent' (Ps. 30:12: *dāmam*). Silence is particularly fearful, since it signifies death and the descent into Sheol: 'The dead do not praise the Lord, nor do any that go down into silence' (Ps. 115:17: *dūmāh*). The prophet Isaiah similarly abjures silence as the negation of his divine calling: 'For Zion's

---

[7] *Theological Dictionary of the Old Testament*, vol. 3, ed. Johannes Botterweck and Helmer Ringgren (William B. Eerdmans: Grand Rapids, Michigan, 1978), p. 260.

sake I will not keep silent', but the prophets are more inclined to the language of *ḥāšāh* and *ḥārēš*, perhaps underlining the greater emphasis upon prophetic speech as a conscious act entailing personal courage and will (Isa. 62:1: *ḥāšāh*; cf. Isa. 62:6: *ḥāšāh*; Jer. 4:19: *ḥārēš*).

It is in the Book of Job however that the metaphor of silence comes most richly into play. Here we can see a tension between *ḥārēš* and *ḥāšāh*, as refraining from complaint, and *dāmam* as the reverent acceptance of the divine will. Initially Job did not 'charge God with wrongdoing' and 'sin with his lips' on account of his grievous losses (Job 1:22; 2:10), but his long struggle to be silent (6:24: 'Teach me and I will be silent': *ḥārēš*) is finally lost when he says 'I will no longer restrain my mouth; I will speak in the anguish of my spirit' (7:11: *ḥāšāh*).[8] Silence, at that point, would be death for Job (13:19: *ḥārēš*). In a series of eloquent speeches Job protests his innocence to God, although he knows that his own mouth will nevertheless condemn him (11:20). Still, he commands his critics, Eliphaz, Zophar and Bildad to be silent so that he may speak (13:13: *ḥārēš*). It is only when God himself finally speaks 'out of the whirlwind' (38:1) that Job falls silent: 'See, I am of small account; what shall I answer you? I lay my hand on my mouth. I have spoken once, and I will not answer; twice, but will proceed no further' (40:4–5). Although the word is not used at this point (but note 'I lay my hand on my mouth', and also 30:27: 'my innards are in turmoil and are never still: *dāmam*), this passage marks the restoration of *dāmam*, which is the appropriate silence to be maintained by human beings in the face of God's pronouncements, whether as words or revelatory actions. This word is used for the respectful silence which others maintained before Job prior to his fall from grace: 'They listened to me, and waited, and kept silence for my counsel' (29:21: *dāmam*). He was like a 'king among his troops' (29:25), even nobles and princes were silenced before him (29:9–10). Job's 'word dropped upon them like dew' (29:22). From this perspective therefore, the story of Job is an account of how this privileged man underwent a transformation from being one to whom *dāmam* was offered by those around him to one who himself, despite his calamities, finally discovered a silence of respect, expectation and awe before the divine presence as, again, *dāmam*. Silence as *ḥārēš* is in this case an intermediate stage, and ironically it is only because Job failed to maintain *ḥārēš* before God (unlike his counsellors who are finally rebuked by God) and spoke out to him from his heart that God finally replied like 'thunder' (37:2), instilling in Job a *dāmam* of reverence and peace.

---

[8] This usage of *ḥāšāh* does indeed show that there is some considerable overlap with *ḥārēš*.

The Hebrew words for silence that we have analysed so far all belong to the field of *molchanie* rather than *tishina*. Indeed, one of the most striking aspects of linguistic imagery in the Old Testament is precisely the absence of divine *tishina*. The first Genesis narrative is taciturn on the silence that precedes the *fiat*, although we are told of the 'formless void' which was the earth and the 'darkness' that 'covered the face of the deep' (Gen. 1:2). Just as silence means death for the Psalmist, or for Job, so God's final silence would mean cosmic annihilation: 'If he should take back his spirit to himself, and gather to himself his breath, all flesh would perish together, and all mortals return to dust' (Job 34:14–15).[9] Indeed, the threat that God's *molchanie* (his passing wrath) might become *tishina* (wholesale destruction of all that is) is intrinsic to the eschatological terror of the later prophets.

It is the relative absence of silence as *tishina* that makes the use of the Hebrew word *d^e mām āh* (דְּמָמָה) so interesting. This noun appears only at three places in the Old Testament, but in each case it is closely associated with the presence and speech of God. The first occurrence is when Elijah meets God: 'Now there was great wind, so strong that it was splitting mountains and breaking rocks in pieces before the Lord, but the Lord was not in the wind; and after the wind an earthquake, but the Lord was not in the earthquake; and after the earthquake a fire, but the Lord was not in the fire; and after the fire a sound of sheer silence (*d^e mām āh*)' (1 Kings 19:11–12).[10] God, who has passed before Elijah, then speaks, commissioning him to anoint Hazael as king over Aram and Elishah as prophet in his place (1 Kings 19:13, 15–16). The contrast between the silence on the one hand and the wind, earthquake and fire on the other establishes the transcendence of Israel's God, clearly distinguishing him from deities of the elements. It suggests an impersonal *tishina*, or 'tranquillitas' (which is an alternative rendering of *d^e mām āh*).[11] But the silence is immediately followed by the sounding of a voice, as we find again in the second occurrence of the word, when Eliphaz describes a divine theophany (Job 4:16).[12] We are left therefore with an unresolved interplay between silence as absence of noise on the one hand and silence as a mode of God's speech on the other, since the God who inhabits the silence is a God who speaks.

---

[9] Speech is linked with life and the holy spirit in Job at 27:3–4 and 33:3–4 (cf. Gen 2:7).

[10] The translation of this term has given difficulty over the ages. It appears in the LXX as 'αὔρα', meaning 'breeze' or 'puff of wind' and in the Vulgate similarly as 'aura', in all three places.

[11] *Konkordanz zum Hebräischen Alten Testament*, ed. Gerhard Lisowsky (Stuttgart, 1958), p. 367.

[12] In the third and final occurrence, the word is again contrasted with the force of the elements (Ps. 107:29). The stillness is the result of divine action, but on this occasion there is no voice.

Hebrew words for silence are characteristically linked with notions of stupefaction, stillness and rest: if speech is associated with action and will in the Old Testament, then silence with inaction, the refusal to act, or a state of rest. Not so for the Greeks. In Greek texts from the classical and early Christian periods, we shall consistently find an association between silence and the mind, silence and transcendence; and we shall meet it in the main as a noun and not a verb. For the Greek then, *tishina* predominates over *molchanie* in matters of religion. But both Plato and Aristotle sit lightly to the notion of silence altogether. Indeed, how could the loquacious Socrates ever be an advocate for the cessation of διαίρεσις, with its intimate link to διάνοιἄ? In a brief passage from the Sophist (238c), Socrates speaks of non-being as that which is ἄρρητος, which cannot be spoken of, and at the same ἄλογος, standing outside rationality. In other words, the silence of non-being is a mark not of its sublimity but rather of its nonsensical character. And Aristotle, likewise, is not enamoured of silence. In a passage from the Problems (948b22) the Philosopher discusses the silence of the fearful, suggesting that the body is chilled and the air sinks down, away from the mouth, towards a lower orifice.[13] With heroic pragmatism, and as an inspiration to all empiricists, Aristotle therefore equates silence with the breaking of wind.[14]

In the work of Philo, we begin to see an interesting confluence of Greek and Semitic ideas on silence. As a Hebrew, he is keenly aware of the interaction of speech and silence, stating of the latter that it 'is a power, sister to the power of speech', and he understands the place of an awed silence in the presence of the divine (cf. *dāmam*).[15] But as a Greek, he invests silence with cognitive properties, pointing towards *apatheia* and transcendentalism: 'Our beings are sometimes at rest, at other times subject to impulses or, as we may call them, ill-timed outcries. When these are silent, we have profound peace, when it is otherwise we have relentless wars.'[16] Philo refers to the 'outcries of pleasure', 'the voice of desire', the 'cry of the passions', which is 'full-toned and sonorous'[17] and

---

[13] Raoul Mortley, *From Word to Silence*, vol. 1 (Bonn: Hanstein, 1986), pp. 117–18.

[14] How fortunate, we may feel, that Aristotle did not know the Hebrew word *d‘māmāh* [LXX: αὔρα], and that the LXX translators of this ambiguous term did not know Aristotle!

[15] 'The Confusion of Tongues', l. 37, *Philo*, vol. 4 (London: William Heinemann, 1932), p. 31. I am indebted to Mortley for these quotations from the work of Philo. The motif of silence in the mystery schools and their links with the Greek philosophical tradition are usefully surveyed in Odo Casel, 'De philosophorum Graecorum silentio mystico', in *Religionsgeschichtliche Versuche und Vorarbeiten*, Band 16, Heft 2, Verlag von Alfred Töpelmann in Giessen, 1919.

[16] 'On Drunkenness', l. 97, *Philo*, vol. 3, (London: William Heinemann, 1930), p. 369 (translation slightly adapted).

[17] Ibid., l. 102.

their 'thousand tongues and mouths'[18] and continues: 'when the subject of that experience says that he feels that in the camp of the body all the sounds are the sounds of war, and that the quietness (ἡσυχία) which is so dear to peace has been driven far away, the holy word does not dissent'.[19] This is the beginning of what will become a major tradition firstly in the Neoplatonists and then in the Christian monastic fathers, for whom silence marks the end of passion and the return of the mind to its origins in transcendental silence. In monastic tradition, extending from Evagrius and Origen to the great figures of fourteenth-century Rhineland and sixteenth-century Spain, and beyond, silence has been a primary Christian metaphor for detachment from the world. It denotes both our passing beyond entanglements through the passions, which have material entities as their objects, and our rising above the complicities of cognitions, which again are inherently inclined to focus upon objects in the world, thus restricting the transcendentalism that is innate to the nature of mind. In the early Christian centuries, this trend is matched by a tendency among the Gnostics to divinise silence as σῑγή, from which all speech is a descent. In the Valentinian systems, speech represents the beginning of the world, as it does for the Hebrews; but altogether in contrast with the ontology of the Old Testament, the focus here is upon the divine silence from which speech emerges and from which it represents a descent and a departure, rather like the emergence of multiplicity from the purity of the Neoplatonic One. The religious spirit is called to rise above the material world therefore, above language itself, in its return to the silent source of all, where alone it can find peace. Silence in this sense lends itself to appropriation in cultic form. It becomes coterminous with the hiddenness of truth, and thus, in its cruder forms, supports a hierarchy of those who dispose over its secrets. Already in the Greek tragedies (above all in Oedipus Rex), silence conceals truths; the initiate of the Greek mysteries is one who maintains a secretive and cultic silence, and Christian developments of silence in this sense, as Origen's 'mystical' or 'hidden' dimensions of Scripture for instance, will constantly risk appropriation back into cults of silence through Christian gnosticism, apocalypticism and a hierarchy of privileged knowledge.

Apophaticism in its classical Christian forms is decidedly the prod-uct of Greek ways of thinking. We began with a distinction between 'reference' and 'address', arguing that in the Genesis tradition, the world is called into being through reference (the divine optative 'let it be' still

---

[18] Ibid., l. 103.   [19] Ibid., l. 104.

fundamentally refers) and ourselves in our personhood through address (blessing and command).[20] It is largely through address that the profoundly mysterious nature of God is conveyed in the Old Testament: in God's self-naming as the enigmatic 'I am that I am' at Exod. 3:14 or the equally difficult God of 'graciousness' and 'compassion' at Exod. 33:19. It is within the relationality established by the self-naming of God and the naming of Israel in relation to himself as self-naming God that the mystery of God is experienced by his people. How is God to be understood, for as he himself says: 'my ways are not your ways, and my thoughts are not your thoughts' (Isa. 55:8)? It is *dāmam* which serves as the affirmation of God's will in this Hebrew context, however unfathomable it may appear. In early Christian tradition, however, apophasis frequently appears to stand within the domain not of address but of reference. It is therefore easily confused with other contemporary non-Christian forms of silence and denial. For instance, an early Latin translation of Ignatius' letter to the Magnesians substitutes for 'proceeding from silence (σῑγή)' (1 Magn. 8:2) the phrase 'not proceeding from silence', in the belief probably that a silence prior to the Word had suspiciously Valentinian connotations.[21] The proximity of Christian apophasis to Neoplatonism is apparent also in the predominance of terms such as *hesychia* and *apatheia* in the spiritual writings of early Christian monks. And Plotinus, who is the greatest of the Neoplatonist thinkers, is emphasising the place of silence in his own transcendental metaphysics of the One just at the moment when the Church is attempting to think the new Christianity within the terminology and concepts of the Greek philosophical systems. It is only in silence, for Plotinus, that we can approach the One, imitating within ourselves the same transcendence beyond language and being which is the very essence of the Ineffable and the Alone.[22] Clearly there is a risk here that reference will overcome address, and that a transcendentalism born of apophatic reference will subvert the original Judaeo-Christian notion of a God who speaks.

But it is easy to forget the extent to which belief in Christ necessarily promotes a metaphysics and linguistics of address, which may remain however unthematised as such. The classical statements of Greek patristic apophasis stand squarely within a context of liturgy and naming. The opening chapter of Pseudo-Dionysius' *Mystical Theology*, for instance, itself contains strong elements of address, and must be seen alongside the liturgical practices and thinking of the Divine Names: 'Trinity! Higher

---

[20] See notes 4 and 5.
[21] 'Silence', *Dictionnaire de Spiritualité*, vol. 14, Paris: Beauchesne 1990, col. 835.
[22] Ennead VI, 8.

than any being, any divinity, any goodness! Guide of Christians in the wisdom of heaven! Lead us up beyond unknowing and light, up to the farthest, highest peak of mystic scripture, where the mysteries of God's Word lie simple, absolute and unchangeable in the brilliant darkness of a hidden silence . . .'[23] Even a rigorously apophatic thinker such as Meister Eckhart, much later in the tradition, cannot be seen to be operating with apophatic reference to the exclusion of address, since the God in whom he believes, who is a God of thorough-going negation, *ihtes nihtes* ('nothing of anything'), reproduces himself constantly in the soul. The individual is therefore in the most profound sense addressed by God through the *gotesgeburt* or birth of the Word in the ground of the soul.[24] Christian apophatic language is not pure reference therefore, but rather reference which has been transformed by divine revelation as address. In its liturgical practices and reading of scripture, the Christian community creatively remembers and celebrates the incarnation of the Word of God. It is this sense of presence as address which controls the deep foundations of Christian speech, tying language-use in to a *relation* of faith and calling language back to a celebratory recognition of its own origins in the divine creativity of God. The Christian who lives in a world of God's creation, and who sacramentally recalls God's own entry into the condition of createdness, speaks in a way that recalls Bakhtin's concept of 'addressivity', whereby language itself, whether as conversation or reference (speaking with or speaking of), is governed by a foundational relationality, exercised by the self towards the incarnate Word and towards the world, which was made through and in the Word.

In the second part of this chapter, we come to the thematic development of silence in three modern texts. For all the displacements and conceits of modernity, Judaeo-Christian silence as reference and address can still exercise a powerful fascination upon the religious imagination and function as a potent and creative mode of textual presence. The first such text is taken from René Girard's study *Resurrection from the Underground: Fyodor Dostoevsky*, in which Girard sets out his view that 'extreme negation' is 'the only Christian art adapted to our time, the only art worthy of it', since this art 'does not require listening to sermons, for our era cannot tolerate them. It lays aside traditional metaphysics, with which nobody, or almost nobody, can comply. Nor does it base itself

---

[23] 'The Mystical Theology', in *Pseudo-Dionysius. The Complete Works*, ed. and trans. Colm Luibheid (New York: Paulist Press, 1987), p. 135.

[24] See Oliver Davies, 'Die Rhetorik des Erhabenen: Sprachtheorie bei Meister Eckhart', in G. Steer and L. Sturlese, eds., *Lectura Eckhardi: Predigten Meister Eckharts von Fachgelehrten gelesen und gedeutet* (Stuttgart: Kohlhammer Verlag, 1998), pp. 97–115.

on reassuring lies, but on consciousness of universal idolatry'.[25] Girard
views Dostoevsky's text therefore as a kind of revelation, 'the revelation of nihilism', in the service of an art of Christian revelation.[26] That
'underground' is defined as 'the law of our own desire', in which 'mimetic
desire is failed selfishness, impotent pride that generates the worshipful
imitation of idols unrecognised as such, because they are hated as much
as they are revered'.[27] This underground, which Girard invites us to
compare with Dante's *Inferno*, is one in which 'the Other exercises a
force of gravitation that one cannot conquer except in opposing it with
a pride denser and heavier, around which this Other will be constrained
to gravitate'.[28]

Girard, of course, understands that apotheosis of the self in terms of a
mimetic rivalry, which is expressed in Dostoevsky's world at the level of
'doubling' and reduplication, often linked with duplicity. Girard points to
the role of the double as *Doppelgänger* in Dostoevsky's works, most notably
in the early short story *The Double*. He points also to the parallelisms
or representational exchanges which occur between radically opposed
figures such as the saintly Prince Myshkin and the wicked Stavrogin. Most
memorably, Girard reflects upon roulette, and the passion for gambling,
as the primary exemplum and metaphor for this exchange. In the rapid
changes of fortune/s of the wheel, 'miserly prodigality' and 'wasteful
avarice' become the 'moments of a dialectic' which 'succeed each other
very quickly and cease to be distinct. At each spin mastery and slavery
are at stake. Roulette is the abstract quintessence of alterity in a universe
where all human relations are affected by underground pride.'[29] The
way out of this cycle of violence, in which the other is always a rival to
be hated and imitated, seems straightforward enough. Girard tells us

Dostoevsky's art is literally prophetic. He is not prophetic in the sense of pre-
dicting the future, but in a truly biblical sense, for he untiringly denounces the
fall of the people of God back into idolatry. He reveals the exile, the rupture,
and the suffering that results from this idolatry. In a world where the love of
Christ and the love of the neighbour form one love, the true touchstone is our
relation to others. It is the Other whom we must love *as oneself* if one does not
desire to idolize and hate the Other in the depths of the underground. It is no
longer the golden calf, it is this Other who poses the risk of seducing humans in
a world committed to the Spirit, for better or for worse.[30]

[25] René Girard, *Resurrection from the Underground: Fyodor Dostoevsky*, trans. James G. Williams
(New York: Crossroad, 1997), p. 137.
[26] Ibid., p. 82.   [27] Ibid., pp. 155, 157–8.   [28] Ibid., p. 74.
[29] Ibid., p. 77.   [30] Ibid., p. 129.

This passage can be paralleled by another in which again the appeal is to intersubjectivity as a way of defining the self, and to love of the other as a form of personal–spiritual liberation from the constraints of mimetic violence:

the Self is not an *object* alongside other selves, for it is constituted by its relation to the Other and cannot be considered outside this relation. It is this relation which the effort to substitute oneself for the God of the Bible always corrupts. Divinity cannot become identified either with the Self or with the Other; it is perpetually part of the struggle *between* the Self and the Other.[31]

But in the world of Girard–Dostoevsky there is more to the critique of idolatry than an Augustinian appeal to the discernment of love. The pride and malice which constitute this idolatry specifically replicate themselves as *representational mimesis.* Here we seem close to the thought of Gilles Deleuze, for whom traditional forms of representation are trapped in a fourfold affirmation of identity, and who makes, in his work *Difference and Repetition*, an impassioned plea for a new kind of thinking which will, for the first time, accommodate 'difference' and restore what he calls 'the *genitality* of thinking'.[32] There is therefore for Girard an epistemological violence at work, an arrogance of the self, which manifests as representation and thus constitutes the mimetic structures of culture itself. This approaches the heart of Girard's critique of culture and of human identity as it informs and is formed by images in conflict, contesting the same representational space. Those images themselves become models, both expressing and propagating patterns of competitive, or to use Girard's word, 'idolatrous', human behaviour.

Although at this point Girard himself explicitly advocates radical altruism as the way out of the remorseless round of representational exchange, predicated upon violence, a further liberating possibility seems to come into view in his discussion, at this same point in the text, of the encounter between Dostoevsky's Grand Inquisitor and Christ. In Girard's words, 'the Christianity that the Inquisitor describes is like the negative of a photograph – it shows everything in a reversed manner, just like the words of Satan in the account of the temptations'.[33] The Inquisitor 'sees all, knows all, understands all', but cannot accept Christ's love: 'What to do in this case but to reaffirm the presence of this love?' Girard asks, and

---

[31] Ibid., p. 94.
[32] Gilles Deleuze, *Difference and Repetition*, trans. Paul Patton (London: The Athlone Press, 1994), p. 266.
[33] Girard, *Dostoevsky*, p. 130.

continues: 'Such is the sense of the kiss that Christ gives, wordlessly, to the wretched old man.' I want to pause with the word *wordlessly* here ('sans mot dire', in Girard's French original).[34] Dostoevsky's Russian text is interesting at this point. The word which is repeated through this passage is in fact *molchanie*, our interpersonal 'silence', and its verbal forms around the root *molchit*, 'to be silent'. We can see the force of this word at work in the opening line of the relevant paragraph, which contains the perfective form *umolk*: 'The Inquisitor fell silent.' He waits a while for the prisoner, Christ, to answer him. His falling silent, then, is answered by Christ's silence, and we are told the silence (*molchanie*) of Christ troubles or disturbs the Inquisitor.[35] So oppressive does Christ's silence become that Dostoevsky tells us the Inquisitor would be happy to hear anything at all, even something 'bitter and terrible'. And then suddenly Christ kisses him on his bloodless, ninety-year-old lips. Crucially he does so *molcha*, a present gerund form, meaning literally 'maintaining silence', 'not speaking'.[36] As a verbal form, this is a much more powerful notion than 'wordlessly'. It suggests communicative agency: a positive act of not speaking, of remaining silent. It is, incidentally, the same word which is used when Alyosha kisses Ivan, at the end of this passage.[37]

Within the contexts of the Grand Inquisitor scene, with its reminiscences of Mt 26:63, it would appear that Girard's ethical answer to the cycle of violence as 'loving the Other as yourself' is matched by a representational answer, which is the introduction of language not as reference and representation but as interpersonal communication. In terms of our original distinction between *tishina* and *molchanie*, reference and address, within the linguistic cosmology laid out in Genesis, we can gloss this as the retrieval of a secularised function of reference, fatally prey to the personal and representational rivalries of mimetic violence, back into the language of address. That representational rivalry is signalled even in Dostoevsky's text as the return of 'the dreadful Tower of Babel', which will end in conflict, destruction and 'cannabilism'.[38] It is this which Dostoevsky's Inquisitor intends to dismantle by the 'magical' power of the Church. And the latter, the language of address, is configured negatively – as silence (for anything else in the world of Girard–Dostoevsky would simply fall back into representation). By placing silence, which is a non-sign, at the centre of the narrative flow,

[34] René Girard, *Dostoïevski du double à l'unité* (Paris: Librairie Plon, 1963), p. 153.
[35] F. M. Dostoevskii, *Sobranie Sochinenii*, vol. 9 (Moscow: Gosudarstvennoe Izdatel'stvo Khudozhestvennoi Literatury 1958), p. 330: 'ему тяжело его молчание.'
[36] Ibid.   [37] Ibid., p. 331.   [38] Ibid., pp. 318 and 324.

Girard–Dostoevsky can arrest the ceaseless reproduction of representations which foster and reflect mimetic violence, or 'cannibalism'.

Here then we find a reversal of the usual semiological movement from silence to the sign, which occurs as the non-sign of silence is invested with meaning through its contexts in language: what we now have is a movement from the sign to silence, which disrupts the replication of signs and disallows the appropriation of silence into its contextual structures. Interpersonal silence now becomes the Other to mimetic rivalry between signs, marking its transcendence and its limit. The fact that it is Jesus who maintains that silence, who refuses the sign, powerfully reinforces Girard's point that underlying representational violence is the gravitational force of the Other as rival, a structure of pride, conflict and violence which can be overcome only by a refusal to speak which is simultaneously an expression of love for the other.

A second contemporary text which is of interest with respect to silence and speech is Jacques Derrida's article *On How not to Speak: Denials*. The theme of this piece is explicitly that of a discussion of the difference between negativity as deconstruction and negativity as apophasis, or negative theology. In the first few pages of these penetrating and personal reflections (in what he himself calls his most riskful and autobiographical work),[39] Derrida shows himself to be acutely alert to the danger of 'the becoming-theological of all discourse' so that 'God's name would then be the hyperbolic effect of that negativity or all negativity that is consistent in its discourse'. He knows that 'if there is a work of negativity in discourse and predication, it will produce divinity' and that it is but a small step from saying that divinity is 'produced' to saying that it is 'productive'. The consequence would then follow that: '[n]ot only would atheism not be the truth of negative theology; rather, God would be the truth of all negativity'.[40] This would be precisely the reversal of the parodic, so pervasively present in modern thinking, into the onto-theism which it disputes, redefined as a negative ontology which reinstitutes Creator and Creation. In order to close out just such a possibility, he points out that negative theology involves an 'ontological wager of hyperessentiality': it is seeking precisely to argue for the 'existence' of God, as more-being or non-being, as origin of being or surplus of being (what we have called the 'affirmation' of apophasis).[41] Deconstruction,

---

39 Sanford Budick and Wolfgang Iser, eds., *Languages of the Unsayable: the Play of Negativity in Literature and Literary Theory* (New York: Columbia University Press, 1989), pp. 3–70. Derrida himself describes his lecture as 'the most "autobiographical" speech I have ever risked' (p. 66, fn. 13).
40 Ibid., p. 6.   41 Ibid., p. 8.

on the other hand, is what Silverson has termed 'armed neutrality'; it has no such hyperessentialist claims. Perceptively Derrida points out too that negative theology is a mode of address, an encomium or hymn, which bears the distinctive trace of the Other to whom it is uttered. It is preceded by a prayer, which is:

not a preamble, an accessory mode of access. It constitutes an essential moment, it adjusts discursive asceticism, the passage through the desert of discourse, the apparent referential vacuity which will only avoid empty deliria and prattling, by addressing itself from the start to the other, to you. But to you as 'hyperessential and more than divine Trinity'.[42]

This prayer Derrida defines as living conversation, and he speaks of it in most un-Derridean terms as language that can never be written:

Does one have the right to think that, as pure address, on the edge of silence, alien to every code and to every rite, hence to every repetition, prayer should never be turned away from its present by a notation or by the movement of an apostrophe, by a multiplication of addresses? That each time it takes place only once and should never be recorded?[43]

But having made his telling points about the difference between deconstruction and negative theology in terms of the hyperessentiality of the latter in the first few pages of his article, which he further develops in his discussion of Pseudo-Dionysius and Meister Eckhart, Derrida concludes with an intensely interesting and provocative reading of the comments on the nature of theology which Martin Heidegger made at the celebrated seminar in Zurich. There Heidegger dwelt specifically on the distinction between *Offenbarkeit* (primordial openness as being) and *Offenbarung* (divine revelation) and noted, within the parameters of his own philosophy, that theology would have to leave the language of being entirely aside. Otherwise the inquiry into *Offenbarung* would simply be assumed into an inquiry into *Offenbarkeit*. Given Derrida's engagement with Heidegger on this point, together with his extensive and sympathetic comments on the post-metaphysical theology of Jean-Luc Marion, it is tempting to ask whether Derrida's ambient exercise in denial and

[42] Ibid., p. 41. The final quotation is from the first line of the prayer or hymn to the Trinity with which Pseudo-Dionysius begins his *Mystical Theology*.
[43] Ibid., p. 62. Intriguingly Derrida continues: 'But perhaps the contrary is the case. Perhaps there would be no prayer, no pure possibility of prayer, without what we glimpse as a menace or as a contamination: writing, the code, repetition, analogy or the – at least apparent – multiplicity of addresses, initiation.'

non-speaking may not enclose the possibility of a final non-metaphysical theism, that is the possibility of a theology which is innocent of the language of being, even being 'under erasure'.[44] Indeed, his view that it is only the intentionality of the speaker which divides deconstruction and Christian apophatic theology may already contain a tacit admission that he now finds himself situated on a ground which is defined as much by the theological object of his critique as it is by his deconstructionist reflections upon it. In other words, since Derrida shows that it is only the matter of intentionality which divides deconstructive negation as 'armed neutrality' and apophasis as Christian affirmation, then it appears finally to be a matter of *choice*. And when you have choice, or our choosing, then is it not only a short step, as he might himself say, to having divine choice, as election? Perhaps finally therefore the insights with which Derrida wrestles in this most provocative piece are bound up with the essentially parodic character of much postmodern thinking, which still retains a powerful link with the thought of Friedrich Nietzsche. Just as Nietzsche parodied Christianity, even as he critiqued it, doing so – to some considerable extent – in the spirit of protest, revival and reformation; so too in this piece Derrida appears to play with the return of deconstructive speech as *écriture* to prayer as living speech, which takes place in the space between human beings and God and which – as pure address and pure relation – deconstructive *écriture*, the extreme language of reference, can glimpse but never grasp.

Our final author is the Jewish poet Paul Celan. Celan was born in 1920, in Czernowitz, then in northern Rumania, and he experienced the Shoah at first hand.[45] Both his parents were murdered by the National Socialists during the deportations in the summer and autumn of 1942. During the 1950s and sixties, Paul Celan became a major figure in post-war German literature since he both wrote powerfully of the Holocaust and seemed to stand squarely within the classical tradition of German lyric. Silence is a theme with which Celan is fundamentally concerned. We meet in him, in the first place, the *Sprachskepsis* ('scepticism about language') which was a general feature of the post-war years. Not only had the German literary community been decimated, but the German language itself had been poisoned. In a speech of 1958, Celan

---

[44] Ibid., p. 58: 'If he [Heidegger] were to write a theology, the word *being* would not be under erasure; it wouldn't even appear there.'
[45] For an overview of Celan's life, and the place of individual poems in it, see John Felstiner, *Paul Celan: Poet, Survivor, Jew* (New Haven and London: Yale University Press, 1995).

spoke of the 'terrible dumbness ... the thousand darknesses of death-bringing speech' which language had passed through.[46] Two years later, in his 'Meridian Speech' given on the occasion of his reception of the prestigious Büchner prize, Celan developed his profound mistrust of the aesthetical properties of art. He reminded his audience that every poem written today had to be mindful of the 'twentieth of January': the date with which Büchner's story *Lenz* begins, but also the date on which the Wannsee Conference took place in 1942, which decided the fate of European Jewry.[47] The second fundamental aspect of Celan's poetological thinking to emerge in that speech was the dialogical character of all poetry. Thus the overcoming of silence which the authentic poem represents is always a speaking with another, perhaps – as Celan suggests – a wholly Other. The poem comes about through an act of individuation, whereby the poet stamps his or her individual history upon the language of art, conceives art through that history, and thus the poem becomes a partner in dialogue, with the reader, the community, the world, with God: 'the poem ... becomes a conversation' ['das Gedicht ... wird Gespräch'].[48] And so, for Celan, the poem is always in a certain sense 'utopian', since it is born from the impossible union of the historical as the 'once and for all' ['das Einmalige'] and tradition and art, with their tropes and metaphors, which are discourses of repetition.[49]

There are multiple forms of silence at work in Celan's poetry. In *Argumentum e silentio*, he speaks, for instance, of 'the word not spoken' or 'the word cut off' ['das erschwiegene Wort'], where he has in mind the accounts of Jews who were singing psalms as they were killed. Celan intends a poetic language here, a poetic word, which 'shed no blood as the poison tooth bit through its syllables' ['dem das Blut nicht gerann, als der Giftzahn/ die Silben durchstiess']. But he is mindful too of the silence which is a forgetfulness, and which he refers to as 'Mohn' or 'poppy': luxurious, ritualised, self-obsessed grief which forgets both the other and history. Somewhere between the two, authentic poetry must be found: 'Fastened to the chain that binds gold and forgetting' ['An die Kette gelegt/ zwischen Gold und Vergessen'], where gold is a cypher for silence.[50] The images he generally uses for his ideal of poetry

[46] Ansprache anlässlich der Entgegennahme des Literaturpreises der freien Hansestadt Bremen, *Paul Celan. Gesammelte Werke*, vol. 3 (Frankfurt am Main: Suhrkamp, 1983), p. 186.
[47] *Der Meridian*. Rede anlässlich der Verleihung des Georg-Büchner Preises Darmstadt am 22 Oktober 1960, ibid., p. 196 and passim.
[48] Ibid., p. 198. [49] Ibid., p. 197–202.
[50] 'Argumentum e silentio', *Werke*, vol. 1 (Frankfurt am Main: Suhrkamp, 1983), pp. 138–9.

are those of snow and ice, and the poem 'Etched away' ['Weggebeizt'],
whose central metaphor is that of such a utopian creation, draws
upon imagery of this kind: 'Etched away from/ the ray-wind
of your language/ the garish chatter of second-hand experience – the
hundred-/ tongued false-/ poem, the noem.// Blown/ out/ free/
your way through the human-/ shaped snow,/ the penitents' snow,
to/ the hospitable/ glacier rooms and tables.// Deep in the crevasse
of time,/ by the honeycomb-ice/ there waits, a breath crystal,/
your irreversible/ witness//' ['Weggebeizt vom/ Strahlenwind deiner
Sprache/ das bunte Gerede des An-/ erlebten – das hundert-/ züngige
Mein-/ gedicht, das Genicht.// Aus-/ gewirbelt,/ frei/ der Weg
durch den menschen-/ gestaltigen Schnee,/ den Büsserschnee, zu/ den
gastlichen/ Gletscherstuben und -tischen.// Tief/ in der Zeitens-
chrunde,/ beim/ Wabeneis/ wartet, ein Atemkristall,/ dein unums-
tössliches/ Zeugnis.//'].[51]
   In the first stanza, the poet is evoking and dismissing precisely the kind
of poetry which he rejects in his Meridian address: it is not 'language'
but 'chatter', and it is a 'Mein-gedicht', where 'Mein' suggests both the
garrulous self-reference of inauthentic poetry and the archaic usage as
'false'. That would not be so much a 'poem' ['Gedicht'] as a 'noem'
['Genicht']; and we should note the internal rhyme at this point, for
it is certainly intended as part of the poet's critique of a mendacious
aestheticism.[52] The poet's true path must lead him through a landscape
of snow, shaped as human bodies, crouching as if in penance.[53] But
there is a kind of hospitality there; the poet is expected. In the final
stanza we see in the crevasse of time, in the honeycomb-ice, a crystal
of breath, which is the poet's 'irreversible witness'. This refers to a new
poetry which is formed out of a language that has itself gone through the
'thousand darknesses', which has 'died in the throat', and which, formed
of crystalline breath, has become a testament to the dead that shall not
pass away. Poetry here then is founded at a point between *ḥārēš* and
dāmam. The former would be the refusal of speech and thus of dialogue
and, finally, of existence itself. Here Celan parallels the Psalmist who
fears that he might fall into the 'silence of death'. *Dāmam*, on the other

---

[51] 'Weggebeizt', ibid., p. 31.
[52] Compare Celan's comments in the Librairie Flinker document of 1958 on the extent to which the 'Musikalität' of modern poetry has nothing in common with 'Wohlklang' or 'harmony' (Antwort auf eine Umfrage der Librairie Flinker, Paris, 1958, in *Werke*, vol. 3, p. 167).
[53] 'Büsserschnee' is a technical term which translates 'nieves di penitentes' and refers to the distorted shapes, frequently resembling bowed human forms, which result from the melting and refreezing of snow masses in high mountain regions (cf. 'sun spikes').

hand, would be the silence of witness as remembrance, and it would be a kind of reconciliation. Indeed, within the intensely Jewish contexts of Celan's life and thought, his 'crystal of breath' ['Atemkristall'] is in a sense reverential silence at a catastrophe, and it thus plays a similar role to the *dāmam* of Job's own journey. Job failed to maintain the silence of *ḥārēš* on the way to a new *dāmam*; Celan on the other hand finally resists *ḥārēš* and can therefore begin the process of healing that will lead to *dāmam*. But at the same time, we should remember that Celan's *ḥārēš* and *dāmam* are *poetically enacted* silences, generated from within the multiple interactions of words. Just as language is hypostasised as 'the strangled word', so too Celan's silences are specifically silences of the text.

The second and final poem by Celan which I wish to discuss manifests silence in quite a different way. It is not founded upon the extreme austerity of form and image of 'Etched away', which is the fracturing and reduction of language to a minimum: 'poems on the edge of silence', as Celan called them. Bitingly satirical, the poem *Tenebrae* is an exercise in negation and denial, and thus corresponds, albeit it indirectly, to apophasis, as a way of affirming through denying. The poem reads: 'We are near, Lord,/ near and at hand.// Gripped already, Lord,/ clawed into each other as though/ the body of each of us were/ your body, Lord.// Pray, Lord,/ pray to us,/ we are near.// Wind-skewed we went there,/ went there to bend/ over hollow and crater.// To be watered we went there, Lord.// It was blood, it was/ what you shed, Lord.// It shone.// It cast your image into your eyes, Lord./ Eyes and mouth are so open and empty, Lord./ We have drunk, Lord./ The blood and the image that was in the blood, Lord.// Pray, Lord./ We are near.//' ['Nah sind wir, Herr,/ nahe und greifbar.// Gegriffen schon, Herr,/ ineinander verkrallt, als wär/ der Leib eines jeden von uns/ dein Leib, Herr.// Bete, Herr,/ bete zu uns,/ wir sind nah.// Windschief gingen wir hin,/ gingen wir hin, uns zu bücken/ nach Mulde und Maar.// Zur Tränke gingen wir, Herr.// Es war Blut, es war,/ was du vergossen, Herr.// Es glänzte.// Es warf uns dein Bild in die Augen, Herr./ Augen und Mund stehn so offen und leer, Herr./ Wir haben getrunken, Herr./ Das Blut und das Bild, das im Blut war, Herr.// Bete, Herr./ Wir sind nah.//'].[54]

There are three key motifs at work in this poem. The title itself, *Tenebrae*, refers to the liturgy of Holy Week, evoking not only the darkness of Celan's 'night', a figure which is suggestive of the 'thousand darknesses' of the age, but which also specifically recalls the death of Christ. This

---

[54] 'Tenebrae', *Werke*, vol. 1, p. 163.

is a theme which Celan takes up elsewhere. He likes to align the dead Jews of the Shoah with the crucified Jesus, who is for him a purely human victim of violence, and whom he seeks to reappropriate back into an exclusively Jewish tradition.[55] Thus Celan is able subtly to answer Christian anti-Semitism, while at the same time accessing the resources of crucifixion imagery for his scenes of death. The first and final lines support a further motif however, which is a refutation of the line from Ps 145:18: 'The Lord is close to those who call upon him . . .'[56] This is an attempt to contest the transcendence of God himself, by pronouncing that he is the one who should pray to humans ('Pray, Lord,/ pray to us,/ we are near' [///]), and by reducing him to the most immediate and graphic forms of murdered Jews ('as though/ the body of each of us were/ your body, Lord' [///]). This exchanges the theme of deification of man, which Celan knew through his acquaintance with Kabbalistic tradition, for a grotesque anthropomorphosis of God; and maintains the play upon crucifixion imagery. The reference to being 'watered' in the central part of the poem serves to portray the Jewish people as beasts of burden, while the notion of drinking satirises God's promise that he will give his people water to drink 'in the desert' (Isa. 43:20) and suggests the 'cup of wrath' which, in the Hebrew Scriptures, stands for God's punishment of his people. It is this same image moreover which appears in Christ's prayer to the Father in the Garden of Gethsemane. Celan's Jews drink blood, introducing eucharistic resonances, heavily satirised: for they drink not God's blood, shed for them, but their own blood, while the features mirrored in the blood are those of a dead man. Thus the anthropomorphosis of God is complete.

For all its virulent satire, *Tenebrae* cannot be seen as being anything other than a powerfully religious work. There is sense that Celan can only speak to God in this way at this time; no other speech is possible. The fact that he does speak to him, for all the complex interweaving of savagely satirical deconstructions, does however serve to establish the principle of dialogue: for in his own words the poem intends another – even the wholly Other. Thus the poem becomes in some extraordinary sense a kind of psalm of apophasis, which – as a psalm – is necessarily worked out within a language of address. If he is to speak, then the poet must affirm God, and if he is to affirm God, then he must praise him in the only way possible: as a dead man who drinks his own blood.

[55] See, for instance, 'Mandorla' and 'Hinausgekrönt' (pp. 244, 271–2).
[56] See also Ps. 34:18: 'The Lord is near to the brokenhearted, and saves the crushed in spirit.'

Silence is central to all three of our contemporary pieces, which can be seen to be drawing extensively upon the thematics of silence in earlier Judaeo-Christian tradition. What we have sought to argue is that the uses of silence differ significantly, and that as a non-sign it gains signification from the signs which surround it and in which it is embedded. In other words, it signifies by other signs. This finally is the fate of silence. The motif of silence is easily assimilated from one context into another therefore, and so offers an extraordinarily powerful and flexible instrument for dialogue. As a sign which refers through other signs, we can say that silence constitutes the *possibility* of discourse and utterance, and with that, the possibility of a new way of speaking and of understanding the world. A Christian community which remembers the place of silence as apophasis, not beyond but precisely within the liturgical and credal affirmations of Christian faith, is better able to engage in dialogue with the multiple silences of the world: the silence of those whose anger is directed against God, those who are indifferent about God, those minorities whose voices are not heard in the stridency of contemporary media coverage and political debate. An understanding of silence will enable such a community better to listen to the voice of the other, thus allowing its own speech to be more deeply formed in responsibility before the other. It will allow it also to be more attentive to the stirrings of the Spirit, within and across human language, from which it draws life. And by understanding the place of silence within the speech of Christians, that community will learn not to trust too easily and too glibly the sweet cadences of its own voice.

Select bibliography

Bakhtin, Mikhail, 'From Notes made in 1970–71', in *Speech Genres and other Late Essays*, trans. Vern W. McGee (Austin: University of Texas Press, 1986), pp. 132–58.

Beierwaltes, Werner, Balthasar, Hans Urs von and Haas, Alois, *Grundfragen der Mystik* (Einsiedeln: Johannes Verlag, 1974).

Bonaventure, *Itinerarium Mentis in Deum*, in Philotheus Boehner and M. Frances Loughlin (eds.), *The Works of St Bonaventure*, vol. II (New York: The Franciscan Institute, 1956).

Bonhoeffer, Dietrich, *Christology* (London and New York: Collins, 1971).

Buckley, Michael J., *At the Origins of Modern Atheism* (New Haven and London: Yale University Press, 1987).

Celan, Paul, *Gesammelte Werke*, 5 vols., ed. Beda Allemann, Stefan Reichert, Rolf Bücher (Frankfurt am Main: Suhrkamp, 1983).

Certeau, Michel de, *The Mystic Fable*, trans. Michael B. Smith (Chicago: Chicago University Press, 1992).

Clément, Olivier, *The Roots of Christian Mysticism* (London: New City, 1993).

Davies, Oliver, *Meister Eckhart, Mystical Theologian* (London: SPCK, 1991).

'Thinking Difference: a Comparative Study of Gilles Deleuze, Plotinus and Meister Eckhart', in Mary Bryden (ed.), *Deleuze and Religion* (London: Routledge, 2001), pp. 76–86.

Derrida, Jacques, 'How to Avoid Speaking: Denials', trans. K. Frieden, in H. Coward and T. Foshay (eds.), *Derrida and Negative Theology* (New York: State University of New York Press, 1992).

On the Name, Thomas Dutoit, ed., trans. David Wood, Thomas Leavey and Ian McLeod (Stanford: Stanford University Press, 1995).

Fiddes, Paul S., ' "Where Shall Wisdom be Found?" Job 28 as a Riddle for Ancient and Modern Readers', in John Barton and David Reimer (eds.), *After the Exile. Essays in Honour of Rex Mason* (Macon: Mercer University Press, 1996), 171–90.

Participating in God. A Pastoral Doctrine of the Trinity (London: Darton, Longman and Todd, 2000).

Ford, David F., *Self and Salvation. Being Transformed* (Cambridge: Cambridge University Press, 1999).

Gerrish, B. A., ' "To the Unknown God": Luther and Calvin on the Hiddenness of God', *Journal of Religion*, 53 (1973), 263–92.

Girard, René, *Resurrection from the Underground: Fyodor Dostoevsky*, trans. James G. Williams (New York: Crossroad, 1997).

Gregory of Nyssa, *The Life of Moses*, trans. Everett Ferguson and Abraham Malherbe (New York: Paulist Press, 1978).

Hume, David, *Dialogues Concerning Natural Religion* (Harmondsworth: Penguin Books, 1990).

Jaworski, Adam, *The Power of Silence. Social and Pragmatic Perspectives* (London: Sage Publications, 1993).

Silence. Interdisciplinary Perspectives (Mouton de Gruyter: Berlin and New York, 1997).

St John of the Cross. Collected Works, trans. K. Kavanaugh and Otilio Rodriguez (Washington: ICS, 1979).

Katz, Steven T. (ed.), *Mysticism and Language* (New York: Oxford University Press, 1992).

Labbé, Yves, 'La théologie négative dans la théologie trinitaire', *Revue des sciences religieuses*, 1993, 4, 69–86.

Lossky, Vladimir, *The Mystical Theology of the Eastern Church* (London: 1957).

Louth, Andrew, *The Origins of the Christian Mystical Tradition* (Oxford: Clarendon Press, 1981).

McGinn, Bernard, *The Foundations of Mysticism* (New York: Crossroad, 1991).

The Growth of Mysticism. Gregory the Great through the Twelfth Century (New York: Crossroad, 1994).

The Flowering of Mysticism. Men and Women in the New Mysticism – 1200–1350 (New York: Crossroad, 1998).

McCabe, Herbert, *God Matters* (London: Chapman, 1987).

McIntosh, Mark A., *Mystical Theology* (Oxford: Blackwell, 1998).

Meister Eckhart. Die deutschen und lateinischen Werke (Stuttgart: Kohlhammer, 1936–).

Michaels, Anne, *Fugitive Pieces* (London: Bloomsbury, 1998).

Miquel, Pierre and Dupuy, Michel, 'Silence', *Dictionnaire de Spiritualité*, vol. 14, Paris: Beauchesne, 1990, 829–59.

Mortley, Raoul, *From Word to Silence*, 2 vols. (Bonn: Hanstein, 1986).

Olivetti, M. M. (ed.), *Filosofia della Rivelazione* (Rome: Cedam, 1994).

Pseudo-Dionysius, *The Complete Works*, trans. Colm Luibheid (New Jersey: Paulist Press, 1987).

Sells, Michael A., *Mystical Languages of Unsaying* (Chicago: University of Chicago Press, 1994).

Soskice, Janet Martin, *Metaphor and Religious Language* (Oxford: Clarendon Press, 1985).

Steiner, George, *Language and Silence* (London: Faber, 1967).

Turner, Denys, *The Darkness of God. Negativity in Christian Mysticism* (Cambridge: Cambridge University Press, 1995).

'The Darkness of God and the Light of Christ: Negative Theology and Eucharistic Presence', *Modern Theology*, 15:2 (April 1999), 143–58.

Ward, Graham, *Barth, Derrida and the Language of Theology* (Cambridge: Cambridge University Press, 1995).

    'Kenosis and Naming: Beyond Analogy and Towards *analogia amoris*', in Paul Heelas (ed.), *Religion, Modernity and Postmodernity* (Oxford: Blackwell, 1998), pp. 233–57.

Williams, Rowan, *The Wound of Knowledge* (2nd rev. edn, London: Darton, Longman and Todd, 1990).

    Teresa of Avila (London: Geoffrey Chapman, 1991).

Index